Instructor's Manual and Test Bank

FOCUS on College Success

Constance Staley
University of Colorado, Colorado Springs

Prepared by

Catherine Andersen
Gallaudet University

Constance Staley

WADSWORTH
CENGAGE Learning™

Australia • Brazil • Japan • Korea • Mexico • Singapore • Spain • United Kingdom • United States

WADSWORTH
CENGAGE Learning

For product information and technology assistance, contact us at
Cengage Learning Customer & Sales Support,
1-800-354-9706

For permission to use material from this text or product, submit all requests online at **www.cengage.com/permissions**
Further permissions questions can be emailed to
permissionrequest@cengage.com

ISBN-13: 978-0-534-63867-2
ISBN-10: 0-534-63867-8

Wadsworth
25 Thomson Place
Boston, MA 02210
USA

Cengage Learning is a leading provider of customized learning solutions with office locations around the globe, including Singapore, the United Kingdom, Australia, Mexico, Brazil, and Japan. Locate your local office at: **international.cengage.com/region**

Cengage Learning products are represented in Canada by Nelson Education, Ltd.

For your course and learning solutions, visit
academic.cengage.com

Purchase any of our products at your local college store or at our preferred online store
www.ichapters.com

Printed in the United States of America
1 2 3 4 5 6 7 11 10 09 08

TABLE OF CONTENTS

CHAPTER RESOURCES by Catherine Andersen

TEST BANK by Catherine Andersen

ADDITIONAL RESOURCES by Constance Staley

INTRODUCTION

by Constance Staley

> "Teaching is the greatest act of optimism." ~*Colleen Wilcox*

So you're going to teach a first-year seminar? Great! What an opportunity to get to know your students in a small class format, refine your teaching skills, and enhance your own learning! Many instructors say teaching a first-year seminar has changed the way they teach *all* their classes and that, perhaps for the first time, they truly understand a fundamental truth of best practice: high expectations *and* high support. Perhaps you're new to the course, or you may be a seasoned instructor using *FOCUS on College Success* for the first time. You may be working with "traditional" first-year students or non-traditional adult students. Regardless, teaching this multi-disciplinary skills course can reinforce something you already know: that teaching is about relationship-building. Unlike large lecture classes, in a first-year seminar you have the luxury of doing just that. Some say that building relationships with students today is more essential than ever. Countless books and articles have been written about today's college students. What does the literature say about them?

> "Millennials [born between roughly 1980 and 1994] have grown up with more choices and more selectivity in the products and services they use, which is why they do not have, for example, a generational music…. They rarely read newspapers—or, for that matter, books. They are impatient and goal oriented. They hate busywork, learn by doing, and are used to instant feedback. They want it *now*. They think it's cool to be smart. They have friends from different ethnic backgrounds. They want flexibility—in the classroom and in their lives. 'To get this generation involved, you have to figure out a way to engage them and make their learning faster at the end of the day. Is it possible to do that? I think the answer is yes, but the jury is out.'"[1]

While this description may or may not fit your experience, many of us with decades of teaching experience know that things have changed. It's become more challenging, many instructors believe, to "compete" with television, the Internet, movies, music, and all the distractions available in our culture (hence the title of this textbook, *FOCUS*). Engaging students requires increased effort and creativity, and students want more from us, like ready access and quick results. That's why I believe teaching is more challenging than ever; however, along with the challenges comes greater potential for fulfillment. That's why I wrote *FOCUS on College Success*: to help you in your search to "figure out a way to engage them and make their learning faster at the end of the day." *FOCUS* is rich with options for you and filled a variety of built-in features for your students. Just as students learn differently, instructors teach differently. We each have our own styles and methods, but we also eagerly pursue ways to do it better. A first-year seminar course is "all about them" (meant in the best sense of the phrase) and how much

---

[1] (2007, January 5). How the new generation of well-wired multitaskers is changing campus culture. *Chronicle of Higher Education*. Available at http://chronicle.com/weekly/v53/i18/18b01001.htm

they can learn and *apply*, not only in your course, but in all their classes and their careers beyond college.

One of my graduate students asked me recently, "Why do you care so much about teaching? Why have you devoted your career to becoming the best teacher you can be?" I thought about it for a moment and replied, "My motives are selfish. I care so much about teaching because that is how I learn." She nodded in recognition and smiled.

As I thought about writing the introduction for Catherine Andersen's Instructor's Resource Manual for *FOCUS*, one of my favorite stories of all time came to mind:

> The huge printing presses of a major Chicago newspaper began malfunctioning on the Saturday before Christmas, putting all the revenue for advertising that was to appear in the Sunday paper in jeopardy. None of the technicians could track down the problem. Finally, a frantic call was made to the retired printer who had worked with these presses for over forty years. "We'll pay anything; just come in and fix them," he was told.
>
> When he arrived, he walked around for a few minutes, surveying the presses; then he approached one of the control panels and opened it. He removed a dime from his pocket, turned a screw ¼ of a turn, and said, "The presses will now work correctly." After being profusely thanked, he was told to submit a bill for his work.
>
> The bill arrived a few days later, for $10,000.00! Not wanting to pay such a huge amount for so little work, the printer was told to please itemize his charges, with the hope that he would reduce the amount once he had to identify his services. The revised bill arrived: $1.00 for turning the screw; $9,999.00 for knowing which screw to turn.

~Anonymous

Teaching *is* the greatest act of optimism, as the Colleen Wilcox quotation asserts at the beginning of this introduction, not because today's students are so challenging to teach, but because we believe in the power of students to learn. We know that we can help them discover "which screw to turn" as learners. Underneath it all, we have confidence in our students, who will build a future for us, our children, and our society. We have faith in the power of higher education to transform lives. And finally, we believe in ourselves as *we* learn to become better teachers from *them*.

What is this course about?

> "The great end of education is to discipline rather than to furnish the mind; to train it to the use of its own powers rather than to fill it with the accumulation of others." ~*Tryon Edwards*

A first-year seminar course is about many things: helping students understand themselves and teaching them how to successfully navigate the first year of college. They will learn about how they learn and what motivates them. They will identify campus resources and understand that using these opportunities effectively will help them to succeed. They will comprehend the benefits of managing time and money, and the consequences of not doing so. They will develop specific academic skills such as thinking critically and creatively, reading, writing, and speaking, as well as enhance specific study skills such as memory techniques, note-taking, studying, and taking tests effectively. They will learn about choosing majors and careers, and ways to develop life-long skills in managing relationships, valuing diversity, and working toward wellness.

Bloom asserted many years ago that teachers have three types of goals: *affective, behavioral*, and *cognitive*. As opposed to upper-level discipline-based courses, for example, which emphasize the cognitive domain primarily, in first-year seminars, affective, behavioral, and cognitive goals are more equally weighted. Instructors work to cultivate attitudes and beliefs in first-year students, to foster behaviors that will lead to academic success, and to help them learn about learning from a variety of vantage points and in a variety of ways. Many faculty are most comfortable working in the cognitive domain because, after all, we are subject matter experts: psychologists, mathematicians, or historians, for example. An upper division philosophy course will operate heavily in the cognitive domain. However, research dictates that we must operate in all three domains, despite the specific course content being taught, and in a first-year seminar, instructors must be comfortable with all three types of teaching and learning goals.

Ultimately, first-year seminars are about *metacognition*: "Metacognition is about having an 'awareness of [your] own cognitive machinery and how the machinery works.' It's about knowing the limits of your own learning and memory capabilities, knowing how much you can accomplish within a certain amount of time, and knowing what learning strategies work for you."[2]

Why is the course important?

> "The task of the excellent teacher is to stimulate 'apparently ordinary' people to unusual effort. The tough problem is not in identifying winners: it is in making winners out of ordinary people." ~*K. Patricia Cross*

Some academicians undervalue skills courses of any kind. Theory always trumps skills in their minds. And as a multidisciplinary skills course, a first-year seminar is even more suspect.

---

[2] [Staley, C. (2009). *FOCUS on College Success*. Belmont, CA: Wadsworth; Melchenbaum, D., Burland, S., Gruson, L., & Cameron, R. (1985). Metacognitive assessment. In S. Yussen (Ed.), *The growth of reflection in children*. Orlando, FL: Academic Press.]

However, the first year of college is the foundational year. If students are successful in the first year, their chances of graduating are greatly enhanced. Often, students' grades in their first-year seminar courses are predictive of their overall first-term success. As Chapter 1 of *FOCUS* asserts to student readers, "In short, the weight of evidence indicates that FYS [first-year seminar] participation has statistically significant and substantial, positive effects on a student's successful transition to college….And on a considerable array of other college experiences known to be related directly and indirectly to bachelor's degree completion."[3]

First-year seminar instructors (and motivated students) understand the value of connecting with other students and an instructor who is invested in their success, of honing academic skills, and of applying what they learn across all their courses. First-year seminar courses are about making "winners" out of *all* students who will internalize and apply what they learn.

How is a first-year seminar different from other academic courses? How is the course organized?

> "In teaching it is the method and not the content that is the message...the drawing out, not the pumping in." ~*Ashley Montagu*

First-year seminar courses come in all shapes and sizes. According to the 2006 national survey conducted by the National Resource Center on the First-Year Experience and Students in Transition:

Models
- 60 percent of reporting institutions offer extended orientation seminars
- 28 percent offer academic seminars with generally uniform content across sections
- 26 percent offer academic seminars on various topics
- 15 percent offer pre-professional or discipline-linked seminars
  22 percent offer basic study skills seminars
- 20 percent offer a hybrid
  4 percent offer some "other" type of first-year seminar

(Note: Percentages are rounded off; some schools offer more than one type of seminar.)

Course Objectives (regardless of the model)
1. Develop academic skills
2. Provide an orientation to campus resources and services
3. Self-exploration/personal development

Course Topics
1. Study skills
2. Critical thinking
3. Campus resources

---

[3] [Pascarella, E. T., & Terenzini, P. T. (2005). *How college affects students: A third decade of research*. San Francisco: Jossey-Bass, p. 403.]

4. Academic Planning/Advising
5. Time management

[For further information, see http://www.sc.edu/fye/research/surveyfindings/surveys/survey06.html]

You'll notice that *FOCUS* covers thirteen different, multifaceted topics that are known to contribute to student success, including those identified as the most common components of first-year seminars nationally. Each chapter is grounded in research (documented in endnotes so that citations are not intrusive), and the learning system and features, which are part of the book's infrastructure, are carried throughout the text. Students may not even realize the extent to which they are being motivated, challenged, and supported as they develop as learners.

There is no one right way to teach a first-year seminar although themes contributing to success may be found across institutions and programs. What then makes a first-year seminar successful? According to Randy Swing, Senior Fellow for the Policy Center on the First Year of College, the answer to that question is *engaging pedagogy*: "If your seminar intends to produce learning outcomes in critical thinking, writing, reading, and oral presentation skills; connections with faculty; or time management skills, then a critical first step is to ensure that seminars are delivered with a high level of engaging pedagogy"… a variety of teaching methods; meaningful discussion and homework; challenging assignments; productive use of class time; and encouragement for students to speak in class and work together."[4]

First-year seminars must include many different ways to get students engaged in course material. Because so many students are multimodal and kinesthetic learners today, we must be creative in designing ways to engage them. Engagement is a primary underlying goal of the *FOCUS* experience—"drawing out, not pumping in"—as is building a community of learners who understand the value of this unique course in their current and future success.

Instead of simply discussing the chapter each week, change the format from time to time: set up a debate; actually do the alcohol poisoning simulation in Chapter 5; divide the class into smaller groups, and let each class group teach a chapter; or "VARK" a chapter and let groups teach portions based on their common learning style preferences; employ a community-based service-learning project; bring in a panel of professionals representing different careers; follow some of Catherine's activity suggestions, or try one of the new activities I've developed for inclusion later in this manual. As I've often said, a steak dinner may taste good, but would you want the same meal every evening for a month? Vary how you spend your class time, so that students are curious about what to expect and come to class ready to be engaged.

---

[4] [Swing, R. (2002). http://209.85.173.104/search?q=cache:q8hFMHQ-354J:www.csuchico.edu/vpaa/FYEpdf/First_Year_Initiative_Benchmark_Study.pdf+Randy+Swing+%22engaging+pedagogies%22&hl=en&ct=clnk&cd=2&gl=us; http://209.85.173.104/search?q=cache:q8hFMHQ-354J:www.csuchico.edu/vpaa/FYEpdf/First_Year_Initiative_Benchmark_Study.pdf+%22first-year+seminar%22+%22engaging+pedagogies%22&hl=en&ct=clnk&cd=2&gl=us]

Am I qualified to teach the course?

> "Effective teaching may be the hardest job there is." ~*William Glasser*

Institutions have different rules about qualifications, but if you have been invited to teach a college success course, you are undoubtedly qualified. Someone has recognized your teaching expertise and your ability to build relationships with learners. No one has an advanced degree in College Success, but as a faculty member, student affairs professional, or adjunct instructor, you yourself have been academically successful. If you are a faculty member, remember that regardless of whether you teach chemistry, sociology, or geography, for example, most college professors have not received instruction on the practice of teaching even though they are well versed in their disciplines. If you are a counselor or advisor, you bring a helpful skill set to this course, and if are teaching as an adjunct, you have real-world experience to bring to the classroom.

Teaching, as the quotation above notes, is difficult. Good teaching is at times downright exhausting. But noting the outcomes, accepting the gratitude of thankful students, and observing their future success is more than worth the effort. Attend the first-year seminar faculty training sessions provided by your institution. Use your first-year seminar colleagues for support, exchange reflections about the *FOCUS* features and activities that have worked well, and share new ideas. Work together as a group to develop a mission statement, rubrics, and a set of desired, intentional learning outcomes. And as you're advised later in Catherine Andersen's chapter-by-chapter guide, make notes to yourself about what you've learned in teaching each topic, and record what you may want to do differently next time. Record these observations while you're teaching the course, so that when you teach it again, you won't have forgotten.

How should I communicate with my students?

> "The most important knowledge teachers need to do good work is a knowledge of how students are experiencing learning and perceiving their teacher's actions." ~*Steven Brookfield*

The quality and quantity of communication with your students are essential to your students' success and your satisfaction with your teaching experience. Consider these suggestions:

- **Set guidelines**. Will you accept text messages? Will you give students your home or cell phone numbers? Will you communicate via Facebook, MySpace, or neither? Will you hold virtual office hours? Will you require students to communicate via your institution's e-mail system, as opposed to all the other options available (yahoo, gmail, etc.) Will you expect a certain level of grammatical correctness, even in informal messages? Will you require a tone of mutual support and "professionalism"? Will you encourage your students to check their e-mail accounts daily (at a minimum)? Think beforehand about the best ways to develop relationships with your students, and let them know how you'd like to communicate with them.

- **Praise, when it's warranted**. You've experienced it: you open an e-mail message from a student that says, "I really enjoyed class today. I'd never thought about many of the things we discussed. Thanks for being such a great teacher." Do the same for your students, either face-to-face or electronically. It only takes a few seconds to write a student a message like this: "Wow! The presentation you gave in class today was brilliant. I could tell how much time you invested in researching the topic and creating your PowerPoint slides. Thanks for all your hard work!" Positive reinforcement goes a long way.

- **Respond right away**. If at all possible, take quick action when it comes to your students' success. Recently I received an e-mail from a student that read, "Professor Staley, I've been traumatized by something that happened recently in my home town. I can't continue. Today I'm going to drop all my classes, forfeit my scholarship, and leave school." When I got that e-mail, I placed a few phone calls and wrote back, "Dear _____, This is a very important decision. Let's talk about it before you do anything. My Assistant Director and the Dean will meet you in your financial aid advisor's office in an hour." The group rallied around her, and today she's in school and doing well. That one moment in time was critical. Of course, it's not always possible to respond quickly. Had I been busy in meetings or otherwise away from my computer, this student's future might have been very different. But sometimes timing is critical in getting students over a hump.

- **Be persistent**. If a student is missing in your small class, give him a call on your cell phone, and pass the phone around so that all his classmates also invite him to class. Knock on his residence hall door. I once staged an "intervention" when I heard that one of my students didn't have his assigned presentation done, so he was playing hacky sack with his friends outside the building instead of coming to class. The entire group went outside and "captured" him and brought him to class. When he turned around and saw 16 people approaching him, he said, "But I don't have my assignment done" to which the group replied, "Come to class, anyway!" He was deeply touched by this gesture of support, came to class, and never missed again. You may not go to such extraordinary measures with more mature students, but in this case, our wayward first-year student learned his lesson. Experiences like this one have contributed to my philosophy in this course: Remember that first-year students are "under construction," so go the extra mile.

- **Pay attention**. If you begin to notice that one week a student is hyperactive and the following week, this same student seems deeply depressed, take note. If this up and down behavior becomes a pattern, see if you can find out why. Behavior like this could be a sign of problems at home, drug use, or a mood disorder. Intervention may be required. If need be, ask the student if she'd like you to walk her over to the Counseling Center. You may feel that you are being intrusive or that it's inappropriate for teachers to "go there." However, my personal philosophy after many years of teaching is that we must pay attention to what gets in the way of learning, and if students need help, it's our job to help them get it. You may not be a trained counselor, and it's not appropriate to solve students' problems for them. But as an administrator I met recently likes to say, "There's a difference between *caring* and *carrying*." Of course, not all students will accept your help, but you will know that you have tried.

- **Provide meaningful, specific, frequent, and timely feedback.** One of students' biggest pet peeves is instructors who take forever to return assignments, appear not to have read students' papers, or provide minimal feedback: "B" with no explanation or rationale, for example. It's a two-way street, they believe, and if they're expected to invest in their coursework and turn in assignments promptly, they expect the same from us. Instead of simply marking a paper with a "B," provide rubrics in advance for why assignments deserve particular grades and provide specific critiques: "This paper does a good job of addressing the major goal of the assignment, which is to choose a position on a controversial topic and support your position. But the assignment asks for specific types of evidence from a minimum of three books, four journal articles, and five web sites…, etc." Students need regular feedback from you in order to know how to improve their work and grow academically.

What do I need to know if I'm teaching this course for the first time?

> "Teaching can be compared to selling commodities. No one can sell unless someone buys… [Yet] there are teachers who think they have done a good day's teaching irrespective of what pupils have learned." *~John Dewey*

It is my personal belief that college success happens when three sets of goals intersect: *academic* goals, (students') *personal* goals, and (class and campus) *community* goals. In my mind, it looks like this:

(Note the activity on page 210 related to this point.) This belief is at the core of first-year seminars, and in my view, instructors must adopt it and base their teaching and interaction with students on it.

As you prepare to teach a first-year seminar for the first time, read, study, and learn as much as you can about effective teaching and about today's learners. Check out the online resources listed in the Additional Resources at the back of this manual, for example, The Boyer

Commissions' "Reinventing Undergraduate Education," or the American Association of Colleges and University's report, "Greater Expectations," or their publication, *Liberal Education*, or the Jossey-Bass magazine/journal called *About Campus*. When you begin to look, you'll see that illuminating resources are everywhere.

Use this manual and the online *FOCUS* Resource Center. Get to know your colleagues, and your students, individually and collectively. Watch out for non-cognitive variables that get in the way of learning. And above all, make sure learning is taking place. Do "One-Minute" papers (or index cards) at the end of class to find out what students valued most and what's still confusing. If you're insecure, ask for volunteers from your class to act as the course "Board of Directors." Meet with these representatives, get feedback from them about how things are going, or if your institution uses peer mentors, solicit that input from him or her. Consult the Teaching and Learning Center on your campus. It's possible that experts there can come to class to observe your teaching, invite you to faculty workshops on best practices in teaching, or provide you with materials to read. Generally speaking, help is only a phone call, an e-mail, or a jaunt across campus away.

How can I rejuvenate the course if I've been teaching it for years?

> "One new feature or fresh take can change everything." ~*Neil Young*

After teaching any course for a number of years, many instructors find themselves searching for new ways to do things, whether the course they want to update is a discipline-based course such as math or literature or a first-year seminar course. Among other goals we have in this quest is our own need to keep ourselves fresh, engaged, and up-to-date. Refresh your memory about things you already know, like Chickering and Gamson's now 20-year-old "Seven Principles of Best Practice." Good practice:

1. encourages student-faculty contact.
2. encourages cooperation among students.
3. encourages active learning.
4. gives prompt feedback.
5. emphasizes time on task (as opposed to multitasking, perhaps?).
6. communicates high expectations.
7. respects diverse talents and ways of knowing.[5]

Because of the comprehensive coverage of topics, the built-in activities, and its integrated learning system, *FOCUS* will most definitely play a role in reinvigorating your course. It may help you see topics you've taught before differently. As writer Thomas Higginson notes, "Originality is simply a pair of fresh eyes." One of the intentional strategies used in the *FOCUS* learning experience is helping students not only discover *what* to do, but *how* to do it, *why* doing

---

[5] [Chickering, A. W., & Gamson, Z. F. (1987). Seven principles for good practice in undergraduate education. *The Wingspread Journal*, *9*(2). See also AAHE Bulletin, March, 1987.]

it is important—and then actually doing it! With new resources at your fingertips, you will undoubtedly find yourself considering new approaches to teaching your first-year seminar. The preface of your Annotated Instructor's Edition of *FOCUS* outlines each new feature, point by point, and the role each one plays in first-year seminar big challenges: retention, engagement, motivation, credibility, and varied learning styles.

Beyond the natural innovations that come with using a new text, you may reinvigorate your course by deliberately deciding to infuse it with a specific innovation, either in your own section of the course or across the entire program. Here are three examples to consider.

- **Service-Learning:** *FOCUS* discusses service-learning in several different places (including a full-page featured box on p. 348). If your students could benefit from real-world writing experiences, for example, pair each one with a senior citizen in the community to co-author the elder's "memoirs.". If you have a preponderance of students with text anxiety, have them teach chapter 9 on test-taking to middle school children through a newly launched community-based program. Allow students to select a *FOCUS* chapter and design a service-learning experience of their own within parameters you set. Somehow linking the requirement to the text or particular features of your campus or community will communicate the value and relevance of service-learning, so that students see the integral role it plays (as opposed to seeming like busywork). Or consider using a term-long activity such as "Reflecting on Service: 5 C's Journals" in *50 Ways to Leave Your Lectern* (p. 92) to connect the classroom and the community-based service-learning project through journals. Many schools have added service-learning to their programs with excellent results. While you must think through grading this type of activity and deciding how much of the course it should be worth, service-learning is as excellent way to encourage students to bond with one another, particularly if they work in groups, and come to value the application of what they are learning in your class.

- **Peer Mentors:** If your program does not yet employ the assistance of peer mentors, this is another possible innovation with potentially broad-based positive results. Former first-year seminar students with strong academic and leadership skills (from sophomores to graduate students) can be nominated by their first-year seminar faculty, apply competitively for, and be selected to work with each section of the course. These students should be trained, ideally through a class on teaching and learning in which the specifics of your program and the issues that relate to your current first-year students can be discussed. Often first-year students connect with these role models, and they can serve in a liaison capacity, becoming a valuable aid to retention.

- **Faculty Development:** Although this theme has run through many of the suggestions in this introduction, faculty training cannot be overemphasized. First-year seminar instructors typically come from a variety of academic and professional backgrounds. Training helps them move beyond the "borders" of their disciplines and focus on students. Over time faculty can become increasingly specialized in the intricacies of their research. However, coming together with faculty and staff from across the campus to focus specifically on teaching and learning can change the way they teach *all* their courses. Strong faculty training programs are almost always behind strong first-year seminar programs, and most institutions, I'm convinced, could benefit in many ways by doing more.

How does this course relate to my discipline?

> "Systems thinking is a discipline for seeing wholes. It is a framework for seeing interrelationships rather than things, for seeing patterns of change rather than static 'snapshots.'" ~*Peter Senge*

If you teach courses in another discipline, and you're teaching a first-year seminar for the first time, you may be wondering how the two intersect. Although they may seem miles apart to you, there may actually be more commonalities than you think. And of course, the best practices of teaching apply to both. As you'll read in *FOCUS*, knowledge is interconnected, and a variety of disciplines are included in the textbook. If you are a math teacher, you will resonate with the section in Chapter 9 on test-taking and math anxiety; if you teach composition or communication, you will feel at home in Chapter 10 on speaking and writing. If you teach health sciences, you will see much of the research from your discipline explained to students in Chapter 13 on wellness. If you teach psychology, you'll notice that Chapter 1 of *FOCUS* begins with the work of Stanford psychologist Carol Dweck. If you are a student affairs professional, you will see elements of student development theories underlying everything in the book.

No matter which other discipline you teach, underneath or alongside the content is "advice" you give your students about how to master course material. Use your knowledge of this "hidden curriculum" and draw upon it in your first-year seminar course. Further, while a first-year seminar course is unique, don't be reluctant to touch on your disciplinary expertise. Students will be curious about other aspects of your job, the interrelationships between its various components, and why you wanted to teach a first-year seminar in addition to everything else you do.

Throughout *FOCUS*, the "static snapshot" of each chapter is woven together into an integrated "system" for better learning. And you will be interested, as Peter Senge notes in his quotation above, in the "patterns of change" in your students.

How will the course be different if I teach non-traditional versus traditional students?

> "The learner should be actively involved in the learning process." ~*Malcolm Knowles*

Malcolm Knowles coined the term "andragogy," meaning the study of adult learning, as an equivalent to pedagogy. According to Knowles, these four issues are critical:

1. **The need to know**—adult learners need to know why they need to learn something before they will learn it.
2. **Learner self-concept**—adults are self-directed learners.
3. **Role of learners' experience**—adult learners have a variety of life experiences in which to ground their learning.

4. **Readiness to learn**—adults are motivated learners because they recognize the value of learning in dealing effectively with life situations.
5. **Orientation to learning**—adults prefer to see the practical value of applying learning to their everyday lives.[6]

You will note that *FOCUS* is designed to reach learners of all ages. Several of the *FOCUS* Challenge Cases involve adult learners, learners of different ethnicities, and learners at community colleges versus four year institutions. My goal was for every student reader to see him or herself reflected somewhere in the book.

Perhaps the greatest difference in using *FOCUS* to teach adult learners will be where you place emphases in the course, which examples you use, and how you design basic assignments and activities, using *problem-based learning*. For example, if you allow students to choose topics for their papers, traditional students may choose to research binge drinking or Greek issues on campus. Nontraditional learners may choose to research a current *problem* or challenge for which they're seeking a solution: buying a first home or finding day-care options in your town. Adult learners may be more motivated and focused, as faculty sometimes note, but they must still deal with myriad complexities in their busy lives. They will want to share their backgrounds with class members and take practical applications that relate to their own lives from your course.

How can I get involved with my students if I'm a part-time instructor?

> "Communication works for those who work at it." ~*John Powell*

If you are teaching a first-year seminar as an adjunct professor, particularly if you don't have an office on campus, you will need to capitalize on class time and rely on technology to connect with your students. But you can also be creative: hold your office hours in the school's cafeteria or library. Meet your class as a group for pizza, or if you're comfortable, invite them to your home to pick apples from the tree in your yard and bake a pie, for example. Just as you stay in touch with "long-distance" friends and relatives you care about, vow to do the same with your students. It's entirely possible to bond in ways other than those involving face-to-face contact.

How should I evaluate students? Isn't the point of a college success course to help students succeed?

> "Success on any major scale requires you to accept responsibility...in the final analysis, the one quality that all successful people have...is the ability to take on responsibility."
> ~*Michael Korda*

This is an important question, one with which first-year seminar instructors often struggle. How should I grade a student who doesn't come to class or turn in assignments, despite my attempts to

---

[6] [Knowles' Andragogy. Available at http://www.learningandteaching.info/learning/knowlesa.htm]

contact him or her? How much leeway should I give students in turning assignments in late? How do I balance *challenge* and *support*? These are common questions, and the assumptions behind these questions are the reason that some non first-year seminar faculty assume that first-year seminars are simply "hand-holding" classes in which all students receive "A's," regardless of their performance, when instead, first-year seminars are well-thought through, structured learning experiences in which expectations for college success are made clear and overt.

The answer to your own personal questions about balance will likely come with experience teaching the course. But what are we teaching students about their futures when we excuse them from responsibilities or when we give them amnesty from assignments that are documented in the syllabus from the beginning of the term? Emergencies notwithstanding, what lessons will they learn? Are their bosses likely to say, "That's OK, Wilson, I understand you've been busy. Why don't you take another week on the Jones project even though we were supposed to close the deal tomorrow?" Probably not.

It is clear that first-year seminar instructors walk a tightrope. My advice to instructors is to "clamp down supportively." As one expert in the field notes, "If we have minimal expectations for what beginning students can and will do, we set in motion a self-fulfilling prophecy." If we dumb down first-year seminar courses, students will "live down" to our expectations. I believe it's important, instead, to "challenge up."

Again, this is where your colleagues should work together to achieve consistency across sections of the course and resolve sticky issues. Engage in discussions. Develop standards across sections. Generate rubrics for grading: what *is* an A paper, a B paper, and so forth? Hold "norming" sessions in which all first-year seminar faculty grade the same set of papers and discuss their rationales. You may find that a chemistry professor, a sociology professor, and a history professor grade the same papers very differently, which will generate further discussion about practices and priorities.

Finally, a word that is often associated with evaluation is assessment; however, the words are not synonymous. Assessment is a concept that has generated countless books and articles with multiples theories and practices behind it. As a first-year seminar instructor, your focus is to evaluate your students work with the ultimate goal of helping them succeed.

Whatever the model used, what are the desired learning outcomes of a college success course?

> "The classroom is a microcosm of the world; it is the chance we have to practice whatever ideals we cherish. The kind of classroom situation one creates is the acid test of what it is one really stands for." ~*Jane Tompkins*

As you have read here, some first-year seminar courses are extended orientation courses, some are discipline-based, some are interdisciplinary, some are gateway to general education courses. Regardless of which model is used, the goals are similar, and it's best if you and your colleagues articulate these exact goals together. It has been my great fortune (and ultimate learning experience) to work with faculty at many, many institutions over the years, to have many questions put to me, and to learn a great deal from many other first-year seminar instructors. Whatever the specific goals are for your institution, the goals for *FOCUS* as a multifaceted learning experience for your students have been identified here, throughout the Annotated Instructor's Edition's preface, and in all the support materials available to you. My final suggestion in this Introduction to Catherine Andersen's Instructor's Resource Manual is that you remember this last quotation by Jane Tompkins above, mount it in your office, and observe the way you live it every day.

USING *FOCUS*'S ADDITIONAL SPECIAL FEATURES

By Constance Staley

FOCUS on College Success has many unique features available via the text book, as well as the text's online Resource Center to enrich the learning environment in your classroom. These features not only "VARK" the *FOCUS* experience to engage all types of learners, but they provide you as an instructor with options. You will undoubtedly prefer some features over others, based on your teaching style and the particular characteristics of your students. After you teach with *FOCUS* once, you will very likely find your favorite features to use. But the following year, you may have a very different group of first-year students and will need to select different features that will appeal to them. While many of these features are described elsewhere, such as the preface of the Annotated Instructor's Edition, they are listed here for your consideration, too.

 ## *FOCUS* Challenge Case Studies

- **Why should I use this feature?** The *FOCUS* Challenge Cases are, according to one reviewer, "the most realistic case studies I have come across." Students often respond: "How does this book know so much about me?" Why do they evoke such responses? Each *FOCUS* Challenge Case is based on an actual student or a composite of students I have worked with directly over the years. The stories are based on these students' experiences. After many years of teaching, instructors learn how to "get into first-year student's heads." And if we can't figure out a particular student, we ask, "What's going on?" Most first-year students struggle with something, even if they are gifted academically. Occasionally, a student may ask why the case studies are negative or primarily about problems. Research shows that negative role models help people learn. When things are going swimmingly, there is less cause for self-examination and discussion. Using real students in the book, on the Resource Center web site, and as guests on the mock television shows (described below) provides a highly kinesthetic, real-life learning experience for your students. These thirteen students (my own students at UCCS) are the *FOCUS* cast, and readers will see them in photos throughout the book. If your students are experiencing similar problems as those described in the *FOCUS* Challenge Cases, they will learn that they are not alone. And the safety of discussing someone else's issues always helps students learn more about themselves.

- **How can I use this feature?** Case studies are excellent discussion generators. Generally, students are interested in other students. Ask your students to come to class ready to discuss Gloria or Derek or Anthony by jotting down answers to the "What Do *YOU* Think?" questions immediately after the case, or put students in pairs or groups to discuss these questions. At the end of each chapter, students are asked to revisit the case, based on what they have learned by working through the chapter, by responding to a section called "*NOW* What Do You Think." Their opinions may have changed, based on new information they have learned. Something that seemed like a simple fix may be seen more realistically now, and students will have an opportunity to apply what they have just learned, which provides reinforcement.

Entrance and Exit Interviews

- **Why should I use this feature?** Many institutions (perhaps even yours) spend thousands of dollars each year on commercial instruments to collect data about their students. Other institutions cannot afford such expenditures, have never found an instrument that suits their needs, or have never initiated this practice. For these reasons, *FOCUS* comes with its own built-in pre- and post-instruments to measure students' *expectations* of college at the outset, and their *experience* of college at the end of the course. The instruments appear in the text in the front and back matter for pencil and paper administration, on the text's Resource Center web site for online administration, and via clicker technology with JoinIn on TurningPoint. Some of the questions are general in nature (How many hours per week do you expect to study for your classes?) and some are specific to *FOCUS* content, asking students which chapter topics they're most interested in and which they expect to be most difficult to apply. Not only will you learn about your students and their individual and collective characteristics, but you will be alerted to students who may need additional support or intervention . Students will learn about themselves, and your institution may wish to collect these data broadly about the entering class each year.

- **How can I use this feature?** Ask your students to fill out the Entrance Interview at the beginning of the course, either via technology or on paper. Alternatively, send it out before the course begins, along with summer reading materials or a welcome letter from your institution. Or if your first-year seminar program uses peer mentors, ask them to conduct actual one-on-one interviews, using the instrument and write down interviewees' responses. Do the same thing with the Exit Interview at the end of the course. The annotated versions of the Entrance and Exit Interviews in the Annotated Instructors' Edition give the rationale for each question and comparison guidelines for the two instruments so that you can note changes in individual students over the term.

"Inside the *FOCUS* Studio" Mock Television Shows

- **Why should I use this feature?** According to Neilsen Media Research, the average college student watches 3 hours and 41 minutes of television per day. The VARK Learning Style Questionnaire categorizes television as kinesthetic, the preferred learning style of many of today's college students. *FOCUS* has devised an alternative way to deliver content by creating short, mock television shows, based on Bravo's 13 time Emmy-Award nominated program, "Inside the Actors Studio."

[See http://www.bravotv.com/Inside_the_Actors_Studio/] James Lipton's (Dean Emeritus of Actors Studio's MFA drama program) insightful interviews of actors from stage to screen are "replicated" with Constance Staley as host and *FOCUS* cast members as guests. Episodes appear, along with discussion questions, in "YouTube" style on the text's Resource Center web site for Chapter 1 (Gloria Gonzales, "Building Dreams, Setting Goals"), Chapter 7 (Kevin Baxter, "Developing Your Memory"), Chapter 11 (Kia Washington, "Building Relationships, Valuing Diversity"), Chapter 12 (Ethan Cole, "Choosing a College Major and a Career"), and Chapter 13 (Anthony Lopez, "Working toward Wellness"). Scripts were written by New York comedy writer Matthew McClain, and a short comedy segment appears as part of each episode amidst content coverage for these chapters. The episodes were co-produced by Matthew McClain and Constance Staley in the television studios at the University of Colorado, Colorado Springs.

- **How can I use this feature?** The television shows are excellent ways to introduce the chapters or to review them, since each episode generally covers the "You're About to Discover" bullets at the start of that chapter. You may show episodes in class, or ask students to view them at home and answer the questions on their own to discuss later in class.

 MP3 Format iAudio Chapter Summaries

- **Why should I use this feature?** Today's students are wired for sound. Whenever you see them walking across campus, they're either on their cell phones or have their earplugs inserted. Some of their instructors podcast lectures as a way of re-viewing or pre-viewing (or in this case, listening rather than viewing) course content. Again, written by Matthew McClain, these approximately four-minute summaries (the length of a song, roughly) reinforce *FOCUS* content. Traveling home on the subway or pumping gas at the station, students can listen to them to get each chapter's "big ideas" by downloading these segments from the text's Resource Center web site.

- **How can I use this feature?** You may use this feature however you wish: by asking students to listen to the podcasts immediately after class, for example, while ideas are fresh, as they prepare for quizzes, or before reading the chapter so they know what to watch for. The options are limitless. While aural learners may be most benefited by this feature, all students can use them to reinforce their learning since they are chapter content summaries.

 Challenge Yourself Online Quizzes

- **Why should I use this feature?** Simply put, preparing for quizzes enhances learning and helps assure that students are doing assigned reading. However, Challenge Yourself Quizzes are different from most. Students can select from among three levels of challenge. Questions are graduated by cognitive complexity (Bloom's Taxonomy): Level 1 deals with *knowledge* and *comprehension*, Level 2 with *application* and *analysis*, and Level 3 with *synthesis* and *evaluation*. (While the model has been used as a guide, individual questions do not always adhere strictly, and some questions obviously cross categories.) First-year seminar courses teach self-direction and self-advocacy, and the lesson here is that students should adjust the level of challenge to their own mastery skills, but that they should always continue to keep themselves motivated to rise above it.

- **How can I use this feature?** You may use this feature as you see fit, depending on the academic skills of your students. If your students don't read particularly well or you are working with probationary students, for example, you may start by asking students to respond to Level 1 questions (and perhaps report their scores to you via e-mail), but also indicate that the point of Challenge Yourself Quizzes is just that—to challenge yourself. Eventually, they should move beyond their comfort zones and try more challenging questions.

Team Career Exercises

- **Why should I use this feature?** Employers are unanimous about the fact that many of today's students graduate with technical expertise in their disciplines, but they are less adept at using "soft skills," like communication, collaboration, and teamwork. Available at the Resource Center web site, *FOCUS* Team Career Exercises are creative applications of chapter material that are to be done in small groups or pairs, typically outside of class. The side benefit of the actual content learned about the workplace and careers, of course, is that students will need to work together to accomplish them. In each chapter, Team Career Exercises are referenced immediately after the "Create a Career Outlook" box.

- **How can I use this feature?** Assign these activities as homework and debrief in class or have students choose, for example, three Team Career Exercises to do with an ongoing group over the term and keep a learning log about their experiences.

When Moms and Dads Go to School (book for non-traditional students' children)

- **Why should I use this feature?** As a working woman who went back to school for both a master's degree and Ph.D. with two young children at home, I am particularly sensitive to the needs of non-traditional students. The challenges of raising a family while juggling academic courses and a job are overwhelming at times. *When Moms and Dads Go to School* is a picture book for children that explains the ups and downs of life as an adult student and parent. I have tested it with five-year olds, and they grasped the concepts very well.

- **How can I use this feature?** Students who are interested may download the book from the *FOCUS* Resource Center web site or read it to their children on screen.

 Orientation Materials

- **Why should I use this feature?** Many institutions struggle with organizing orientation programs for incoming first-year students and their families. How do we make sure our institution is well represented? How can we make certain students are engaged? Is too much information being presented, or too little, or the *right* information? What should be done about overly assertive parents? One suggestion, which appears in more detail on the *FOCUS* Resource Center web site in a downloadable pamphlet on orientation programs, is to conduct student and parent orientation sessions by grouping them by particular topic choices and using color PDFs of *FOCUS* Challenge Cases to generate discussion (students and money management, Chapter 3; students and wellness, Chapter 13, etc.).

- **How can I use this feature?** When families sign up for orientation dates, ask them to register for particular mini-courses of interest (based on *FOCUS* chapters). You may wish to divide student and parent groups so that discussions can be directed more easily and train faculty and staff to facilitate these discussions.

Common Reading Accompaniment or Chapter 1 of *FOCUS* as Stand-Alone Summer Reading

- **Why should I use this feature?** Many schools send a book or reader to incoming first-year students over the summer to serve as an initial common academic exercise. If a book is selected, the author of the book is sometimes invited to speak at an opening convocation ceremony. Although there are many ways to conduct a summer reading program, and even if your institution doesn't have one, consider sending a color PDF of the first chapter of *FOCUS* to each incoming student, along with a welcome letter or book before school starts. (Contact your Wadsworth sales representative for details.) You may also wish to include a copy of the *FOCUS* Entrance Interview to collect data about students' initial expectations of college. Ask students to fill in these materials, mark up Chapter 1 with questions and comments, and bring them as completed assignments to their first class. Many institutions report that students complete initial reading assignments—their first college homework ever—with vigor and arrive at school ready to go.

- **How can I use this feature?** Encourage students to mark up the chapter, fill in the exercises and activities on the color PDF, and come to class prepared to discuss Gloria Gonzales and the chapter's content. Doing so is an excellent way to launch the *FOCUS* experience and assure that students are engaged from day one.

DESIGNING A SYLLABUS WITH *FOCUS*

By Constance Staley

"The syllabus—what students eagerly await on the first day; a record of the class; one of the only artifacts to remain after the students move on. Your syllabus represents both an end and a beginning—a final product of your course planning and a valuable way to introduce yourself and the course to your students… Research indicates that outstanding instruction and a detailed syllabus are directly related."[1]

What should a syllabus include?

Here's a checklist to consider:

Basic Information
__ course title/number/section, days and times taught, location of class
__ semester and year course is being taught
__ your name and office number, office location, e-mail, phone number
__ office hours
__ web site address or group e-mail addresses

Course or Section Description
__ goals/objectives/value of the course

Course or Section Texts/Materials
__ text: title, author, edition
__ where texts can be bought
__ other necessary equipment or materials (e.g., sticky notes or dots)

Course Schedule/Weekly Calendar
__ dates of all assignments and exams
__ dates when readings are due
__ holidays and special events (e.g., field trips, guest speakers)

Course or Section Policies
__ attendance/tardiness
__ class participation (if you choose to assign points)
__ late/missing assignments
__ academic dishonesty
__ explicit grading criteria
__ expectations/grading standards
__ accommodation for missed quizzes, etc.

---

[1] [Sinor and Kaplan, Center for Research on Learning and Teaching. Available at http://www.crlt.umich.edu/gsis/P2_1.html]

Other Handouts or Information Relevant to Your First-Year Seminar Course
__ availability of outside help (e.g., tutoring services, language labs, Writing Center)
__ unique class policies
__ a short bio about you
__ a written introduction or worksheet for the icebreaker
__ questions to answer so that you can announce the class profile the following week: "In this section, we have three athletes, one biology major, four musicians…"
__ color, art, symbols, a version of the syllabus cut up as a puzzle—be creative!
__ Entrance Interview from *FOCUS* for students to return to you

Credit Hour Variations and *FOCUS*

If your first-year seminar course is a three-hour course, you can capitalize on many of the *FOCUS* features. Because each chapter is rich, decide what has the most value for your students, and you'll be able to maximize all *FOCUS* has to offer and tailor the learning experience to your particular class. If your course is a one or two-hour course, consider these options:

- Use a custom edition of the book, eliminating chapters you have not covered traditionally, such as "Speaking and Writing" or "Working Toward Wellness."

- Use the entire book, but selectively, in this manner: determine six essential chapters, and then allow your students to vote as a group on two more chapters to cover as course material. Giving students a voice can be important. (Or take a look at the results of question 16 on your students' Entrance Interviews, which asks them about their interest in each chapter of the text.) Students who wish to read more may elect to. (For example, when I have tried this in a one-credit course, some students have said things like this: "I'd like to read the relationships chapter on my own, even though the class has not selected it, because I'm having trouble with a relationship right now. Is that OK?")

- Divide the class up into six groups based on *FOCUS* features, for example:
    a) Challenge→Reaction boxes
    b) Insight→Action boxes
    c) C Factor: "Cultivate Your Curiosity"
    d) C Factor: "Create a Career Outlook"
    e) C Factor: "Control Your Learning,"
    f) MBTI feature: "Your Type Is Showing."
  Make these "permanent" groups throughout the course, if you wish, with several groups reporting each week on these features.

- Divide the class by VARK learning style preference groups, and since the largest proportion of students, statistically, is likely to be multimodal, group them by their highest VARK score, even if it is only slightly higher. Get students involved in "VARKing" the course by presenting material in their group's learning modality.

- Omit several chapters, formally, but ask student groups to present highlights of these chapters in class. For example, if you omit chapters 3, 10, 11, and 13, divide the class into four groups, and designate one week on the syllabus for group presentations on these chapters. You may be amazed by what students come up with!

- Put selected portions of the course online. *FOCUS* materials will be available for use with Blackboard or other Cengage courseware options.

- Bypass a few features, based on the characteristics of your group and your own preferences. For example, if you have used the MBTI in the past and consider yourself well versed in it, have your students do the SuccessTypes Learning Style Type Indicator (or the full MBTI) and cover all the "Your Type Is Showing" boxes, and as a trade-off, elect not to cover something else. Few instructors cover every single option exactly as presented in every single textbook they use. Instead they tailor course materials to their own strengths and interests. That is always an instructor's prerogative, and I encourage you to adapt *FOCUS* materials to your needs and those of your students.

A sample syllabus for a 16 week semester follows. (Note that the syllabus is designed to keep students focused—before, in, and after class!) For a trimester or quarter-based course, a course with fewer contact hours, or a course for at-risk, developmental, or probationary students, for example, omit the "After Class" assignments or consider the suggestions above.

Sample Syllabus (16 week semester, maximum challenge level)

Course: College Success 101

1

BEFORE CLASS
<u>Read</u> Chapter 1: Building Dreams, Setting Goals
<u>Watch</u> Inside the *FOCUS* Studio, Episode 1
<u>Complete</u> Exercise 1.2 (The Ideal Student) and bring your results to class.

IN CLASS
<u>Complete</u> Exercise 1.1 as a group and discuss chapter highlights.

AFTER CLASS
<u>Complete</u> Exercise 1.3 (Your Academic Autobiography) and submit your essay as an e-mail attachment
<u>Listen</u> to the iAudio file for Chapter 1.

2

BEFORE CLASS
<u>Read</u> Chapter 2: Learning about Learning
<u>Complete</u> Exercise 2.1 (VARK Learning Styles Assessment) and bring your results to class.

IN CLASS
<u>Complete</u> Exercise 2.2 (SuccessTypes Learning Style Type Indicator) and discuss chapter highlights.

AFTER CLASS
<u>Complete</u> Exercise 2.3 (VARK Activity)
<u>Listen</u> to the iAudio file for Chapter 2.

3

BEFORE CLASS
<u>Read</u> Chapter 3: Making Use of Resources: Finances, Technology, and Campus Support
<u>Complete</u> Exercises 3.2 (Your Monthly Budget) and 3.3 (Create a Spending Log) and bring your results to class.

IN CLASS
<u>Complete</u> Exercise 3.1 (*Picture* Success) with your teammates and post your results online. Discuss chapter highlights in the remaining time.

AFTER CLASS
<u>Complete</u> Exercise 3.4 (Group Ad) with your teammates. (Hint: Use some of the images you gathered for Exercise 3.1.) Your ad will be aired during the next class session.
<u>Listen</u> to the iAudio file for Chapter 3.

4

BEFORE CLASS
Read Chapter 4: Managing Your Time and Energy
Complete Exercise 4.1 (Term on a Page) and bring your results to class.

IN CLASS
Complete Exercise 4.2 (So Much to Do—So Little Time) and discuss chapter highlights.

AFTER CLASS
Complete Control Your Learning: Your Toughest Class
Listen to the iAudio file for Chapter 4.

5

BEFORE CLASS
Read Chapter 5: Thinking Critically and Creatively
Complete Exercise 5.1 and bring your results to class.

IN CLASS
Complete Exercise 5.3 (Rocky Mountain State University Case Study and Simulation). Discuss chapter highlights in the remaining time.

AFTER CLASS
Complete Exercises 5.4 (Decision Style Inventory) and 5.5 (Creative Potential Profile) and email your results.
Listen to the iAudio file for Chapter 5.

6

BEFORE CLASS
Read Chapter 6: Engaging, Listening, and Note-Taking in Class
Complete Exercise 6.2 (How Well Do You Listen?) and bring your results to class.

IN CLASS
Complete Exercise 6.1 (One-Way versus Two-Way Listening) and discuss chapter highlights.

AFTER CLASS
Complete Exercise 6.3 (Note-Taking 4-M) and e-mail your results.
Listen to the iAudio file for Chapter 6.

7

BEFORE CLASS
Read Chapter 7: Developing Your Memory
Watch Inside the *FOCUS* Studio, Episode 2
Complete Exercise 7.1 and bring your results to class.

IN CLASS
Midterm Quiz - Use your iAudio chapter summaries to study! Discuss chapter highlights.

AFTER CLASS
Complete Exercise 7.2 (VARK Activity)
Listen to the iAudio file for Chapter 7.

CLASS FIELD TRIP WEEK

8 **BEFORE CLASS**
Read Chapter 8: Reading and Studying
Complete Exercise 8.1 (What Is Your Reading Rate?) and e-mail your results before class.

IN CLASS
Complete Exercises 8.2 (A Press Conference with the Author) and 8.3 (Marginal Notes)

AFTER CLASS
Complete Exercise 8.4 (You Are What You Read!) and e-mail your response.
Listen to the iAudio file for Chapter 8.

9  **BEFORE CLASS**
Read Chapter 9: Test Taking
Complete the "Your Type Is Showing" activity on page 269 and bring your results to class.

IN CLASS
Discuss chapter highlights.

AFTER CLASS
Complete Control Your Learning: Your Toughest Class
Listen to the iAudio file for Chapter 9.

10 **BEFORE CLASS**
Read Chapter 10: Writing and Speaking
Complete Exercise 10.1 (Dearly Departed) and bring your written example to class.

IN CLASS
Complete Exercise 10.2 and discuss chapter highlights.

AFTER CLASS
Complete Exercise 10.3 (VARK Activity)
Listen to the iAudio file for Chapter 10.

11  **BEFORE CLASS**
<u>Read</u> Chapter 11: Managing Relationships, Valuing Diversity
<u>Watch</u> Inside the *FOCUS* Studio, Episode 3
<u>Complete</u> Exercise 11.1 (What's Your Conflict Style?) and bring your results to class.

IN CLASS
<u>Complete</u> Exercises 11.2 (What's the Difference?) and 11.3 (Circles of Awareness) and discuss chapter highlights.

AFTER CLASS
<u>Complete</u> Activity 11.4 (VARK Activity)
<u>Listen</u> to the iAudio file for Chapter 11.

12 **BEFORE CLASS**
<u>Read</u> Chapter 12: Choosing a College Major and a Career
<u>Watch</u> Inside the *FOCUS* Studio, Episode 4

IN CLASS
<u>Complete</u> Exercise 12.1 (Think Tank) and discuss chapter highlights.

AFTER CLASS
<u>Complete</u> Exercise 12.3 (Get a Job!) with your assigned teammates and e-mail your results.
<u>Listen</u> to the iAudio file for Chapter 12.

13 **BEFORE CLASS**
<u>Read</u> Chapter 13: Working toward Wellness
<u>Watch</u> Inside the *FOCUS* Studio, Episode 5
<u>Complete</u> Exercise 13.1 (Wellness Survey) and bring your results to class.

IN CLASS
<u>Complete</u> Exercises 13.4 ("How Do I Love Thee?") and 13.5 (Which Dinner Would You Order?) and discuss chapter highlights.

AFTER CLASS
<u>Complete</u> Exercise 13.3 (Workplace Stress Survey) and e-mail your results.
<u>Listen</u> to the iAudio file for Chapter 13.

SERVICE-LEARNING (OR RESEARCH, ETC.) STUDENT PRESENTATIONS

FINAL QUIZ, COURSE CRITIQUES, PIZZA, AND GOODBYES

(Add items from syllabus checklist above.)

FOCUS ON COLLEGE SUCCESS

CHAPTER RESOURCES

By Catherine Andersen

CHAPTER 1: BUILDING DREAMS, SETTING GOALS

1. Why is this chapter important?

This chapter sets the foundation for student learning: self-understanding. The desire to learn more about what makes us tick is a fundamental human trait, and students are no exception. But often students lack self-insight and are not always realistic about the personal and academic investment required to get a college degree. In a recent Noel-Levitz study (National Freshman Attitude Study, 2007) of the attitudes of nearly 100,000 entering college students, 95% of these students had a strong desire to complete their education, with almost 75% indicating they would welcome help in developing their test-taking skills, 66% wanting career guidance, and 48% indicating they would like help in math. But, these same students often don't access the support services provided on campus or approach their teachers for needed help. Nationally, only a little more than half of students who enter college finish.

As instructors, we must help students learn more about themselves, so that they can reach their reported goal: attaining a college degree. Follow students' interests and get them thinking about who they are, about their attitudes, values, and behaviors, and help them make connections between these things and college success. Sometimes we assume "they get it"—that is, they understand college success skills conceptually. But understanding and acting on that knowledge are two different things. Remember that most of the students who enter college want to succeed. We have to help them to understand themselves, and turn their desires into real behaviors that propel them toward the finish line.

This first chapter of *FOCUS* launches a series of self-assessments and reflection tools, all aimed at helping students better understand themselves. Using the recurring 4 C-Factors of intrinsic motivation that appear throughout the book will help students focus on what motivates them and why, distinguish the difference between dreaming about something and taking the steps needed to actually achieve their goals. They will learn that *insight* is not enough, but that they have to take *action* to achieve positive change. For some students, even the eventual realization that their dream may not be realistic can be a positive learning outcome in the long run. Without first understanding the "self," students cannot move on. Thus, this chapter is critical for establishing the framework for the rest of the course/text. For many students this chapter provides the "aha" moment that initiates an action-oriented first term.

2. What are this chapter's learning objectives?

> ➤ How this book will help students learn
> ➤ What motivates students
> ➤ How students' attitudes can sabotage them
> ➤ How beliefs about students' intelligence can affect college success
> ➤ What separates *performers* and *learners*

- ➢ What core values say about us
- ➢ Why students should distinguish between dreams and goals
- ➢ How students can develop goals that work
- ➢ What it takes to succeed in college

3. How should I launch this chapter?

One great way to start the semester is to mail a copy of the entrance interview and a color PDF of Chapter 1 from *FOCUS on College Success* with your welcome letter to students or your institution's common reading selection over the summer. (Color PDFs can be ordered from Wadsworth. See your sales representative for details.) Students can mark up the chapter, familiarize themselves with the book's format, and arrive at your first class ready to go! And you will get their true initial responses about what they expect college to be like on the Entrance Interview—before they've even started classes. You may even consider using color PDFs at orientation sessions to break up students and parents into discussion topics (Financial Management: Chapter 3), (Motivation: Chapter 1), (Wellness: Chapter 13), etc.

Regardless of whether or not you follow that suggestion, it's important to think about what you'll do on the first day of class. Most instructors are somewhat nervous—as are students! Perhaps it's your first time teaching this course, or you may be a seasoned instructor determined to challenge yourself to do something a little different this year. Your students may be unusually quiet since they don't know you or the other students. Like Gloria Gonzales in the Chapter 1 *FOCUS* Challenge Case, they may not think they need this course, or believe they are not going to get useful information from it. If so, you clearly face a challenge, but there is plenty of evidence that suggests that student success courses like yours make a difference in students' persistence toward attaining a degree and in their overall success in college. *FOCUS* was designed as a multifaceted, multi-modality learning experience to try to engage *all* students through podcasts, mock television shows, exercises, self-assessments, discussion prompts, reflective tools, and, of course, the written word.

Here are some pointers about how to get you and your class comfortable, engaged, and connected. In this first chapter, as in all chapters, you will focus on getting students to understand the chapter's content, and more importantly, to apply it, not only in this course, but in all of their classes. By completing the exercises, reflecting on their responses, and sharing with others, students will gain insight into themselves. Once *insight* is gained, the challenge will be to help students take *action*. Action can be in the form of a verbal or written commitment to do something to change their behavior for the good—and then to do it and report back on the results.

Here are some tips to begin with:

- **Familiarize yourself with the entire book.** Also, read ahead to Chapter 11 on Emotional Intelligence (EI). While students will not learn about this until Chapter 11, as an instructor, you will learn that EI is the foundation for student change. And regular EI research annotations in the instructor's edition will clarify the ties between emotional intelligence and college success.

- **Don't allow students to skip the Readiness Check at the beginning of each chapter**. This activity will help students focus on whether they are ready to read and learn. Students using trial versions of *FOCUS* reported that Readiness Checks become a habit, one that they also perform, not just before they begin to read, but also mentally before class begins. This habit also extends to their other courses, which is one of the activity's intentional goals. The chapters end with a Reality Check that compares students' expectations at the beginning of the chapter with the actual experience of reading and responding to the material. The potential contrast helps students develop a more realistic approach to learning.

- **Make sure students are comfortable with you and with each other** by using Exercise 1.1 "We'd like to get to know you," or some similar activity.

- **Make an e-mail distribution list for the class,** including your e-mail, so that students have ways of contacting you and each other. Let students know how and when they can see or contact you. To help students learn your e-mail address, you might require them to send you an e-mail describing the most interesting thing they learned about someone or something in the first class session. You can begin the next class with a summary of what students sent you. Consider holding your normal office hours in places other than your office: the student cafeteria, campus coffee shop, or library, for example. If you're willing to interact via Facebook or MySpace, accept instant messages, text messages, or engage in online chats, let them know that as well.

- **Engage in the activities yourself.** If you elect to do the "We'd like to get to know you activity,"** presented on page 6 of this chapter in class, join in. When students see you participating, they become more motivated to participate themselves and see you as a student-centered teacher.

- **Help students find peer support.** For example, in "We'd like to get to know you," in addition to having students simply introduce themselves or a classmate based on information they learn about each other, students can find someone who has the exact or similar answer to one of their questions. This "mate" can become the person they introduce to the class (if they introduce each other, rather than introducing themselves). A discussion could follow about commonalities (and differences) among class members. Knowing that they're "not alone" is very reassuring to new students.

- **Have students take one of the self-assessments from the chapter, and take the self-assessment yourself and tell the students your scores**. As much as they want to know about themselves, they also want to know about you. Discuss your scores as a group, and how all these scores will affect your work together throughout the course. Making abstract ideas more personal gets students more involved.

4. How should I use the *FOCUS* Challenge Case?

Each chapter begins with a *FOCUS* Challenge Case about a real student (or a composite of several students) that depicts a challenging situation college students often face. The *FOCUS* Challenge Case is an integral part of the chapter and an excellent way to begin discussing the chapter's content. Typically, students can pinpoint another student's mistakes and from there begin to consider and compare their own experiences. Case studies are a non-threatening way to apply each chapter's content.

In Chapter 1, we meet Gloria Gonzales, a student who dream of becoming a famous fashion designer. She enters her first class, thinking she knows everything she needs to know. School is not a top priority, and she is a first generation college student. Even though her family thought Gloria's older sister was the "smart one," she dropped out of college and is now out in the workforce earning money. Gloria plans to work about 35 hours a week while in school (a potential risk factor) at the store in the mall, where she is a really successful sales person (not necessarily a skill indicative of potential talent as a fashion designer). Everyone said college was the "right thing to do," so she enrolled without much forethought or planning. Her parents want her to become an engineer who will have a secure career, but Gloria has other ideas about her future.

You can use this *FOCUS* Challenge Case to discuss some of the issues Gloria faces. You may not know it yet, but there may be several students in your class who share some of Gloria's issues. Case studies are ways that students can "detach" and discuss, listen to other student's views of the issues, and identify with parts of the story.

Use the Gloria Gonzalez story to get students to begin opening up and refer back to Gloria whenever you can. Ask students which of Gloria's qualities they see in themselves. Have them answer the "What Do *You* Think?" questions and pair up to discuss their responses, or ask students to work through the questions in small groups. Encourage students to debate their opinions within the group. Consider using the Continuum Activity (described later here) to get them out of their chairs and place themselves along an imaginary continuum to check their responses against those of other students.

Show the Chapter 1 "Inside the *FOCUS* Studio" episode in class. In addition to reading the *FOCUS* Challenge Case, show the Chapter 1 mock television show (available on the Online Resource Center). These talk shows are based on the Emmy-Award winning Bravo series, "Inside the Actor's Studio," and the first episode stars Debbie, who plays Gloria Gonzales in the book. The "Inside the *FOCUS* Studio" shows include brief comedy sketches, based on the chapter's content, and cover the chapter material in substantial depth, using a kinesthetic learning modality. Since many or even most of today's learners are kinesthetic, they will likely respond favorably to this format.

5. What important features does this chapter include?

Readiness and Reality Checks

At the beginning of the chapter, students complete a Readiness Check and at the end, they complete a Reality Check. It is important to help students compare their expectations with their actual experience. Often students succumb to an "optimistic bias" and hope that something won't take as much time and effort as it actually will. "Reality Testing" is a critical aspect of Emotional Intelligence. A writing assignment or class discussion can be used to share students' pre and post chapter results.

Challenge → Reaction → Insight → Action prompts

Throughout the book students will be reminded about the learning system used in every *FOCUS* chapter: The Challenge → Reaction → Insight → Action system. Keep reminding students about this learning "chain reaction." Students need to understand that learning is different for each individual because it is based on what someone already knows about a subject.

Discuss the Challenge → Reaction prompts in helping students assess what they already know, and if they don't know much about the topic coming up, that's understandable. That's why students are in college! If they know a great deal about what's coming, they're in a good position to learn even more. Remind students that Challenge → Reaction prompts shouldn't be skipped. (If they are reluctant to write in their books, suggest they use sticky notes.) And C → R prompts not meant to intimidate students who don't know the answers. Often there isn't a single correct answer, but several possible ones. They are truly challenges (and it can be fun to think of them as a contest with yourself!) to see how much they already know and how much they can learn. C → Rs demonstrate that learning is taking place.

Use Insight → Action prompts as you think best: as discussion generators, as threaded discussion questions for the entire class, or as written or e-mailed journal assignments. Based on the reading level skills of your group and your course objectives, require students to complete all the Insight → Action questions or choose one or two. This system is repeated throughout the text and students will continue cycling back to the first step as they encounter new challenges. Whenever appropriate connect students' discussion to this model.

Self-Assessments

Another important and really valuable feature of the text are the variety, range, and immediate applicability of self-assessments. The AIMS assessment in this chapter sets up the book's C-Factors. Other activities—for example, "Your Academic Autobiography"—are great self-assessments. Take some time for students to share their stories with others. Often, students don't realize that others are in the same situation and finding commonalities can help your group bond.

C-Factors

Each chapter of *FOCUS* contains features related to the four aspects of intrinsic motivation: curiosity ("Cultivate Your Curiosity"), control ("Control Your Learning"), career outlook ("*FOCUS* on Careers" and "Create a Career Outlook"), and challenge ("Challenge Yourself Online Quizzes"). These built-in features are intended to increase students' intrinsic motivation. Use them well!

FOCUS on Careers

This feature highlights a career related to the chapter's content. If students become really "hooked" on the information presented in the chapter, they can begin thinking about particular careers that may be possible fits for them. In this chapter, we meet psychologist Erik Sween, who helps clients build dreams and set goals.

6. Which in-text exercises should I use?

Three exercises are built into this chapter. Here are descriptions of why the exercises have been included, how much time each one will probably take, and how you might debrief them.

EXERCISE 1.1 WE'D LIKE TO GET TO KNOW YOU

Why do this activity?
This activity helps to create a classroom climate where students know each other, feel comfortable and included, and become willing to get involved.

What are the challenges and what can you expect?
This is a relatively easy activity and students enjoy getting out of their seats and interacting. Students should fill out the exercise and then it can become the basis for classroom introductions.

How much time will it take?
It should take between 20-25 minutes and the only materials needed are the students' textbooks.

How should I debrief?
It's a good idea to ask students the following question when they are done: did anything they learn surprise them? For example, someone might say that they were surprised to learn that "X" was working full time. Or that "Y" was a retuning student, or that "Z" was commuting from a distance. If no one volunteers, be sure that you include something that surprised you. Conclude by talking about why it's important to build a community of learners at the start of the term.

EXERCISE 1.2 THE IDEAL STUDENT

Why do this activity?
This activity helps students identify behaviors that lead to student success and then commit to them. You can also use this activity with students to identify the learning outcomes that you want them to have for this course (as well as what *they* want to learn in the course) and can serve as the "contract" they have with you. Throughout the course, especially at mid-term, remind students of the contract they created and ask them whether or not they are meeting their goals and if not, why.

What are the challenges and what can you expect?

It's important that this first "homework" assignment be turned in, showing students that you expect them to do assignments and that you will hold them accountable. Students quickly pick up on the classroom climate, and if they are assigned an activity that does not have an accountability component, they may conclude that some assignments in the course can be written off as "busywork."

How much time will it take?

It should take between 20-25 minutes and the only materials needed are the students' textbooks (or you may simply read or e-mail the assignment to them).

How should I debrief?

Ask individual students to share their lists, and then make a master list as a class. Ask students to copy down the master list and put their initials next to each item they will promise to try to do during the term. Complete the activity by having them create a similar list for "The Ideal Teacher" (you!) and sign the items you will promise to try to do. Many of the behaviors students identify will be related to self-regulation and emotional intelligence (described in more detail in the Chapters 8 (Reading and Studying) and 11 (Building Relationships, Valuing Diversity).

EXERCISE 1.3 YOUR ACADEMIC AUTOBIOGRAPHY

Why do this activity?

This activity is designed to help students reflect upon their educational experiences, to help them identify themes in their academic life that have made them the student they are, and to help them think about how these behaviors might help or hinder them in college. The assignment also gives you an initial, baseline assessment of students' writing skills and alerts you to any non-cognitive variables that might interfere with students' learning.

What are the challenges and what can I expect?

Students enjoy looking back to early reading and writing experiences. Often, they have not thought about this for a long time. Encourage students to look for themes that describe them as learners: some kind of reoccurring behavior, such as loving to read, struggling to sit still, or succeeding based on their connection with particular teachers, and how these factors might influence their work in college. Ask students to include specific times and places in their examples, such as primary school, middle school, and high school, or particular subjects. Be sure that students don't simply submit a string of facts, but that they do some interpretation and speculation about how particular events affected them.

How much time will it take?

This is a homework assignment that should take students about an hour.

How should I debrief?

Students really benefit from hearing how other students responded to this activity and often can identify with each other. Students might be assigned to read another student's paper and report to the group two significant facts that seemed to have shaped the way the student learned. Or if students write about sensitive issues—difficult home situations, for example—you may wish to keep their papers confidential.

7. Which additional exercises might enrich students' learning?

<u>Getting to Know You</u>
Class activity
Materials needed: flip-chart paper, markers, masking tape
Time: 30-50 minutes
Goal: To help students to get to know each other and create a comfortable classroom environment
Students circulate around the room and write on sheets of posted flip chart paper with the same headings as in Exercise 1.1. For example, one sheet of paper would have the heading "I'm happiest when…" and students would add their responses to that paper. Then you may post individual students beside each list and read it to the entire class after everyone has had a chance to post all their responses.

<u>Think/Pair/Share</u>
Class activity
Materials needed: none
Time: 10-20 minutes
Goal: To get students discussing, involved, and engaged with the course material
Sometimes it's difficult to get a discussion going in class. This think/pair/share activity provides a mechanism for all students to get involved and can be used for any topic.
- **Think** individually about why the information is important, how it connects to student success, and why it was included in the text. You may wish to have them jot down their ideas. (3-5 minutes)
- **Pair** up with the student next to them and discuss their responses. The pair will then decide on one or two issues to bring up to the group (3-5 minutes).
- **Share** with the class their responses, and as a group the class will discuss some common themes. (5-10 minutes).

<u>"Trading Places"</u> by Staley, C. (2003) originally based on "Trading Places" in Silberman, M. (1995).
Class activity
Materials needed: pad of sticky notes
Time: 10-20 minutes
Goal: To help students identify a positive quality, characteristic or experience that that they have that Gloria may or may not have
Ask students to write a positive characteristic or descriptive word about themselves on a sticky note and put it on the front of their shirt. Next, students are to walk around the room "hawking" their characteristics, and trading with others to gain something that they may not have. At the conclusion of the activity, have students discuss why they chose particular attributes, or traded them, and whether or not Gloria appears to display these. Discuss the impact of these attributes on college success.

Focus Learning System
Class Activity (or an out-of-class assignment where students work in groups)
Material needed: Old magazines, tape, markers, and flip charts
Time: 20-30 minutes
Goal: To help students understand the Challenge → Reaction → Insight → Action System
In groups, have students describe some challenge that they may encounter during college. Using photos from magazines, ask students to select faces of individuals that represent how they identify a *challenge*, another photo of a facial expression that represents their *reaction*, one that represents *insight*, and the final photo representing *action*. Using only these four photos as prompts, the groups share their challenge and subsequent responses and behaviors with the class.

"The Human Continuum" (based on Staley, C. (2003))
In-class activity
Materials needed: none
Time: 10-20 minutes
Goal: To help students place themselves on a continuum to predict their AIMS score
The following is an activity that asks students to predict their AIMS scores. However, the continuum is an activity to have students quickly respond to most any prompt related to course material.

- Identify one side of the room as one pole (High AIMS scores - 100-125) and the other side as the opposite pole (low AIMS scores –below 75) with the remaining scores in the middle.
- Ask group members to take a position that they believe will most likely represent their score.
- Ask each member individually to explain why he or she will probably score as predicted.
- Then ask students to fill out the instrument. They may be surprised because they believe themselves to be more intrinsically motivated than revealed by the instrument. Remember that actual scores on the instrument may get at sensitive issues. Having students report out is probably not a good idea, but this activity can be illuminating.
- Remind students that having a high level of intrinsic motivation is not necessarily a guarantee that they will be successful. They must translate their motivation into action.

8. What other activities can I incorporate to make the chapter my own?

In many ways, *FOCUS* teaches itself. It contains built-in activities, discussion and reflection tools, and a variety of features to motivate and engage students. Beyond what appears in the student edition, the instructor's version of the text is annotated. The annotations in each chapter provide helpful background information for you and contain a variety of suggestions for five ways to enrich the chapter. Separating the annotations into five categories helps save you time because you can scan for what you need as an instructor:

1) **Teachable Moments** (places to capitalize on a particular learning opportunity)
2) **Activity Options** (additional exercises to introduce or emphasize content)
3) **Sensitive Situations** (alerts signaling relevant in-class discussion topics that may generate possible controversy, embarrassment, or discomfort among certain students)

4) **Emotional Intelligence (EI) Research** (research on EI that reinforces a tie between an emerging vital research area and college success)
5) **Chapter Crossover** (places to look ahead or look back at related content in other chapters to reinforce learning)

If you are familiar with additional research about teaching and learning, capitalize on what you know in addition to what appears in this Instructor's Resource Manual. For example, research indicates that instructors have a short window of time to actively engage students in learning. If students are not engaged early on, it may be impossible to reverse the situation. The more engaged students are, the more likely they will be to remember and apply what they learn.

Included here, all in one place, are Activity Options taken from the Annotated Instructor's Edition. Reflection, discussion, and writing or presentation opportunities are ways in which students can become active learners.

ACTIVITY OPTION (p. 5): As they read *FOCUS*, students will get to know Gloria Gonzales and all the other *FOCUS* Challenge Case students who appear in photos throughout the book as they navigate their way through college. Take some time early on for your students to get to know each other. Later in the chapter, there will be an activity to incorporate, but early on it's important to set the tone in class. A simple get acquainted activity is for students to write something on an index card or piece of paper that includes their name, where they are from, possible major, and a unique fact about themselves. Collect the index cards, and redistribute them. Have students read the card they received and try and guess which person in the class is described on the card.

ACTIVITY OPTION (p. 5): Hand students cards that state something that might cause a student to lose focus in school. Cards may include items such as these: your roommate blasts the DVD all day, your grandmother is ill, your books cost more money than you expected, your babysitter's last day is Friday, and so forth. Depending on the size and composition of the class, make as many cards as you need. Ask students to hold up cards that cause students to lose focus, but situations they can change and refocus. Ask them how the hypothetical student can re-focus. Sometimes students will say that they cannot change a situation, but with foresight and planning, they actually could.

ACTIVITY OPTION (p. 6): Be sure that you do this Exercise 1.1 along with your students. Remember, they want to get to know you too. Pair up students and have them share their information with a partner. Have the partner introduce the student to the class and report on two or three items (from the activity above) that were really interesting about the student they just met. Another activity, similar to Activity Option on p. 5, is called "You Would Never Guess." Ask students to write something on an index card that no one would guess about them (non-embarrassing items that are appropriate). For example, a student might write on a card "I am one of nine children," "I played Annie in our high school play." Collect the cards and read them aloud. Have students guess who it might be.

ACTIVITY OPTION (p. 8): This activity has been adapted using Staley's (2003) "Spending Time." This activity can help students see the cost of missing class. Have students add up the cost of their tuition, room, board, books, (any expense related to school) divided by the number of hours they are in school (number of weeks times the number of hours they are supposed to be in class). Have students calculate the cost of missing a single class.

ACTIVITY OPTION (p. 9): Have students respond to the following challenge: It's Friday, and a student has a ten-page paper due on Monday. His roommate has invited him home for the weekend and the student wants to go. What are the possible reactions, insights, and actions related to this situation?

ACTIVITY OPTION (p. 13): Give each student 10 sticky notes. Ask students to write one phrase on each paper to fill in the blank: Successful students _____. Repeat this prompt ten times, each time giving the students only seconds to fill in the blank. On the board, write "student has control" on one side and "Student has no control" on the other. Have students put their sticky notes under the heading they believe is true of their statement. Some students believe that they have no control on issues that they really do. Let students lead the discussion

ACTIVITY OPTION (p. 15): Ask students to work in groups to decide what a student might do in this situation described by Daniel Goleman in his book *Emotional Intelligence: Why It Can Matter More Than IQ* (1994): Although you set yourself a goal of getting a B, when your first exam worth 30 percent of your final grade is returned, you received a D.

ACTIVITY OPTION (p. 16): Divide students up so that at least two students are assigned to each of the eight ways to adjust attitude. Ask students to describe a real-life example related to the numbered point they have been assigned.

ACTIVITY OPTION (p. 20): Ask students to call out loud the names of their most challenging courses. Make a list of the top five most challenging courses in the group. Ask for suggestions on how the C-Factors and intrinsic motivation apply. Have students share what they plan to do to be motivated in these challenge courses. Remind students that *plan* and *follow-through* are the key words. Success (all A's) doesn't just happen.

ACTIVITY OPTION (p. 22): Ask students to answer the following question: "If I could spend one day with someone who has died, who would it be?" Have students share their choice and explain why. This activity demonstrates what values really seem to be important to that individual. Suggest reading Mitch Albom's book *For One More Day* (2006).

ACTIVITY OPTION (p. 24): Put students in groups of three or four and assign each group two letters of the word *FOCUS*. Ask students to think of successful student behaviors that begin with the letters they are assigned. Ask them how these behaviors connect to goal-setting. As a class, make a banner to hang in the classroom with the word *FOCUS* with successful student attributes under each letter.

ACTIVITY OPTION (p. 24): Have students write a letter to themselves, their parents, loved ones, or a friend listing their goals for the semester and what they will do to meet them. Provide envelopes for students and seal their letters and return these to your students at the end of the term to see if they met their goals. Have them write a paragraph about why they did or did not meet their goals upon return of the envelopes.

9. What homework might I assign?

Generating Goals
Have your students create three goals for this semester that pass the *FOCUS* test: (1) **Fit** (2) **Ownership**; (3) **Concreteness**; (4) **Usefulness**; and (5) **Stretch**. Then, have them identify three obstacles that could prevent them from reaching their goals—and how they would work around these obstacles.

"A Letter for Later" by Staley, C. (2003).
Goal: To help students describe their own behavior, set goals, make predictions, and to see whether or not they met their goals and if not, why not. (Described briefly earlier.)
Have students write a letter to themselves answering some of the important questions in this chapter. Students are to describe who they are and what they want to become. They should describe what motivates them and their values, dreams, and goals. In addition, ask them to respond to the phrase "If it is to be, it is up to me," and how they might enact this phrase in all their classes during the term. Do they think they will make smart choices, set realistic goals, be able to monitor themselves, and create their own futures? If so, describe how, and if not, why. Students will place this letter in a sealed envelope and give it to you to return the envelope to the students at the end of the term. Responding to their original impressions could become the basis of their final class writing assignment.

Journal Entries
One: Have students write a one page journal entry, or send you an e-mail reflecting on the Readiness Check. You might prompt students by asking them to choose the three questions they responded to with the lowest numbers and how these questions relate to success in college. Ask students to explain if they have any control over their ability to improve their score on these items and to discuss why or why not.

Two: Have students write a one-page journal essay or send you an e-mail describing one situation in which they were extrinsically motivated and one in which they were intrinsically motivated and how they felt about each. Ask them to connect the different kinds of motivation to college success.

Three: Ask students to write a journal comparing their original response to the *FOCUS* Challenge Case about Gloria Gonzales, "What Do YOU Think?" with their final impression after reading the chapter to the "NOW What Do You Think?" section.

Four: Use the Insight → Action prompts as journal or blog assignments.

10. What have I learned in teaching this chapter that I will incorporate next time?

CHAPTER 2: LEARNING ABOUT LEARNING

1. Why is this chapter important?

Changing behavior requires that you first know become aware of what you are currently doing. As an instructor, do *you* know how you learn? Do *you* know what your personality type is and how that impacts your teaching? Information in Chapter 2 is vitally important to you, too. In this chapter, both you and your students should fill out *all* the assessments that appear for your own benefit, but you should pay particular attention to two primary instruments that will reappear as potential assignments (VARK Activities) or regular informational features ("Your Type Is Showing") in every chapter:

- The VARK, based on information input and processing—Visual, Auditory, Read/write, and Kinesthetic (sensory modalities)
- The Success Types Learning Style Type Indicator, an MBTI based instrument

After discovering their learning and personality style using these two instruments, students will have opportunities to reinforce their preferences and try different approaches in every chapter. VARK activities appear in each chapter of *FOCUS*, and by the end of the book, students will have been able to try twelve different approaches to their strongest preference so that they develop the skills to translate between the "language" used by their instructors and their own VARK learning preferences, a critical skill for college success. Since features related to these two instruments reappear throughout the book, this chapter is a strong foundation for the rest of the text.

As you will see in this chapter's *FOCUS* Challenge Case about Tammy Ko, students often encounter instructors and situations in which they will need to understand how they learn in order to study and prepare for exams appropriately. As instructors, we can't adapt to every single learning style in a class (although we can certainly try to reach them all by varying our assignments and teaching methods). Students must learn to assume responsibility for adaptation themselves.

This chapter is also important because in addition to learning about themselves, it gives students an opportunity to learn about learning and the brain and multiple intelligences. Students may find it fascinating to discover how they can create conditions that are optimal for learning, and "ah-ha" moments may happen when students realize that what works for one person may not work for another. And, above all, when they understand that they have the control over their learning, students are more confident that they can succeed. The response is transformed from "I can't learn because the teacher is boring" to "Okay, this isn't working; what can *I* do about it?"

Also, in this chapter students will begin to see the pattern of the text repeated from Chapter 1. The chapter begins with a *FOCUS* Challenge Case, then a Readiness Check, followed by a number of Challenge → Reaction → Insight → Action prompts and the recurring C-Factors—all parts of the infrastructure of the book. These C-Factors (challenge, control, curiosity, and career outlook) that appear throughout the book, will help students focus on what motivates them and why. As you and your students work through the text, it will be important to reference your students' AIMS score from Chapter 1. If a student has low to moderate intrinsic motivation, it is especially important to re-emphasize the C-Factors. Remind students that it's not enough to have the *insight*; they must take *action* to achieve positive change. So taken together (the 4C's and the Challenge → Reaction → Insight → Action prompts), these features will help students see that by understanding what makes them tick, and by doing something about it, they are much more likely to have positive learning outcomes in all their courses.

2. What are this chapter's learning objectives?

> ➤ How learning changes the brain
> ➤ How people are intelligent in different ways
> ➤ How students learns through their senses
> ➤ How an individual student's personality affects learning style
> ➤ How to become a more efficient and effective learner

3. How should I launch this chapter?

You're most likely past your first week or so of class. Congratulations! Remember that research shows that these first few weeks can make or break the way that students connect to you and to each other. According to one study, students make assessments about instructors within the first five minutes of the first class (in this study, even *before* the syllabus was distributed). Furthermore, their initial reactions held until the end of the term!

If you encourage IMs or text messages, are you receiving them from students? Are your students e-mailing you? Have students come to meet with you, one-on-one? If students have not responded to you or contacted you *and* they are not showing up for class, it's important to take action. Contact them directly by phone or e-mail, and if they don't respond, do some quick intervention. Be persistent! Check with their academic advisor to find out if they are attending other classes. If your institution has an "early alert" system for students, now would be a good time to sound the alarm. Remember: first-year students are "under construction," so go the extra mile! In addition to making sure that students are coming to class and are engaged, here are some things to think about for this chapter.

- **Make sure students know each other's names.** You probably already know everyone's name in the class, but students may not know each other. You can do a brief check by asking students to name a person in the room and something they remember about them. Chances are students remember at least something about everyone. By doing it this way, you don't put anyone on the spot by asking them to name everyone in the group. When a student names a person and says something about him or her, then it becomes that person's turn to name another. Do this until everyone is named. Make sure that you jump in and help out if it seems like a few people are left without anyone remembering their names. If you have a sense that someone might be left out, you should introduce those students—or start the activity yourself by naming a person that seems isolated from the other class members. If you have a large class, ask students to take out a sheet of paper, fold it long ways to make a "table tent," and write their name on it so that everyone learns everyone's name. Students are gratified and appreciative when others remember their names and details of their identities.

- **Control Your Learning: Your Top Ten List for Each Class.** This is a great activity to get students to zero in on the classes they are taking this semester. It's a reflective activity that asks students to describe their classes and compare them to the optimal conditions for learning that are listed in the text. Don't pass up this activity. It's a great way for students to apply what they are learning. It also might help them identify a class in which they have to make some changes or get extra help. This activity also works well as a topic for a one-on-one office visit with you.

- **Help students find support.** This might be the time and place to ask students if they need help. After the "Control Your Learning" activity, students might be a bit more aware of the realities of their college experience. Most college students need one kind of help or another at some point in college. Students who need help, but can seem to find the time or have the courage to take advantage of campus resources often become retention statistics. Preview the support services available on your campus (a topic covered in Chapter 3). They may have learned about them during orientation, but sometimes if you don't need information at the time, you don't pay close attention. Now is a time to share some information about where they can go for help. Also, see if there are common concerns in the class. Students find comfort in knowing they are not alone. Find out if there are students who are doing well in classes where others are not and connect them with each other for informal tutoring from which both "teacher" and "student" can benefit. Help students taking the same classes to form study groups. Academic and social integration are two key components of a successful college career.

- **Remember the Readiness Check at the beginning of the chapter and the Reality Check at the end**. These activities help students focus on whether they are ready to read and learn. Again, students piloting *FOCUS* reported that Readiness Checks become a habit, one that they also perform, not just before they begin to read, but also mentally before class begins. This habit also extends to their other courses, which is one of the activity's intentional goals. The chapters end with a Reality Check that compares students' expectations at the beginning of the chapter with the actual experience of reading.

- **Going beyond the book.** Check with your Career Center staff, or academic advising center to see if they are able to give students the full Myers-Briggs Type Indicator. This tool will give students a more in-depth look at their personality type. Also, encourage students to look online at the vast resources about their personality type. They can simply type in the four letters, ENFP, for example, and get a wealth of information about how they learn and interact and careers that might be appealing to them.

The VARK and the Success Types Learning Style Type Indicator are both available online (web sites are available in *FOCUS on College Success* in Chapter 2). Here are several web sites that can help interpret MBTI scores http://www.mbtitoday.org/typechars.html; www.typelogic.com; http://www.murraystate.edu/secsv/fye/m-b.htm

4. How should I use the *FOCUS* Challenge Case?

Just as in Chapter 1, the chapter begins with a *FOCUS* Challenge Case about a real student (or a composite of many students) that depicts a challenging situation college students often face.

In this chapter, we meet Tammy Ko, a student who was one of a high school class of seventeen students. At first glance you would think that Tammy has it all together. She was successful in high school, thinks she knows her intended career, takes an introductory course in Criminology (based on her career goals), and attends classes and studies. But, her instructor, Professor Caldwell, is not at all what she expected. She is frustrated, not doing well on tests, and questioning whether or not this is the career for her. It is guaranteed that this is a situation many of your students will face at least once in their college careers. By using this *FOCUS* Challenge Case, students will begin to see the connections between who they are as learners, and how this knowledge connects to their success in college.

Use Tammy's story to get students to begin opening up and refer back to Tammy whenever you can. Ask students if they think that Tammy will have challenges in college and what those challenges will be. As a part of a group discussion, ask students if they have encountered this situation in college. Most likely they have. It's important that this discussion does not become a course complaint session or an instructor-bashing one. What's really important is that students come to understand that *they* are the ones who will have to make adjustments.

5. What important features does this chapter include?

Readiness and Reality Checks
In the beginning of each chapter students complete a readiness check and at the end, they do a reality check. It is important to help students compare their expectations with their actual experience, because, among other things, it helps them to more accurately predict how long an assignment will take. Your students may not be experienced at reading difficult texts, which may make this chapter more challenging for them as it introduces metacognitive theories (without calling them that). A writing assignment or class discussion can be used to share students' pre and post chapter results. You might even ask students to e-mail you a short reflection about their expectations and the realities they have come to understand by the end of the chapter. When students are able to go over material more than once and reflect, they begin to hardwire information.

Challenge → Reaction → Insight → Action prompts

Throughout the book, students will be reminded about the learning system used in *FOCUS*: The Challenge → Reaction → Insight → Action system. This learning system is part of the fundamental infrastructure of the text. For example, an Insight → Action prompt in this chapter asks students to remember learning highs from their past and asks what made these learning experiences so memorable. In a Challenge → Reaction prompt, students are asked to respond to questions about their views on learning. What is learning? This activity challenges students to explore their beliefs about learning and can lead to in-class discussions or reflective writings about why they think or react the way that they do. This chapter is filled with these types of activities. Because this learning system is woven throughout the entire book, make sure you spend a little extra time on these so that they become a very natural anticipated activity for all the remaining chapters.

Self-Assessments

This chapter has three key assessments: the VARK Learning Styles Assessment, the Success Types Learning Style Type Indicator, and an informal instrument on Multiple Intelligences. Your students may not completely comprehend how to apply their results to their coursework. Here is a good opportunity to use your own results in a "teachable moment." Connect your learning preference, personality type, and multiple intelligences to your past learning experiences. There may even be a correlation between your chosen discipline and your results! In addition to these instruments, there is a self-assessment on a student's classes and optimal learning conditions. Also, students should begin to start connecting who they are with who they want to become. As students go through the text, each chapter presents a personal interview with a person in a certain career and highlights for students the most common MBTI preferences for that occupation through the "Create a Career Outlook" feature.

It's important to tell students that career type profiles can be based on each of the four MBTI scales individually or on the 16 MBTI types. Most often data are reported by actual types, as is done in the chapters. However, data vary by how and where they are reported. It's important to tell students that if their type profile does not match the most common one, they should not necessarily be discouraged from pursuing that particular career. They should realize that they may have a "minority" type in that career field, should they enter it, but that other factors should be considered in making their decision as well.

C-Factors

If you recall, each chapter of *FOCUS* contains features related to the four aspects of intrinsic motivation: "Cultivate Your Curiosity", "Control Your Learning", "Create a Career Outlook", and "Challenge Yourself Online Quizzes" at the end of each chapter. Some of the C-factors are more prominent than others depending on the content for each chapter. Before much learning takes place people have to be curious about something. Many of the readings and activities cultivate curiosity, but a great one for this chapter is "building a better brain." Wouldn't we all like the answer to that challenge? The point is that we can make our brains work better, and we want students to be curious enough to wonder how. Throughout the book students are asked to control their learning and think about their toughest class. Because this chapter is about learning, the focus is on what student can do to take control of their learning.

More often than not, perhaps, students have more control than they think they do. The "Create a Career Outlook" is a great feature for each chapter and here we meet Neil Fleming, University Professor and creator of the VARK Learning Style Questionnaire. Generally, students are interested in learning more about the creator of an instrument they are now using like the VARK. They might be interested in why *you* chose college teaching as a career. Students will begin to make connections between themselves and careers, since they will be asked questions such as "What would you find most challenging about this type of career?" and "What would you find most satisfying about this type of career?"

6. Which in-text exercises should I use?

Three exercises are built into this chapter. Here are descriptions of why they have been included, how much time each one will probably take, and how you might debrief them.

EXERCISE 2.1 VARK LEARNING STYLES ASSESSMENT

Why do this activity?
This activity helps students understand their preferred learning modality. By simply knowing the way they prefer to learn, and by using that preference in a variety of ways, learning will seem easier and certainly more efficient. Make sure you take this assessment, too. You may learn something about yourself that you suspected and now will get confirmation about.

What are the challenges and what can you expect?
All of us are curious to learn things about ourselves. This activity is easy, and students will enjoy adding up their final scores to see which of the learning styles they prefer. Many students will fit into the category of multimodal (having a preference for more than one modality). These students have more flexibly in learning than those students who have a strong preference for a single modality. However, to truly believe they have mastered material, multimodal learners will feel have to make use of all their preferred modalities.

How much time will it take?
This activity should take about 20-30 minutes depending on how much time you spend debriefing.

How should I debrief?
It's always a good idea to ask students when they are done, if anything they learned by taking the assessment surprised them. Most likely students will feel validated about they way they learn. Most students agree immediately with their results although some may need more time to think about it. Ask students to share a learning experience that they feel was a good match for their learning style. See if you can get them to articulate exactly what the experience was like, why they think it is indicative of their preference(s), and what was especially positive about it. Be sure that you refer to the Figure 2.2 on page 55 which lists general strategies, study strategies, and exam strategies for each of the styles. Fleming believes that people taking the VARK are in the best position to judge the accuracy of their scores, and that students should learn in college by engaging in "variations on a theme," using their preferred modalities in a variety of ways.

EXERCISE 2.2 THE SUCCESS TYPES LEARNING STYLE TYPE INDICATOR

Why do this activity?
This activity helps students identify how their personality type influences the way they learn, as well as which career choices might best fit them. Throughout *FOCUS* there is a short feature called "Your Type Is Showing," and students must complete the assessment in order to understand this feature. Additionally, often career or counseling centers on campus offer the full MBTI. If they do, encourage students to take it. Their results will be similar if not the same, but the full instrument provides considerably more depth. Just like the VARK, this activity is easy and fun and provides another piece of information to help students understand the way they learn best. The activity is also helpful for students to learn about how their personality type connects with majors and careers.

What are the challenges and what can you expect?
There are probably only a few challenges you can expect when doing this activity. First, students may think that this is not a true picture of them. Remind students that this is a self-assessment and that they answered the questions about themselves. Also remind them that this is an abbreviated version of a more reliable instrument, taken each year by millions of people around the world. If they don't have a strong preference for a style, the letters alone may not completely reflect their type and they may have tendencies for both preferences. It might also be a little disheartening for some students if they want to pursue a career that does not seem to fit their type. Remind students that within one career, there may be many different jobs and opportunities that best fit their style.

How much time will it take?
This activity should take about 20-30 minutes depending on how much time you spend debriefing.

How should I debrief?
In Chapter 1, hopefully you did the activity on the "Ideal Student." (If not, it's not too late!). If you did, expand on this to discuss how some personality types fit better with some aspects of the ideal student. See if you can get students to talk about their types and how they fit the ideal student, as well as others whose types might be a bit more challenging. Use Tammy Ko as an example. Tammy is mostly likely an extrovert, who prefers teachers who encourage discussion, a sensor who prefers teachers to encourage independent thinking, a feeler who prefers instructors who establish rapport with students, and a perceiver who likes teachers to entertain and inspire. This is *not* the personality type of Professor Caldwell. Get students to talk about similar situations they have been in; the bottom line is to move students toward thinking about *actions* they might take to make the learning situation better.

EXERCISE 2.3 VARK ACTIVITY

Why do this activity?
This activity is designed to help students make connections between their preferred VARK learning modality and an actual assignment. Remind students that the reason they are doing this is to help them understand themselves and make the most of their preferences. If students are multimodal, recommend that they do more than one activity or that they vary activities from chapter to chapter. By the end of the book, students will have been introduced to 12 (because the VARK is in Chapter 2) different ways to learn via their preferred modality or modalities.

What are the challenges and what can I expect?
There are no real challenges in this activity except for the students who are multimodal. may not want to do more than one activity, so you may want to make doing more than one assignment optional for them or vary activities by chapter.

How much time will it take?
This activity can be done outside of class; the only time it takes is the actual debriefing in class, and you can take whatever time you need.

How should I debrief?
Students really benefit from hearing how other students respond to this activity. Ask students what about this activity they enjoyed and why. Let students identify the commonalities that students with like preferences report.

7. Which additional exercises might enrich students' learning?

<u>Who Am I?</u>
Class activity
Materials needed: Index cards with personality types written on them
Time: 30-50 minutes, depending on the size of the group
Goal: To help students identify the behaviors that are typically indicative of particular personality types
In groups of three, students will role play having a meeting over coffee. Each student will be given a card with a particular type—for example, ENFP or ISTJ, etc.—and will act out their role in this casual meeting. The meeting could even be a meeting between a hypothetical instructor and student. After about five minutes the classmates who are observing are to write down the type of each character. It's okay to exaggerate! You might even use this activity for students to disclose who they are! You can guess along with the students. Although it is not possible or even recommended that people try to guess the actual MBTI profile of others, this activity can be a good introduction to types.

<u>Think/Pair/Share Activity</u>
Class activity
Materials needed: none
Time: 10-20 minutes
Goal: To get students thinking about a class they are taking now where there is not a good fit between them and the instructor

Sometimes it's difficult to get a discussion going in class. This think/pair/share activity provides a mechanism for all students to get involved and can be used for any topic.

- **Think:** Individually have students identify a class, where their learning style does not match their professors' teaching style. (Note that a professor's teaching style may not be the same as his or her learning style, but it should be safe to say that learning style influences teaching style to some degree.) Also, students must identify one thing that they can do to help themselves succeed in this class. (3-5 minutes)
- **Pair** up with the student next to them and discuss their responses. The students will decide on one or two issues to bring up to the group. (3-5 minutes)
- **Share** with the class their responses and as a group the class will discuss some common responses that students encounter with their instructors as well as identify some techniques to help them succeed. (5-10 minutes)

<u>Help Wanted!</u>
Class activity
Materials needed: Newsprint for each group of 4-5 students and index cards with an occupation on it
Time: 10-20 minutes, depending on the size of the group
Goal: To help students recognize the skills and personality types connected to success in a career

In groups of four to five students, ask them to develop a help wanted ad with the learning type needed for a particular job. The jobs that each group will be given are artist, political candidate, president of a company, and social worker. Their job is to create a job description that would result in selecting a person who would work well in the job. Students are not to list types, (i.e. ENFP wanted) but to describe the desired behaviors.

<u>Help Is on the Way!</u>
Class Activity (or an out of class assignment where students work in groups)
Material needed: none
Time: 40-50 minutes
Goal: To help students to problem solve a mismatch between a student and instructor

Present students with this challenge. Julia is attending a class on economics. The first day of class, the teacher says "Okay students, you don't have to read your books, but the information in the book is on the midterm and final. In this class, it's all about real world economics. You will set up a business, it doesn't matter to me what kind, and at the end of the semester you must demonstrate your understanding of the key principles of economics as a result of this project. Class is dismissed for today. Come in next Monday with your proposal." Julia leaves the class in tears and tells her roommate "I know I am going to fail, I just don't know what he wants or how even to begin!" In small groups, have students outline what Julia should do to. In addition, have students speculate about the different VARK learning style Julia and her professor might have as well as their Learning Style Type Indicator. Julia can't drop the class or change sections!

8. What other activities can I incorporate to make the chapter my own?

While suggestions and activities are provided for you, this text is so rich that you can use all of the annotations, the Readiness and Reality Checks, the Challenge → Reaction → Insight → Action system in any way that is comfortable for you. Keep in mind the concept of student engagement, and that the more involved the students are the more likely they are to learn.

Scan for particular annotations in the Instructor's Edition for ways to enrich the material for your particular group:

1) Teachable Moments
2) Activity Options
3) Sensitive Situations
4) Emotional Intelligence (EI) Research
5) Chapter Crossover

Included here, all in one place, are Activity Options taken from the Annotated Instructor's Edition.

If you are familiar with additional research about teaching and learning, capitalize on what you know in addition to what appears in this Instructor's Resource Manual. There are so many ways that you can make this chapter your own. For example, if your background is psychology, you have a great deal of information to share with the class about learning styles, motivation, and personality. If you are a business professor, share with your students how certain types make for ideal accountants or others ideal stock market traders. Share with students your background and area of specialty and refer to it in this chapter. You should also be thinking about your own teaching style based on your type. Share this with students and while the best teachers are those who can teach to all types, this is not often the case. Make sure students understand this.

ACTIVITY OPTION (p. 36): Divide the class into two groups: those who consider themselves spontaneous and those who do not, those who like predictability. Ask the two groups to describe the ideal teacher. In addition, ask students to rate Professor Caldwell's teaching on a scale of 1 to 10. After five minutes, ask the groups to read aloud their responses. Generate a list and see if there are differences in their responses and the number they assigned to Professor Caldwell's teaching. There should be differences. Those who like predictability may think that Professor Caldwell is okay and describe ideal teachers as organized. The spontaneous students will most likely describe their ideal teacher and Professor Caldwell differently.

ACTIVITY OPTION (p. 38): Give students lengthy directions for a fictitious assignment that would be due in the next class. Give them instructions about where they would find an article to read about studying in college, and tell them that you want them to write a three- to five-page paper, then change your mind, and make it a one-page essay. Confuse them; change what you want. And then go right on to the next part of the class. See if anyone raises a hand for clarification. Someone should! If not, ask someone to repeat what is due. Discuss some of the strategies, if any, students used to clarify the assignment.

ACTIVITY OPTION (p. 40): One of the most dreaded courses in college is math. In fact, large numbers of students take developmental math when they first enter college. They often say "I will never use this." To help students see that even courses they don't think they need are valuable, begin a brainstorming activity. Ask students to work alone or in groups and brainstorm reasons why it's important to learn math. Give students five minutes and then have them call out their responses while you write them on the board. The group or student with the most credible responses gets a few bonus points on the next assignment.

ACTIVITY OPTION (p. 42): Ask students to work in teams to build a learning tower. Draw a tower consisting of four blocks on the bottom row, three on the third, two on the second, and one at the top. The top block should be labeled "successful student." Students are to fill in what they need to know first before they are successful students. Each row should be a prerequisite to the next row.

ACTIVITY OPTION (p. 43): Determine whether there are any commonalities among the students' responses to this "Control Your Learning" exercise. Which courses do most students find the easiest? Which are the most difficult? Which are the least interesting? Have students share their responses so they can learn from their peers.

ACTIVITY OPTION (p. 46): Have students add up the number of checks they had in each category. Then group students according to their highest numbers. Give each group five minutes to share with each other their favorite classes (present or past). Ask students to find common threads in the classes they identified. Have the groups report to the class and discuss what they do to succeed in classes that they don't enjoy as much.

ACTIVITY OPTION (p. 48): Group students again according to their multiple intelligences (responses from the "Challenge → Reaction" about Multiple Intelligences) and create a sign that indicates the strength of the group (i.e., the intrapersonal group). Assign the groups the task of coming up with careers that a group different from theirs would enjoy and report to the class. Have the group to which the job relates respond to why they would or would not enjoy the job.

ACTIVITY OPTION (p. 50): Ask students to have someone who knows them well fill out the same "Challenge → Reaction" about them. Does their roommate or spouse know that they must have music on to study, for example? Encourage students to share their needs with roommates and family members who may have a different style. The responses will help students see how others perceive them as well.

ACTIVITY OPTION (p. 54): On the board or on a large piece of poster board, list the four modalities (Visual, Aural, Read/Write, and Kinesthetic) and have students write their name and score of their top two modalities. For example, a student might put her name and a 10 under Visual and her name and an 8 under Aural. Are there similarities in the class? Do these students enjoy the same classes? Now ask students to put their dominant multiple intelligence next to their name. Are they beginning to see any patterns? Ask each student to describe one way in which they can use their dominant learning style and strong intelligence to help them in college (if there is not enough time in class, they can e-mail the class with their answer, or bring their response to the next class).

ACTIVITY OPTION (p. 60): Before students fill out the SuccessTypes Learning Style Type Indicator, have them guess their type. Let them know that an "E" learns from doing, an "I" prefers studying in quiet, an "S" likes to memorize, "N's" like to think about the big picture, "F's" relate information to people, while "T's" are logical, "J's" love organized classrooms and clear syllabi, and "P's" don't mind change and going with the flow. After the assessment, see if they were correct on any of the indicators.

ACTIVITY OPTION (p. 62): Have students develop a six-slide PowerPoint presentation for the class describing something they do and explaining why they do it that way based on their type. For example, if they were to describe plans for fall break, would they go with a few people or a group, would it be spontaneous or planned, would they be the leader or prefer someone else to take charge?

ACTIVITY OPTION (p. 66): Ask students to summarize their responses to the Reality Check and send it to you via e-mail. In addition, ask them to tell you the most significant thing they learned about themselves and give a specific example of how they will use what they've learned to prepare for an exam.

9. What homework might I assign?

Your students have gained a considerable amount of information about themselves by now. They know more about how they are motivated, their learning style, their dominant multiple intelligence(s), and their personality type. Using the information they have, have students create a customized learning plan for their toughest course. Their plan should include how they will use their class notes, how they will read their assigned coursework, and how they will prepare for exams.

Who I am, what I know I can and can't do well, and what I am going to do about it
Goal: To help students to describe their own behavior, using their VARK and Success Types Learning Style Type profile
Assign students to do a Power Point presentation similar to the one described in the activity option above. Ask students to present to the class and report on one thing that they learned about themselves from this chapter, describe it in some detail, and identify how it will impact how they learn.

Journal Entries

One: Have students write a one page journal entry, or send you an e-mail reflecting on what they learned about themselves in this chapter. You might prompt students by asking them to choose the three specific things that they learned about themselves. They can list their specific scores, but they must also indicate something that they currently do that reflects that behavior. Ask students to explain what about their particular learning and personality style is a good match for college and what might put them at risk. What do they plan to do about any risk factors that are present?

Two: Have students write a one page journal essay or send you an e-mail describing one situation in which they were really engaged in the class. What made it so? Can they also describe a situation where they were completely disconnected and explain why? How can they take what they learned about themselves in the first class and apply it to the second.

Three: Use the Insight → Action prompts as journal or blog assignments.

10. What have I learned in teaching this chapter that I will incorporate next time?

_____
_____
_____
_____
_____
_____
_____
_____
_____
_____
_____
_____
_____
_____
_____
_____
_____
_____
_____
_____
_____
_____
_____

CHAPTER 3: MAKING USE OF RESOURCES: FINANCES, TECHNOLOGY, AND CAMPUS SUPPORT

1. Why is this chapter important?

When you think about students being successful in college, one of the first things that typically comes to mind is whether students are academically prepared. Of course, that's important, but believe it or not, some of the main reasons that students leave college are not having the money to pay for college, engaging in unhealthy coping mechanisms, not admitting to needing help, and (over)using what students often know best, the computer and Internet. So really, this chapter tackles some of the key non-cognitive components of student success that you may have never thought about. First, let's start with finances.

The *FOCUS* Challenge Case student, Jessica Taylor, may or may not be like one of your typical students. Clearly, she is a young woman of privilege. She has done well in high school and appears ready for college. (Notice the word *appears*!) She immediately applied for four credit cards during campus promos and admits she is a bit nervous about over spending. Credit card debt, whether the student comes from a privileged background or not, is a common problem among college students. Student debt can cause tremendous anxiety and even derail students academically. Students have to learn to manage finances. Recognizing how important fiscal responsibility is to college success, many institutions now offer students free seminars on debt management. Some students need to learn to distinguish between needs and wants; while others have to take a hard look at the way they are managing money and attempting to pay for college, perhaps by working so many hours or by juggling more than one job that they cannot complete their coursework. Check to see what types of services are available at your institution.

Another reason why this chapter is important is to address students engaging in unhealthy behaviors, like abuse of the Internet and excessive shopping. Both seem a fairly harmless, but nonetheless feed right into an addictive personality type. It seems as if these students must not be devoting much time to studying, if they have time for excessive web surfing, checking their Facebook accounts, and shopping, but, often, for students these behaviors begin as an initial stress reliever and then become addicting. The point is, this chapter will help students see what can potentially happen, as well as let them know that there are lots of campus resources to help them deal with all sorts of challenges. They just have to ask for and seek out help! For some students, however, that's sometimes easier said than done.

An underlying question subtly posed in this chapter is who wants to look needy in college? Sometimes students who have struggled before with issues do things like stop taking medications, or refrain from using services for students with disabilities, just because they just don't want anyone to know about their past. For them, college is a fresh start which can quickly turn into a disaster. Yet, even the strongest, most together students are surrounded by temptations which often require intervention and support. This chapter is about knowing why, how, and where to get support on your campus. Make sure that students see getting support as "a normal thing" and not something that weak or needy students do. One way to de-stigmatize getting help is to share your own past experiences. Did you have an area that you struggled with as a first-year student? Be especially aware that young men are much less likely to ask for help than women.

Just like the previous chapter you will see some common activities. The chapter begins with the *FOCUS* Challenge Case, a Readiness Check, followed by a number of Challenge → Reaction prompts, and recurring C-Factors. These C-Factors (challenge, control, curiosity, and careers) that appear throughout the book, help students focus on what motivates them and why. Remember that it's not enough to have the *insight* but one has to take *action* to achieve positive change. This step is especially important for this chapter, because students have to actually *use* the resources available on campus, not just *think* about them, to overcome their particular obstacles.

2. What are this chapter's learning objectives?

➢ What resources exist to help students through college
➢ Why managing finances is so important
➢ Why plastic is perilous
➢ How to get "Fiscally Fit"
➢ How Net life relates to college success
➢ How the Internet can become addictive
➢ What information literacy is and why it's important
➢ Why HELP is not a four-letter word
➢ How to manage a learning disability

3. How should I launch this chapter?

First, remember that this chapter includes potentially sensitive issues. Not everyone wants to admit that they need help, so approach this chapter in ways that depersonalize any private issues. It is almost guaranteed you have someone in your class that has or is struggling with an eating disorder, and the incidence is increasing in men. It is almost guaranteed that someone is in debt, someone has a learning disability, or someone is dealing with anxiety or depression. Be sure you set the tone in your class: all of these issues, while challenging, don't have to cause students to drop out or fail out of college. A large part of college success is knowing about and making use of available resources.

- **By now students should be settling in, and you may begin to see some friendships emerging in the class**. You may also see some students who are sitting alone and struggling. They may be dealing with some of the issues that are addressed in this chapter. However, be sensitive to the fact that introverted students may naturally be reluctant to engage in class; however, this does not necessarily equate to being more at risk. Think about personality issues if (or when) putting students into groups. A sole introvert in a group of extraverts may have a hard time getting a word in edgewise. Create a climate where students are the most likely to be engaged.

- **This is a good chapter for journal writing.** You may find students are more likely to divulge a problem or issue privately to you. In class, they might be talking about "a friend" who has a problem as a disguise. (Or, it really may be a friend they are looking for help to support.) Don't miss this opportunity to give students a chance to share their concerns in a private way. You can simply structure this by doing a slant on the "one minute paper" by asking what they think is the most common problem or most dangerous problem on this campus (of the issues addressed in this chapter) and what they might want to find more out about. The one minute paper is a technique developed by Tom Angelo and Pat Cross. It's a simple assessment that you can use just about any time by asking students to indicate one thing they learned in the class, one thing they are still confused about, and one thing they want to learn more about. You can use your own version, but it should only take about a minute.

- **Remember the Readiness Check at the beginning of the chapter.** Be sure that students are developing the habit of thinking about their own role in the learning process and how to focus on learning new things.

- **Going beyond the book.** As much as students want to know about themselves, they also want to know about you or some situation that you may know about. If you have been teaching for a while, you most likely know of some students who have confronted issues in successful ways. Be careful not to divulge too much information so that you aren't giving away any identities in sensitive situations. Instead, focus on the path to success, rather than the individual. Even if you are new to this course, you have some real life experiences to contribute. You might even check to see if you have any "experts" on campus who could address the perils of the Internet, like social networking or gaming addiction and online predators to emphasize some of the major points of this chapter.

4. How should I use the *FOCUS* Challenge Case?

Jessica Taylor may or may not be like your students. At the beginning of the term, her life was going according to plan: she had made amazing friends, and her high school boyfriend Collin was maintaining their long-distance romance. Now several weeks into the semester, Jessica is facing several challenges: she has too many credit cards, she has spent all her money, her boyfriend is pulling away, and she just got a C- on a test. To make matters worse, Jessica struggled with an eating disorder in high school, but fortunately had the support of her family and others to overcome it. For the time being, Jessica is managing the stress, but she feels pulled back into the one thing she can control—her eating. Like some of your students, perhaps, Jessica feels out of control and does not know where to get help. While the story may sound melodramatic, it is representative of what many college students experience.

Depending on who is in your class, this *FOCUS* Challenge Case may be right on target. Or on the other hand, you may be teaching a class of students from a low income area or adults returning to college. Use the behaviors and challenges, not Jessica the young woman of privilege, as the points of discussion. You don't have to be rich to have credit card problems or spend too much time shopping or the abuse the Internet. The point is that anyone can struggle with issues like these. The question is what to do about it.

5. What important features does this chapter include?

Again, you will see some of the really important recurring themes in this book.

Readiness and Reality Checks
In the beginning of each chapter students complete a Readiness Check and at the end, they do a Reality Check. By this point in the semester, your students may have begun to use the checks in their other classes. Ask them if they are applying the system. If they are not, now would be a great opportunity to encourage them to directly apply what they are learning in this course to their other courses! You might even ask students to e-mail you a short reflection about how (or if) their expectations and realities are beginning to become more consistent.

Challenge → Reaction → Insight → Action prompts
Throughout the book, students will be reminded about the learning system used throughout: The Challenge → Reaction → Insight → Action system. The *FOCUS* challenge is a very important feature of this text. Discuss the C → R: Do students know what types of campus resources are available? Reaction prompts will help students assess what they already know, and if they don't already know about the support on campus, open their eyes to things they never imagined were available.

Insight → Action prompts is where you have to get students to make a move, be incited to act. Think about ways in which you can perhaps build in ways to requirements to use resources. Some of the activity options and suggestions for activities will help you do that. This system is repeated throughout the text and students will continue cycling back to the first step as they encounter new challenges. It is key for this chapter to see a challenge, react to it, develop some insight and then *ACT* !

While there are many different Challenge → Reaction → Insight → Action prompts in this chapter, the Challenge → Reaction prompt on the Internet pros and cons is an important and engaging one for students.

Your Type Is Showing
"Your Type Is Showing" is an important recurring feature of the book. In this chapter students are asked to respond to the relationship between their personality type and managing money. Don't skip over this. Students will find it insightful and helpful.

<u>**Control Your Learning: Your Toughest Class**</u>

In this activity, students identify the most challenging class where they will have to use information literacy skills. The more students can connect what they are learning with a real life class or situation; the more likely they are to retain and apply what they have learned.

<u>***FOCUS* on Careers**</u>

The career focus in this chapter is about an IT Systems Analyst for a Pharmaceutical company. Mr. Hearn states that his biggest challenges are not actually technical; rather, they revolve around time management, creativity, and team work. He recommends that students take advantage of opportunities to apply what they are learning in the classroom to the "real world." After reading the interview, students can ask themselves if they are personally interested in technology as a possible career. This chapter also focuses on a career outlook for an IT Systems Analyst—a computer scientist. They will be asked questions like "Do you have (or could you acquire) the skills this career requires?" and "Are you interested in a career like this? Why or why not?" See if you have any students in your class you are thinking about a career in IT. Make a connection for them with employees on your campus who hold these jobs. Have students visit your IT people and spend a few hours observing what they do.

<u>**Cultivate Your Curiosity: Choose to Choose!**</u>

The curiosity focus in this chapter is about how to effectively manage the myriad of choices available to us everyday, and it's one of the most important things for students to think about among all the "Cultivate Your Curiosity" features in the book. Challenge your students to think about times when they are "maximizers" when they should be "satisficers" or vice versa. Challenge them to apply the four steps for lowering stress associated with constantly being forced to make choices.

6. Which in-text exercises should I use?

There are six exercises built into this chapter. Included here are descriptions of why they have been included, how much time each one will probably take, and how you might debrief them. Since there are a number of somewhat similar activities in this chapter, and especially if you have a class that meets only once or twice a week, consider assigning a few activities as homework, or have students choose one or two activities to complete, as opposed to trying to do them all. For variety, assign all the activities, but to different students, and then have the class discuss the results. This would be a great opportunity to assign groups based on differing learning and/or personality styles. This helps students learn how to effectively work in teams with people very different from themselves.

EXERCISE 3.1 PICTURE SUCCESS

Why do this activity?
This activity helps students learn about campus resources in a fun way. If the weather is agreeable, have students take photos outside. This is a real hands-on activity that students should enjoy. To build community, you might consider putting some students in groups to do this. Consider pairing or grouping students who may not normally hang out together, or assign this activity as homework and have students come to class to present their results. Remind students to get a photo of themselves and their group members. This activity will be a memory from their early college days for sure.

What are the challenges and what can you expect?
You are going to have students who prefer working alone, as well as some preferring to simply look up the same pictures of services on the Internet. Be prepared for a few students that don't understand the purpose of this activity. You might consider doing this during class time, or meet as a group after class hours for pizza to kick-off or end the photo shoot. Also, keep in mind, if you borrow digital cameras from your media center, it's not all that uncommon to lose or break one! Another potential issue is that you might also end up with all of the same resources. Consider giving students a list that they have to find, or have them choose a few resources they must find and photograph out of a hat.

How much time will it take?
The activity could take anywhere from an hour to a full morning or afternoon.

How should I debrief?
Just as you did with other activities, ask students when they are done what they learned by doing this activity. What was a service that they learned about that surprised them? Having students share what they found with others allows students to teach others and to expose the whole class to an array of services (especially if you structured the activity that way to begin with). Think about giving a prize (a gift card to the coffee bar) to the group with the most creative photos!

EXERCISE 3.2 YOUR MONTHLY BUDGET

Why do this activity?
You can bet that you have students in the class who never have done a budget and haven't a clue what one is. They may get the general idea, but to see their exact income versus expenses may be eye-opening. This is especially true for students like Jessica Taylor, the *FOCUS* Challenge Case student, who probably had Mom and Dad taking care of most of her finances. You might suggest students identify how their personality type influences the way that they budget. (Remember the feature "Your Type Is Showing?"). Detailed practical types such as sensors are much more likely to plan and follow a budget than are iNtuitors. That doesn't mean that iNtuitors can't follow a budget; it just might take a bit more discipline. The activity is helpful for students to learn about how their personality type connects with planning and budgeting.

What are the challenges and what can you expect?

Some students may not know much about what things actually cost. They may not know what printer cartridges cost because Mom and Dad always bought them. Or, they may not know because they have never owned a printer until now. A number of students will probably overlook hidden costs like wear and tear on a car when they are estimating transportation. There are tons of hidden fees in credit cards and a good discussion of this is helpful. Is there an expert in the class? If it seems appropriate with your group, have students share what they put down in certain categories for comparisons. For example you might ask for students to raise hands to show who spends more than "x" on a certain category or have students line up from most costly to least for an item. Students who are good money-managers might share their techniques with others.

How much time will it take?

This activity should take about 20-30 minutes, depending on how much time you spend debriefing.

How should I debrief?

Get students to share their reactions about this assignment. Don't probe too much on actual expenses as you need to be sensitive to the possible ranges of income in the class. Use Jessica Taylor as an example. Is she going to get into trouble? Do you think she will tell her parents? Why or why not? What do you think they would do if she told them? If students think that they will bail her out, what are the learning consequences of that? Did Jessica learn? Get students to talk about situations they have been in, and as always, the bottom line is to get students thinking about what *action* they might take to make the situation better.

EXERCISE 3.3 CREATE A SPENDING LOG

Why do this activity?

We have probably all been in a situation where we open up our credit card bill at the end of the month and are surprised at the total. "Wow–I had no idea that I spent so much." We might even begin to review charges and sure enough, they are all yours and by spending a little bit here and there, at the end of a 30 day cycle the bill is huge. This activity helps students see what they spend on a daily basis. They will probably look at the example spending log and pin point where the student could have saved money, but it might be a different story when they see their own. There is research that shows when people record what they eat, they are much more likely to eat less, stay on a diet and lose weight. Share this tip with students so they can apply this strategy to their finances. By using a spending log, students learn how to become fiscally fit.

What are the challenges and what can you expect?

Any time that anyone does a self report, it is subject to interpretation and erroneous information. One thing is clear: this assignment has to be for students, not you. There may be a tendency for students to put down what they think an instructor might want to see as opposed to what is really going on. For sure, there are not many of us who would want to share the details of every morsel we put in our mouths on a daily basis, especially when we are supposed to be on a diet. The same principle operates here. Don't put students in the spot of sharing something that they might not want to divulge. If they volunteer, that's great, but don't push it for everyone. Also, students need to see what one day's worth of spending adds up to over 30 days. A four dollar cappuccino may not seem so bad for a one day spending event, but add it up over 20 times in a month and you have a problem.

How much time will it take?
This activity should take between 30-40 minutes, depending on the number of students in the class.

How should I debrief?
If a few students want to share, let them, but as mentioned, don't press. You might even talk about compulsive spenders and gamblers. Many campuses have support groups on campus that address this. If so, think about bringing someone in to talk about it. Remember: although Jessica may not be your typical student at many institutions, her behavior crosses ages and incomes. In essence, she might be "self medicating" to cope with some other issue that requires attention. Don't hesitate if you feel the need to bring in an expert from your counseling center. You might even survey students, privately, to see if they think this is something important to do.

EXERCISE 3.4 TECHNOLOGY PROJECT: GROUP AD

Why do this activity?
Here is another sample of an activity that helps students learn about campus resources in a fun way. As a group, students will learn how to use technology for a project that helps them share ideas on why the course they are taking is important. (Don't forget to keep these to show your colleagues.) As is suggested in the text, consider an alternative to the project content (about the class) and focus on campus resources or some other topic. It's also a great opportunity for students to present their work to the entire class. Tell students they have "Super Bowl airtime," so you're expecting great things. Or show them an ad from a previous semester so that they have a model to work from. Often, the student groups are very proud of their results.

What are the challenges and what can you expect?
Again, thinking about "Your Type Is Showing," you may have students who prefer working alone, rather than in a group. Some students feel as if they do all of the work, so structure the task by having students have specific roles. One way to address this issue is to have students give you a work plan before they begin. Then at the end of the project, ask every member of the group to assign a "grade" to their team members based on the amount of time and energy they invested in the activity. If you choose to assign doing the ad on benefits of the class, you should get some interesting variations. If you choose to have students work on the campus resources project, assign resources or you may end up with much of the same.

How much time will it take?
This activity should take between 20-30 minutes, depending on the number of students in the class.

How should I debrief?
Just as you did with other activities, ask students when they are done, what they learned by doing this activity. Did they agree that the major benefits of the course were highlighted? Was there a

service that they learned about that surprised them? How sophisticated was the technology? (You may be amazed!) Did students show a variety of technology options? Do you have some experts in class who would be willing to help others?

EXERCISE 3.5 THE CAMPUS LIBRARY: DRAWING A FLOOR PLAN

Why do this activity?
This is a great activity—especially for visual learners—and there is nothing like putting pen to paper to draw what they have learned. Many students today prefer to do all their research online in the comfort of their residence hall rooms or homes. But actually spending time in the library itself can be quite an exciting adventure. Finding one book leads to finding something else of interest, and students can learn the value of asking a reference librarian a question that will save them hours of hunting on their own. This activity helps students learn about campus resources in a fun way. An important aspect of this assignment is asking students to reflect on where in the library they might feel most comfortable. Does this connect with their dominant learning preference?

What are the challenges and what can you expect?
You will definitely have some students who have no intention of studying in the library for a variety of reasons. If you have commuters, they may want to be home. If you have students who have a place in their dorms they may want to spend their time there. However, to give students a real taste of the library (and who knows it may work better then they thought) consider requiring them to spend one hour there, working on an assignment and reflect on they experience. Did they accomplish much? Perhaps more than they would have with the distractions at home?

How much time will it take?
This activity will take the whole class period unless you have students do this out of class, and come back to share. They can also turn this in as a homework assignment. Times will vary depending on which option you choose.

How should I debrief?
The explorer and recorder part of this activity is a fun one. You might see if explorers looked for and found similar things. Did recorders put down things in the same way? Do maps look alike? Also if you chose to require students to spend some time in the library, you need to give students the opportunity to reflect and communicate their experiences. You may just find that you have converted a few students to spending more time in the library.

EXERCISE 3.6 VARK ACTIVITY

Why do this activity?
This activity is designed to help students make connections between their preferred VARK learning modality and an actual assignment. Again, remind students that the reason they are doing this is to help them understand themselves, and make the most of their preferences. If students are multimodal, recommend that they do more than one activity or vary their activities by chapter.

What are the challenges and what can I expect?
There are no real challenges in this activity except for the students who are multimodal. These students may not want to do more than one activity, so you may want to make doing more than one assignment optional for them or suggest variations as noted above.

How much time will it take?
This activity can be done outside of class; the only time it takes is the actual debriefing in class, and you can take whatever time you need.

How should I debrief?
Students really benefit from hearing how other students respond to this activity. Ask students what about this they enjoyed and why. Try and find the commonalties, or rather let students identify the commonalities that students with like preferences report.

7. Which additional exercises might enrich students' learning?

Searching the Web—Even to Learn about your own Campus Library
Class activity
Materials needed: computers
Time: 30-50 minutes, depending on the size of the group
Goal: To help students use the Internet to identify resources both on the web, and in the campus library
In small groups of two to three students, assign groups the task of identifying as many varied, credible resources to do a research paper on the topic of "college student debt" on the Internet. Be sure that students include a varied list of sources, including online database articles through your library as well as web sites. At the end of 30 minutes, have groups report what they found, including the most user friendly search engines and databases.

The Top Five
Class activity
Materials needed: Access to PowerPoint
Time: One hour, depending on the size of the group
Goal: To help students identify the most common resources that students need to access
In small groups of 2-3 (group students differently each time) assign students to identify the top ten campus resources students should know about and access. Students must develop a 6-slide PowerPoint presentation, using a variety of PowerPoint options (to be determined by the instructor) on the top five resources. Included in the presentation should be the name of the

resource, the location, hours of operation, how to contact the person in charge, and why it's important. Students should electronically send copies of their presentations to others in the class.

Under Cover
Out of class activity
Materials needed: computers
Time: 30-50 minutes
Goal: To help students identify Internet profiles of current college students with information that might lead to trouble
Individually, students are to browse a social networking site like MySpace, Facebook, or Second Life and find two profiles that indicate exactly where students will be and when. Have students identify what controls are in place to prevent potentially dangerous situations from developing. Students will also describe what features their chosen social networking site has that may be different from other Internet social networking sites.

8. What other activities can I incorporate to make the chapter my own?

There are many activities that are part of the annotations in the text; you can adapt them to your own style when doing any of them. Part of the way you approach the class will be dependent on your own learning style and personality type. But, you have to keep in mind that your class will consist of students with many learning styles and personality types that are unlike yours. You need to try to find ways to engage everyone.

Share your own experiences when you can. Students do well when they can connect what they are learning with real experiences. Also, you may need to "adjust" some of the activities to place emphasis on a particular type of student you have, whether it is a commuter, a class primarily filled with working parents, or first-generation students. Keep in mind that you also don't know the full backgrounds of students in your class, so vary examples whenever you can.

Included here, all in one place, are Activity Options taken from the Annotated Instructor's Edition.

ACTIVITY OPTION (p. 70): Activity Option Students should take a few minutes to share their responses to the "What Do *You* Think?" questions. In addition, go around the room and ask students to fill in the blank: If I was Jessica's friend, I would tell her .

ACTIVITY OPTION (p. 70): Make up index cards with a typical first-year student challenge, hand one out to each student, or groups of students, and ask them to describe a campus resource that would help students deal with this challenge. How would this resource help? If they were facing this challenge, would they be willing to use the resource they've identified?

ACTIVITY OPTION (p. 72): Put students in teams and assign them specific resources. Have groups create a five-slide PowerPoint presentation to the class about the resource, including where it is located on campus, what hours the resource is available, why they think it might be helpful, for whom it might be helpful, and a quick interview with someone who works there, stating what he or she believes is most important about the resource.

ACTIVITY OPTION (p. 75): Students might want to share how much they spend in a typical day. Group students by their spending from zero to $10, $10 to $50, and above $50. Have the groups identify some things that they could have done without and then share results with the class.

ACTIVITY OPTION (p. 82): As a class, develop some "fiscally fit" ideas. Ask the class to rank the top three practices that they believe are relatively easy to change and would help them stay "fiscally fit."

ACTIVITY OPTION (p. 82): For a "Your Type Is Showing" activity, divide students in the class based on perceivers and judgers (P's and J's). Give each group $100 of play money that they could use when they are off for a long weekend. What would each group do with the money and why? Tell students that they don't have to spend the money if they don't want to.

ACTIVITY OPTION (p. 85): Have students fill in the blank: My worst computer nightmare happened when . Have them share with the class. If no one offers an example, or you only get a few, hand out some index cards with situations like "lost my fl ash drive," "the power went off," "I ran out of paper," for example, and discuss ways to avoid these problems.

ACTIVITY OPTION (p. 90): In small groups, have students examine the fictional ISpy.com web page and decide what parts of the profile should be eliminated to protect one's identity. Have groups share in class what was left on the profile. Could anything still identify this student? Remind students of the benefits of setting their profiles to private on sites like MySpace.com.

ACTIVITY OPTION (p. 90): List the important campus resources on individual index cards and place them in a basket. Have students choose a card and allow them to trade with someone else if they wish. Have students develop a flyer or brochure that they can post online or print enough for the entire class. Students can then vote on which brochure or flyer was the most comprehensive and appealing. By having students create and share the brochures, you're guaranteed that the rest of the class has a list of critical campus resources.

ACTIVITY OPTION (p. 93): Have students list all of the Internet domains (for example, .com, .net, .org, and .edu) and brainstorm which might be the most reliable and credible. What features of a web site might make someone suspicious?

ACTIVITY OPTION (p. 97): Create index cards with one campus resource on each card. Divide the class into two groups for an in-class pop quiz. Hold up a card, and the first group to buzz (they can use cell phones in class!) gets a chance to tell where it's located and what its purpose is. The team that wins gets a prize.

ACTIVITY OPTION (p. 99): Have students develop a slogan on why students should use campus resources. For example, "when in debt . . . don't forget the Financial Aid Center located at _____."

9. What homework might I assign?

Ask students to identify their largest time wasting activity. Some examples might include: (1) social networking sites like MySpace or Facebook, (2) games, 3) television, (4) surfing the Internet, etc. Have students track how much time they are spending on this activity for two or three days. Then challenge them to cut that time in half for the rest of the week. At the end of the week, have students analyze how productive they were toward the end of the week versus the beginning of the week.

Journal Entries

One: Have students write a one page journal entry, or send you an e-mail describing a fictitious student, based on typical issues students in college might face, and identify three possible resources the student should use. Students must describe the student behavior that warrants using a resource, the barriers might the student might encounter to using them, and how would they suggest the student overcome these barriers. Finally, ask the students to identify what would happen if this student chose not to address the issues. Encourage students to identify possible preconceptions our fictitious student might have about students who use campus resource centers. This might help the students (and you!) to identify why they could be reluctant to seek help.

Two: Have students write a one page journal entry, send you an e-mail, or use an online blog (that only you and the student can access) reflecting on what they learned about themselves in this chapter about using resources. Allowing students to blog is a great way to provide flexibility to technology-savvy students or even help technology-reluctant students to become more comfortable with the Internet. Prompt students by asking them to identify three possible times they might use a campus resource and why. Ask students to identify any possible barriers to using one of the resources, and how might they overcome them. Finally, ask students to identify what might possibly happen if they chose not to address the issues.

Three: Use the Insight → Action prompts as journal or blog assignments.

10. What have I learned in teaching this chapter that I will incorporate next time?

_____

_____

_____

_____

_____

_____

_____

_____

_____

_____

CHAPTER 4: MANAGING YOUR TIME AND ENERGY

1. Why is this chapter important?

There is probably no a single topic discussed more often in student success courses than time management. This is a buzz word that we as instructors hear often: "Oh, you teach a course on time management." And often we all at one time or another bemoan our own challenges in this area: "if I just had a few more hours in the day." Poor time management skills are one of the leading reasons why students are not successful in college. What is really important about this chapter is that simply making lists and prioritizing how to manage one's day or week is not the answer to time management. Successful students know what makes them tick, and learn it's more about managing your own behavior—how *you* manage your own time—than what you are doing at any given moment. Have you ever spent hours on a project, but if you honestly analyzed how you spent each minute, the real time the project took maybe a lot less time than you actually expended? Did you count the times you got up for a snack? How about looking out the window? Organizing your closet? Daydreaming about your upcoming break? It's not about the actual time, but what you are doing with the time on the task.

The chapter also makes a unique point among college success texts by discussing the relationship between time management, attention management, and energy management. Managing time becomes much less of a challenge when we manage our energy expenditure—when we are at our best physically, emotionally, mentally, and spiritually. When we're in balance, we're most productive.

Another really critical focus in this chapter is how to identify the common time wasters, and what to do about them. Just as students might have done in Chapter 3 on other subjects, in this chapter students will be filling out logs and forms. Theses exercises aren't meant to be busy work and turned in for a grade, but they can really help students get a solid handle on analyzing where and when they waste time. An important part of this exercise is to understand *how students are feeling during this process*. Are they wasting time because they really don't understand the assignment? Are they frustrated because the assignment is overwhelming? Of course, using the Insight → Action model, it is essential for students to actually change their behavior in order to reduce the amount of time they are wasting.

In addition, in this chapter the awful "P" word (procrastination) will be addressed with some strategies on how to avoid procrastination and just do it! Finally, students will address how to realistically balance work, school, and personal life.

2. What are this chapter's learning objectives?

- ➤ Why time management alone doesn't work
- ➤ How time management differs from energy management
- ➤ How to calculate study hours
- ➤ How to schedule a way to succeed

➤ How common "time wasters" creep in, and how to bust them
➤ How the "P word" can derail anyone
➤ How to realistically balance work, school, and personal life

3. How should I launch this chapter?

This chapter could not come at a better time. In fact, it was planned that way. After experiencing a bit of a honeymoon period when it may have seemed to some students that they could do it all, stress sets in. They might have thought "this is not so bad, I can manage everything" but around week four things begin to pile up. Their courses, which may have begun with review work they recognize from high school, have now taken off into uncharted territory. Now is the time to really tackle time management. And, students are ready to learn more. Begin your discussion of this chapter with a simple show of hands: ask students who is having trouble fitting everything in and managing time. Don't be surprised if all your students raise their hands.

- **Find out if a number of students in your class are taking other classes together.**
  Earlier in the text we discussed the value of working in groups. Especially for those extraverts in your class, working in groups may provide the help they need to get them on the right track. For students who are in the same classes you will find that their approach to the same exam or quiz might be different. This is a good place to talk about quality study time—not just study time in general. Even if students prefer not to work in pairs or groups, students in the same classes can share their plans for how they will approach the upcoming tests and quizzes.

- **Find out how many students have upcoming tests.** Take a few moments to see if anyone has several tests in the next week or so and how they are planning to prepare. Do a little survey in class to see how much time students plan to allot for studying for quizzes that are coming up. You will most likely find variation, so get a discussion going. Students may be surprised to learn how much time good students actually invest.

- **This is a time where you legitimately will find differences in students' schedules, and sometimes they are beyond the students' control.** Like the *FOCUS* Challenge Case student Derek, students' plates are often full. He may be a non-traditional college student, but most students have many outside responsibilities. A healthy step is to acknowledge the fact that there are some things out of our control. Using your good emotional intelligence skills, remind students that the one thing we can change is how we respond to situations. Sure, we could all cut back on an activity or two, but taking care of a sick mother, or working two jobs to support the family is sometimes something students must do. What these students can control is how they handle their challenging, time-consuming situations. Skilled time management and management of energy and emotions are keys to success.

- **Challenge your students to consider their energy management as well as their time management skills.** Often, students are so concerned with scheduling time to study that they forget about their energy management. Challenge students to take breaks during their study times. For example, encourage students not to read for several hours at one time. Instead, encourage them to study in 60-75 minute intervals. At the end of this study session, students should take a 15-20 minute break. This break is a great opportunity for students to grab a snack, walk around for a few minutes, or just relax. Their break should leave students feeling refreshed, which should allow them to easily refocus on their task.

- **Going beyond the book.** There are lots of resources about time management. For example, Steven Covey's book *The 7 Habits of Highly Effective People* (1990) might be one of the books that students in your class have read. Make sure that you tap the resources and knowledge of people in the class, especially if you have some adult learners in your class—ask them to share some of the tips they have learned from the workplace. Workplaces often have sessions on time and energy management, and these students might bring great tools to the table to share.

4. How should I use the *FOCUS* Challenge Case?

Derek Johnson is a student committed to getting his degree. He works full-time in an entry-level marketing position, and he realizes that he has to get his degree in order to advance in his career. Five years after high school, he is ready. Or is he? He has a full time job, a wife, and one child with another on the way. He is heavily involved in singing in his church choir, coaching, and working out every day. He balks about the idea of a 12-page paper, and spends more time worrying about it than actually doing it. Derek seems to think that this 12-page paper is unreasonable. After all, he has a lot to do! Derek doesn't see anything that he can drop from his schedule.

Derek is not alone; most nontraditional students face similar challenges in balancing their responsibilities. It might be a good idea to point out the connection between attitude and motivation that was discussed in Chapter 1 at this point. Ask your students what areas of Derek's life are interfering with his ability to complete his 12-page paper. One way to approach this challenge case is to break your students into groups of two or three. Ask each group to create a plan for Derek that includes all of his responsibilities: completing family tasks, going to his job and completing his project, and completing his paper—all in the allotted four weeks. After ten or fifteen minutes, ask each group to present its plan. You are sure to get different plans, which could help your students find a planning system that works best for them!

5. What important features does this chapter include?

Again, you will see some of the important recurring themes in this book through these features.

Readiness and Reality Checks
This is a Readiness Check that students might be a little more willing to engage in, but they might not yet see the importance. If they are traditional students, they may not share some of Derek's responsibilities; however, they surely have many things to juggle, regardless. After students complete this Readiness Check, see if there are variations in the class responses. Is it

because different students have different levels of things to manage? But the truth is, as any busy person will tell you, you will always make time to finish something that is important to you. While students may think they know a lot about this topic, the reality is that knowing is not necessarily doing. Most students are eager to learn more.

Challenge → Reaction → Insight → Action prompts

By now both you are your students are thoroughly familiar with the Challenge → Reaction → Insight → Action system. There are a number of very important activities in this chapter, most are very short but thought provoking. For example, one challenge is "What is 'time management' and how does it work? Students put down their reaction. While this may seem quite simple, it's a good starting point for discussion. Capitalize on students' self-interest in mastering this chapter, and use the Challenge → Reaction → Insight → Action prompts to spark their interest.

Your Type Is Showing

In this chapter students get to take a self-assessment that will help them make a direct connection between their type and the way they manage time. This chapter even points out how different types use different planning systems. Some personality types are planners and some just are not naturally that way. Make sure students don't just have the attitude "yup, that's me—can't do it." Stress the importance that for most of us there is a need to develop coping strategies since time management is not a naturally occurring habit.

Control Your Learning: Your Toughest Class

This is a really important section for students to do and for the class to discuss. This section connects with procrastination—the "P" word. In this section students are provided with a list of the most common reasons people procrastinate. Have students think of their toughest class and see which of these factors might be the cause of procrastination in a specific course. Often procrastination stems from fear of failure, which means it may relate to their toughest course. Get students thinking about how they might change this behavior.

Cultivate Your Curiosity: Are *You* Caught In The Net?

Have you ever wondered what the fascination is with social networking sites, like Facebook or MySpace? This section of the chapter is essential for students to reflect upon. As these become more and more popular among students, it is vital for educators to know something about Net addiction. Asking your students about the amount of time they personally spend on the internet might become a sensitive situation. One way to depersonalize the discussion is to create a case study of a student who is struggling with a Net addiction. Ask your students to identify the potentially dangerous habits our fictitious student exhibits, then ask them to brainstorm intervention strategies for that student. Refer to the tips in this chapter as a foundation for the discussion.

FOCUS on Careers

In this chapter, we meet Judith Cara, the Community and Government Relations Manager for Intel Corporation. Ms. Cara is responsible for a variety of departments at Intel: managing the local media coverage of the corporation, cultivating relationships with elected officials, implementing Intel's educational programs in her state, and organizing several community outreach events. With so many responsibilities, Ms. Cara admits that being an effective time manager is imperative. She uses an online meeting planner that is accessible to her colleagues. She recommends that students interested in public relations "shadow" a person in that career field. Students will need to think about questions like what types of majors might prepare me well to be a public relations manager? What is the most common psychological type for this profession? Does it match my psychological type? Take a show of hands: who in the class would be happy in this high-energy, fast-paced career field? Why or why not?

6. Which in-text exercises should I use?

There are four exercises built into this chapter. Included here are descriptions of why they have been included, what challenges you might expect, and how you might debrief each one. Many of the Challenge → Reaction → Insight → Action prompts in this chapter are also filled with opportunities to engage students, so if you choose not to do all of the major activities included here, be sure you take a close look at the Challenge → Reaction → Insight → Action prompts.

EXERCISE 4.1 TERM ON A PAGE

Why do this activity?
It's essential that students get to see, on paper, the whole term at a glance. Also, they might now be aware of drop/add deadlines, or they will want to know when these dates are. When students were in high school, their schedules were more structured. They knew that they would be in class everyday, and sometimes they even had a built-in study hall. Some high schools even have hot lines for parents or students to call in about what assignments are due. High schools often build in time management systems for students, but that's not the case in college. Some students are naturally good at managing their schedules, and others not. By seeing the entire semester after using their course syllabi to record tests, quizzes and papers, they might have second thoughts about going away for the weekend, for example, with a heavy week coming up.

What are the challenges and what can you expect?
One of the challenges of this activity is that not every instructor gives a detailed syllabus. Let's hope that is not the case, but if it is, encourage students to ask the professor for more information. The syllabus may say things like "there will be a number of tests and quizzes" that will be determined or TBA listed by assignments. Encourage students to be proactive with their instructors. Check to see if students in your class have the same course and instructors. If students go in pair or groups it may be less intimidating for the students, and more time efficient for the instructor to tell a group of students the same thing. Who knows, it might even spur the instructor on to get more specific about course expectations for students.

How much time will it take?
The amount of time this activity takes will depend on if students do this outside of class time (probably the best option) and report back to the class. If you choose this option, the in-class time is about 30 minutes.

How should I debrief?
You could debrief this activity a number of different ways. You can ask students to work in small groups to see if there are any common challenges. Most likely they will identify mid-term week as a busy one, right before Thanksgiving, and, of course, final exam week. Have each group identify one or two things that they will do to manage these busy weeks. Tell students it's not enough to say they will manage their time. Ask them specifically what they will do. Will they finish a paper before they go out for a few hours on a weekend night? Will they study with friends if they are in the same classes? Or, you might ask students to send you an e-mail to identify the biggest time management challenges they see and what they will do about them. Again, ask students to be specific. Or, you can simply have a class discussion about the benefits of planning. This discussion can lead into one about using planners and the different types available.

EXERCISE 4.2 SO MUCH TO DO—SO LITTLE TIME

Why do this activity?
It's important to show students that they really do have choices in how they spend their time. Like Derek, who didn't seem to think he had much control over his schedule, students think they just can't eliminate things. Also some student put priorities in the wrong place; sometimes putting others' needs before their own. Having students identify the criteria they use to assign items an "A, B, or C" and striking through what's not urgent or important is valuable and because it's not *their* list they might be able to make harder choices and then incorporate the time management principles they've used into their own schedules. Consider having pairs work on this activity together so that they can discuss their choices.

What are the challenges and what can you expect?
There should not be many challenges in this activity. Students simply have to place a letter before each statement or cross it out.

How much time will it take?
It's a quick in-class activity that can discussed immediately in class.

How should I debrief?
Divide the class into four groups and assign each group a letter, A, B or C, and the final "cross out/not urgent or important group." Groups identify and list only the statements they are assigned to. Groups report out and describe why they identified certain statements and other members of the class add or subtract to the list. When students add or subtract, they must identify why. A good class discussion about priorities should evolve.

EXERCISE 4.3 VARK ACTIVITY

Why do this activity?
This activity is designed to help students understand that their preferred VARK learning modality even impacts the way they learn to manage time. You might even bring in a few different planners, and ask students to identify which they prefer and see it there are differences in what students chose, based on their preferences in learning.

> **What are the challenges and what can I expect?**
> You might find that some of these activities take a little more time than others. For example visiting a workplace, or finding just the right program on NPR might not be as easy as color coding a list or writing about it.
>
> **How much time will it take?**
> This really depends on which activity students choose to do and how you debrief it.
>
> **How should I debrief?**
> When students return to class they can group according to the activity they chose, take a few minutes and in one or two sentence describe to the rest of the class what they learned, what was helpful to them, and what was not. If time does not permit, just ask a few students to report what they learned, or have students send you a quick e-mail.

7. Which additional exercises might enrich students' learning?

Just Say No!
Class activity/role play
Materials needed: None
Time: 15 minutes
Goal: To help students understand that they just have to say "No!" sometimes
Ask for two volunteers from the class. One (student A) assumes the role of the roommate, whose parents are in town just for the evening and want to take the roommates out for a really special dinner. The other student (B) has a quiz at 9:00 a.m. and has to study but agrees to go out. Student A's job is to get student B to go out to dinner, and then sight see, and then for coffee, extending the night as long as he/she can. At what point will the student say "no." (Student B is not to be told of the plan to extend the evening.). Ask students if they have even been in a situation like this and what they did about it.

The Ten Minute Teller
Class activity: Discussion after students do this activity at home
Materials needed: Timer
Time: 20 minutes
Goal: To help students break down tasks into small increments and stay focused
Sometimes when tasks are not pleasant or seem as if they will take forever, if they are broken down into smaller segments they seem much more manageable. For homework, ask students to do some activity that they don't want to do. Break it down into three ten- minutes segments. Segments don't even have to be back to back. At the end of 10 minutes, students can take a break or continue. Before they begin the next segment, ask students to take a few minutes to record what they accomplished in the previous segment. Have students come to the next class to discuss what they chose to do, and if the 10 minute segments helped them to stay focused. Did they accomplish more than they thought they would? Once they got going did they feel better? Sometimes just beginning something is all students need to avert procrastinating.

<u>Help Me with My Bad Habits!</u>
Materials needed: nothing
Time: 30-50 minutes, depending on the size of the group
Goal: To help students to identify bad habits they have that cause them to waste time and come up with strategies to help
Divide the class into two groups. Each group is asked to come up with five bad habits for wasting time. For example, a student might be ready to sit down to work on the computer and start to surf the net, or play solitaire. After five minutes each group gives the other group the five habits they identified. It might be a good idea to create a "master" list of all the bad habits. Give each group another five minutes to come up with suggestion on how to "break the habit."

<u>My Favorite Planner</u>
Class activity
Materials needed: Students need to bring in their planners
Time: 30 minutes, depending on the size of the group
Goal: To help students see the different kinds of planners and how people in the class are using them
Ask students to bring their planners to class and take turns coming to the front of the class, and in two minutes describe why they like the planner (or not). Also, ask students to show what they write in their planners. You might bring in the university planner if one is given out to students during new student orientation, for example, and have forgotten that they have it. These planners are helpful since they include dates that are important on a particular campus. Students may be surprised to see that there are day planners, week at a glance, month at a glance, and ones that combine many features. Students must feel comfortable with their planner, and feel that it is helping them. If not, they just won't use it.

8. What other activities can I incorporate to make the chapter my own?

Take full advantage of the activities that are part of the annotations in the text as well as lists and activities in the chapter such as "Ways not to get caught in the Net," "It's too darn nice outside," or "Monitor your schedule every day." Consider assigning students to lead particular activities. You can even break your class into segments—some segments you lead the class, and have students lead other segments. Allowing students to lead the class is one way to engage your introverted students. Plus, you can sit back, relax, and enjoy watching. Think about putting these activity options from the annotations included here on a small sheet of paper and have students pick from a basket. Since control is an important C factor, give students some flexibility in how they interpret their "chosen" activity!

Included here, all in one place, are Activity Options taken from the Annotated Instructor's Edition.

ACTIVITY OPTION (p. 103): Break the class up into groups of two or three so that each group responds to one of the six questions. After working in small groups, ask students to report to the entire class.

ACTIVITY OPTION (p. 107): This is a great opportunity to get students to share with each other the letter grade they gave themselves and why. Pair up students, ask them to share with each other, and then give each other some tip that they think might help with a particular challenge. If time permits, let the entire class share. Students need to understand they are not alone in their challenges, but there are tips to get themselves refocused. You might bring up the topic of "flow." Once you get started and are on a roll, it can feel really good.

ACTIVITY OPTION (p. 112): Give students a chart with times for a full day (twenty-four hours). Have them quickly list their high-energy times. Come together as a group and compare. Are there common times among the group? You should see differences among the students. Now, ask students to volunteer to tell you when they typically study. Are they doing it during peak energy times?

ACTIVITY OPTION (p. 113): Get students out of their seats and lined up based on their personality types. For example, have students line up with strong E's on one end and strong I's on the other. Have them tell each other how they like to plan and what they use to help them plan based on this dimension. Students should be thinking about ways they can move themselves more toward the middle. What do J's do that helps them stay organized? If I am a P, what do I know about myself and what can I learn from a J?

ACTIVITY OPTION (p. 114): Students can share their responses to this "Challenge → Reaction" with each other. If students are willing, you can line them up on a continuum for a quick class check. Have students line up from most hours spent studying to least. Why are they standing where they are? Are some students taking more classes than others? Are some students totally on their own financially? Remind students that time in the library does not always equate with learning. Line up students again with those who stay focused for most of the time they study on one end and those who are distracted throughout the time on the other. Have focused students share their tips with others.

ACTIVITY OPTION (p. 117): Ask students to share with a partner how much time they spend online for things that are not school-related. How many times in the middle of working on the computer for some school-related activity do they respond to an IM or check their e-mail? Often? If this behavior is fairly typical, would they like to change? What could they do to improve their online habits? Give students about ten minutes and then have students report to the group. The goal will be to compare notes on how to improve online habits.

ACTIVITY OPTION (p. 118): This is a great opportunity for students to share with each other their plans for the term. Some students will have lots of details on their calendars while others will have just a few bullets. Pair up students with opposite personality types: S's with N's or J's with P's. What do they learn from each other? Ask students if they have a planner and if they use it every day. Students will begin to see that, like writing their name with the nondominant hand as in Chapter 2, even if something is not natural, with practice they can develop productive habits, like good planning.

ACTIVITY OPTION (p. 125): Make two sets of index cards with the same tasks as listed in Exercise 4.2. Divide the class into two groups and have them decide as a group which time zones to put each task into. At the end of fifteen minutes, have one member of the team report the criteria used to place the cards in the zones to the class, what was eliminated, and what they observed about the different members in the groups. Then give each one of the fifteen cards to an individual student, and have them line up from left to right to indicate how they'd organize the day. They'll likely have to negotiate their positions.

ACTIVITY OPTION (p. 132): The five strategies listed here can help students use real-life techniques to balance multiple things. Write these five techniques on index cards, one per card, and make as many sets as you need so that each student in the class has at least three cards. Hand out the cards and ask students to work in pairs or small groups to come up with real-life examples and solutions for the technique on their card to present to the class.

ACTIVITY OPTION (p. 133): Have students develop a five-slide PowerPoint presentation for the class describing the most important thing they learned in this chapter about managing time and energy. On the second slide they must include one challenge that they're facing and on the third, a specific activity they will do to help them manage the challenge. In the last slide they should describe a possible pitfall they may have to completing the activity and what benefit they will derive if they stick to their plan.

9. What homework might I assign?

Essay
Students can write a two page essay on the follow topic: What I Learned and What Time Management Strategies I Will Incorporate and Why? Goal: To help students to describe some of the challenges they are facing in college, and what information from the chapter they will use.

Journal Entries
One: Have students write a one page journal entry, send you an e-mail, or blog describing something they do to procrastinate. Students must identify a situation when this has happened and what repercussions procrastinating had. Then, ask them to identify an upcoming assignment where procrastination might derail them, and have them describe to you how they plan to overcome the temptation. They can choose from the "Top Ten Procrastination-Busters" list or identify one of their own.

Two: At this point in the semester, students may need some additional motivation. Have students generate a reward system for themselves. Ask students to list five or six activities that they enjoy, but that they don't have time for. Ask students to identify three activities that they must complete this week. These activities could be reading all their assignments, studying for an exam, working on a research paper, etc. Ask them to commit to completing these assignments. If they do, they get three rewards. At the end of the week, have students prepare a three-slide PowerPoint presentation on their experience.

Three: Use the Insight → Action prompts as journal or blog assignments.

10. What have I learned in teaching this chapter that I will incorporate next time?

_____

_____

_____

_____

_____

_____

_____

_____

_____

_____

_____

_____

_____

_____

_____

_____

_____

_____

_____

_____

_____

_____

_____

_____

_____

_____

_____

_____

_____

_____

_____

_____

_____

_____

_____

CHAPTER 5: THINKING CRITICALLY AND CREATIVELY

1. Why is this chapter important?

So what does thinking really mean? According to Staley, thinking is defined as a focused cognitive activity you engage in purposefully. You are focused on something and not simply daydreaming. When thinking critically, we use standards by which to judge things and don't just jump to conclusions and believe everything we read or hear. When we think creatively, we come up with different ways of thinking about the same thing. Creative thinking often uses the words "what if?"

Really, no one can expect first year college students to have fully developed critical thinking skills. In fact, the world is pretty black and white according to most of them. In their minds, there are right ways to do things, and wrong ways, and not too much in between. Sometimes, students have been raised in very sheltered environments; some have been raised in complicated families or even have troubled backgrounds. Students come together from small towns and large cities, and often find that their thinking is challenged. They find out that there are some grey areas in life and that sometimes the context or the situation must be considered. What students experience, read about and study about, require them to use thinking strategies that they may never have used before. But, without making this critical leap from dualistic thinking to critical thinking, succeeding in college will be difficult, if not impossible.

This chapter brings with it some sensitive situations that you should be aware of.

- **Be sensitive to the fact that you will most likely have students who feel very differently about a number of topics based on their age, experiences, and upbringing.** Just like Annie Miller, who feels uncomfortable about not having "answers for things" in class, the level of discomfort around controversial topics is common among first-year students. For some, they have left their comfort zones and the ways they were raised, and their fundamental beliefs may be challenged. Even though their original beliefs may be strengthened through testing in college, they may feel threatened by broaching particular topics. Because your goal is to get students to *think*, be sure that you create a safe climate. Your students should feel that your class is a place to test their thinking and reasoning without judgment or criticism.

- **Be careful how you approach students who demonstrate faulty reasoning.** You may find flaws in students' arguments or faulty reasoning. Instead of directly challenging these students, it's important to make sure that your response is something like "I never thought of it that way—have you ever thought about…?" Just don't make students feel attacked, because then they will shut down. Also, don't let students shoot each other down, but model for them how to disagree and challenge each other appropriately with questions like "what if..?, have you ever thought of…? did you know that…?"

- **Be aware that there are gender differences in how students relate to academia.** As first-year students, males are more likely to interact more with their instructors. However, females are more likely to take notes and study to do well. Later in their academic careers, females rely on other's opinions and collect ideas to construct their own knowledge. Males see the opinions of others as opportunities for debate or challenge. Finally, while females often have their own ideas, they also value the ideas of others. Males tend to process ideas more independently. It is important for you to design a classroom environment that allows both men and women to feel safe, while being appropriately challenged.

2. What are this chapter's learning objectives?

➤ How focused thinking, critical, and creative thinking are defined
➤ Why critical thinking is important
➤ How to use questions to think critically
➤ How a four-part model of critical thinking works
➤ Why reasoning is the foundation for critical thinking
➤ How to analyze arguments, assess assumptions, and consider claims
➤ How to avoid mistakes in reasoning
➤ What metacognition is and why it's important
➤ How to solve problems and make decisions
➤ How to think creatively
➤ How to become a more creative thinker

3. How should I launch this chapter?

A good way to launch this chapter is to get students thinking about thinking! That may sound redundant, but you could begin by asking students to identify the kinds of questions they will answer in college. Questions could range from, what is the capital of Iran; or should stem cells be harvested, to "how important are ethics in today's business world?" Students need to understand that when we make a decision about something, we have facts to take into account, opinions about things, our own experiences, as well as ethical and moral values that underpin how we think and respond.

Think about beginning this chapter with a discussion about the media. How do you know what you see on the news or read in the newspaper is true? If you are not sure, how would you find out?

- **Begin a discussion about why people may have very different responses to the same question.** Ask for a show of hands.
    - Whose hometown is in the same state as their college?
    - Whose favorite color is blue?
    - Whose favorite ice cream is vanilla?
    - Who agrees that small colleges are better than large universities?
    - Does freedom of religion really exist in the U.S.?

Ask students about the differences in these questions. Clearly some questions were just factual. Either their hometown is in the same area as their college or it's not. Favorite ice cream and colors are based on opinions, and it really doesn't matter, does it? Maybe the question of the size of a college gets a little more controversial, but when it comes to freedom of religion, the question becomes much more controversial, and one's response may be rooted in faith as opposed to logic. Students should understand that good critical thinkers are aware of the differences between facts and opinions, and if they come to an emotional response to a question, they are aware of why. For example, someone may know an individual who has been persecuted for religious reasons, or they are horrified (or aren't) that Christmas decorations have become controversial. Challenge students to be active participants in their own thinking: they should be prepared to defend their thinking *process* as much as their opinions.

- **Remember the Readiness Check at the beginning of the chapter.** Instructors could assume that students think they know a lot about thinking. After all, they have graduated from high school, and surely they had to think to get their diplomas. Out of all the Readiness Checks students have completed so far, how interested are they in this particular chapter? Are they less motivated to read it because they believe they already know a lot about thinking or because the chapter sounds too abstract to them?

- **Going beyond the book.** There are a number of terrific opportunities for students to learn more about critical thinking in this chapter. They might even enjoy their logic, ethics, or philosophy classes if they were more prepared for the challenge. This is a good time to talk about some of the skills that are needed in courses such as these. Also, consider getting students to read a bit more about emotional intelligence now. Strong emotional intelligence requires good analytical skills. In order to be realistic about something, which is a critical EI skill, you have to assess what is really happening. To know how to respond effectively to others, you have to know yourself. And effective problem solving is really a trial (and sometimes error), step-by-step approach to figuring out what is important.

4. How should I use the *FOCUS* Challenge Case?

Annie Miller came to college expecting, even welcoming, change. From her large high school and her big city life, she now finds herself in a small college, on the other side of the county in a small town. She is now concerned that she might have made a mistake, because she misses the fast pace of city life. To make matters worse, her Introduction to Philosophy professor emphasized the importance of critical thinking in his very first class. Professor Courtney asks an endless chain of questions, none of which seem to have a *right* answer. Although challenged by the way her professor approaches the class, Annie is actually more attentive and engaged in this class than her others. You might begin by asking the class if Professor Courtney's style is an effective teaching method. What you will probably find is that you will have some differences of opinions in the class. This is a good opportunity to ask the class what is the right answer? There really is not a right answer. And that can be very frustrating for students. Exploring the Socratic method, how it relates to critical thinking, and Annie's reaction to it, might be another good way to launch the chapter.

5. What important features does this chapter include?

Students should be fairly used to the recurring features in the book. You might even be at a point, especially if your class only meets a few hours a week, to begin putting students into groups and assigning some of these features for homework and have them report on different ones in class. For example, you may assign the Challenge → Reaction prompts to Group A, and the "Your Type Is Showing" to Group B. Ask each group to prepare a two to three minute presentation on their assigned activities. As the course continues, keep track of which activities each group has already reported on. If you try this technique, be sure that each team has a chance to do a number of different features.

Readiness and Reality Checks

This Readiness Check may prove to be an interesting one. We might safely assume that a number of first year students have never even thought about thinking, or much less how to do it critically and creatively. They just thought they were thinking! You might consider doing a pre- and post- comparison on this chapter. Guesses are that the Readiness Check at the start is different from the Reality Check at the end.

Challenge → Reaction → Insight → Action prompts

There are a number of very important Challenge → Reaction → Insight → Action prompts in this chapter. The Challenge → Reaction → Insight → Action prompts in this chapter or in any chapter, can be used in quizzes, journals or class discussions. You might even consider taking all of the Challenge → Reaction → Insight → Action prompts, put them is a basket and have students pull them out and respond for an in class quiz. Try doing this in pairs and point out the wisdom of this method of learning in the group. Another way to use these prompts is as a class opinion poll. For example, take the Challenge → Reaction prompt, "What is the difference between *critical* thinking and *creative* thinking?" Ask students to answer this prompt on 3 x 5 index cards and turn them back in to you. Sort the answers into piles, based on similar answers. Then, report back to the class the similarities and the differences in their answers. This could form the basis for an interesting discussion on how multiple answers to a question could all be right!

Self-Assessments: Decision Style Inventory and Creative Potential Profile

In this chapter, students will take a 20 statement Decision Style Inventory and a 25 statement Creative Potential Profile. Remind students that there are no right or wrong answers, but that it's a self report on how they think they would most likely respond to a situation. As a result, they will discover if their decision style is directive, analytical, conceptual, or behavioral and if their creative potential profile is intuitive, innovative, imaginative, or inspirational. It might be fun for students to read the description of the types first and guess which style they are. After they complete the inventory see if their hunches were correct.

<u>Your Type Is Showing</u>
Break your students out into groups based on their Decision Style. Now ask your students what their what their score was on the MBTI like assessment from Chapter 2. Do the students in each group have similar MBTI like scores? I bet there do, since researchers have shown a strong connection between the Decision Style Inventory and the MBTI.

<u>C-Factors</u>
Because of the highly engaging and detailed simulation on alcohol poisoning at Rocky Mountain State University and the two lengthy instruments on decision-making style and creativity profile, the features "Cultivate Your Curiosity" and "Control Your Learning" don't appear in this chapter. However, "*FOCUS* on Careers" and "Challenge Yourself Online Quizzes" are available.

<u>*FOCUS* on Careers</u>
The career focus in this chapter is on Federal Judge, Harold (Hallie) Tyler and careers such as his. Judge Tyler outlines how the duties of judges shift, depending on what particular aspect of the law a judge works with. However, he emphasizes the importance of critical thinking for this profession. He believes that the three most important skills of a judge are to think critically, write well, and decide cases in a timely fashion. Students will need to think about questions like what types of majors might prepare me well for a career like Judge Tyler's? What is the most common psychological type for this profession? Does it match my psychological type? It's clear that not only do judges need to carefully analyze facts; critical thinking is fundamental to this profession. Take a show of hands: who in the class would be find this career satisfying? Who would find it challenging? Why or why not?

6. Which in-text exercises should I use?

There are five exercises built into this chapter. Included here are descriptions of why they have been included, what challenges you might expect, and how you might debrief each one. Many of the Challenge → Reaction → Insight → Action prompts in this chapter are also filled with opportunities to engage students, so if you choose not to do all of these, be sure you take a close look at these Challenge → Reaction → Insight → Action prompts.

EXERCISE 5.1 AND JUST WHY IS CRITICAL THINKING IMPORTANT?

Why do this activity?
This activity is simple and quick and could be done in class. While it's in the format of a brief survey where students respond to statements about why critical thinking might be important, it's really a teaching tool to point out why critical thinking *is* important and what aspects of life it connects to.

What are the challenges and what can you expect?
When you take a look at the prompts they begin with "would you like to….become a better citizen, a better employee" for example. Students might tend to rate them all high. Of course, the point is exactly that. All of the reasons stated are essential reasons for developing critical thinking skills.

How much time will it take?
This activity should take about 30 minutes.

How should I debrief?
Because you will probably find that students score high on most of these, it's probably best to just have a general discussion about how critical thinking applies to all important aspects of life. You might start out by asking students which of the statements is not important. Let's hope they say something like "they are all important reasons for development strong critical thinking skills." If they don't, ask them to defend their answers as to why a particular statement is not important.

EXERCISE 5.2 CRITICAL SEARCHING ON THE INTERNET

Why do this activity?
With the advent of the Internet, there is so much information at our fingertips that it becomes harder and harder to distinguish facts from opinions or even untruths. Students must know how to evaluate what they find on the Internet, understand the different domains, and look at measures, like how current the site is, how to know it's accurate, who the author of the site is and his or her credentials, etc.

What are the challenges and what can you expect?
What you can expect is that while today's students are very technically savvy, they may not be all that aware of how to assess sources.

How much time will it take?
Depending on how you wish to debrief this activity, it could take anywhere from 30-45 minutes.

How should I debrief?
You can debrief this activity by asking students for examples of web sites that were not credible for academic research purposes and then ask them to report the "give-away" clues. If no one volunteers, you might suggest that if web sites are under construction, or web sites contain any kind of typing or grammatical errors that should send up an automatic red flag.

EXERCISE 5.3 ROCKY MOUNTAIN STATE UNIVERSITY CASE STUDY AND SIMULATION

Why do this activity?
Not only does this exercise relate directly to today's traditional students and help identify issues that can spark debate, it's a great example to bring in discussions about binge drinking and the possible consequences. By looking at the letters to the editor from ten different individuals and their reactions to a death of a college student from alcohol poisoning, students get a chance to try to sort out facts from claims, and the criteria for logical explanations versus self-serving motives.

What are the challenges and what can you expect?
You can expect that students will be interested in reading this. They will be pulled into the material and although they may not reveal what they really think since they may believe it's not

what you would want to hear, they will likely be highly engaged. Be sure to reiterate that there are no right or wrong answers, so they will know you are not expecting a particular answer. Emphasize that you really *do* want to know what they think, not parrot back your own ideas.

How much time will it take?
This activity could take up a full class period or at least 50 minutes.

How should I debrief?
Three questions appear at the end of this exercise. Divide the class into three groups and assign them to one of these questions. Have groups report out and lead a discussion. If there is not time in class for this you could ask students to respond to the three questions as a homework or e-mail assignment. Not only is this information relevant for students, it provides great examples for finding faulty reasoning, examining claims versus facts, and evaluating individual's opinions.

EXERCISE 5.4 DECISION STYLE INVENTORY

Why do this activity?
This is just a simple twenty question inventory that helps students gain one more piece of information about themselves. While it is primarily for managers—and students are not yet in managerial positions typically, unless of course you are working with non-traditional students— it does provide a prediction for the way they might eventually manage others and general information about their decision-making styles.

What are the challenges and what can I expect?
Because most students have not yet had much if any managerial experience, some of the questions may be a hard to answer. However, students will most likely score in ways similar to their MBTI types.

How much time will it take?
This could be a homework assignment that you debrief in class. Depending on how much time you wish to discuss, this activity could take 20-30 minutes.

How should I debrief?
Have students read the descriptors before taking the assessment and have them guess their profiles before they take it. Afterwards, ask students if they were correct in their guesses. Take a look at Figure 5.4 and have students discuss their Decision Style Inventory and their MBTI. If there is not time to discuss this, have students summarize this and send it to you in an e-mail

---

EXERCISE 5.5 CREATIVE POTENTIAL PROFILE

Why do this activity?
Just as students learned more about themselves in Exercise 5.4, they will learn about themselves and their creative potential after doing this exercise. Many students believe that they cannot think creatively because they are not "artistic." By exploring their own creative potential, students will gain a greater appreciation for what creativity actually is. It may even encourage them to explore their creative aspects outside of class!

What are the challenges and what can you expect?
There should not be many challenges to this activity. One caution might be to help students continue to make connections about all of the assessments they have been taking. Are they getting a clear picture of how their own behavioral and learning preferences?

How much time will it take?
This activity could take around 20-30 minutes.

How should I debrief?
Although this is mentioned in the text, it warrants a discussion. Remind students that its *motivation* not general intelligence that is the key to creativity. Remember the quote "if you can and you don't, it means you won't." Without challenging themselves to do something with their creative side, they may not develop a key component of their competence..

EXERCISE 5.6 VARK ACTIVITY

Why do this activity?
This activity is designed to help students understand that their preferred VARK learning modality. This activity encourages students to relate their preferred VARK learning modality with particular study skills. Visual learners should use the white space in this chapter to write a personal response to each section of the chapter, while aural learners should discuss the key concepts with a friend. Read/write students will summarize a controversial article, and kinesthetic learners should check out additional resources on thinking.

What are the challenges and what can I expect?
There are no real challenges in this activity except for the students who are multimodal. Again, these students may not want to do more than one activity, so you may want to make doing more than one assignment optional for them or just let them choose one.

How much time will it take?
Because this activity is done outside of class, time spent in class will depend on how you wish to debrief the activity.

How should I debrief?
Just as you did in similar VARK activities, choose how you want students to respond to their experiences—by e-mail, online—in chats, etc. What important is that you vary the way that students respond to the VARK activities.

---

7. Which additional exercises might enrich students' learning?

Critical Thinking—Critical Searching (Adapted from Staley (2003))
Materials needed: Web site links and a comparison chart
Time: 45 minutes to an hour
Goal: To help students critique web sites for academic uses
Ask students to find four web sites that relate to binge drinking for college students. Ask students to assess the four web sites according to the criteria listed on the chart below. Then, ask them to

present the most credible site to the class. Insist that students are able to logically defend their choice.

	Accuracy	Authority	Objective/ Perspective	Currency	Coverage/ Scope	Purpose	Access
1							
2							
3							
4							

The Best News of the Day
Class activity: Discussion in class, after students have reviewed the news articles at home
Materials needed: Two different news articles about of the same incident that you provide
Time: 45 minutes
Goal: To help students see that presenting slightly different information can alter one's perception of the same incident
For homework give students two short articles on the same topic. Maybe your town has more than one newspaper—taking an article from each would be ideal. Or you could use your college paper and the local one, or *USA Today*. Ask students to evaluate which version of the article they preferred and why? Was it because one was more sensational or gave more facts? This should lead into a discussion of what really sells the news. Is it just the facts?

Good Thinkers Please Apply
Materials needed: Large news print and markets
Time: 30-50 minutes, depending on the size of the group
Goal: To understand and describe the thinking skills necessary for success in careers
Divide the class into two groups. Each group comes up with a job description and want ad for a good thinker. Groups put their ads on newsprint for the class to see. Classmates vote on which is the better description. For example, the description might read "Wanted: An individual who is able to help bring our company to the number one position among our competitors in the nation. Applicants must be able to work effectively in teams, understand the steps involved in solving complex problems, etc."

8. What other activities can I incorporate to make the chapter my own?

At this point in the course you probably have a sense for whether you have a group of self starters or students that you have to constantly draw into the conversation. You are probably getting comfortable with the students and now it might be fun to do something a little different. Remember that there are some personality types that don't like change, so make sure you still keep the same activities and assignments that were planned or put on your syllabus.

Included here, all in one place, are Activity Options taken from the Annotated Instructor's Edition.

ACTIVITY OPTION (p. 137): Divide the class into three groups. Choose three of the questions from "What Do *You* Think?" and ask students to work in groups to answer the question and report to the class. As a variation, ask students to do the same for homework and compare answers in the next class or discuss their responses in an online threaded discussion or chat.

ACTIVITY OPTION (p. 141): Give students five minutes to write down this sentence: Thinking critically is "critical" to lifelong success because _____. Have students fill in the blank. Make a class list and come to some conclusions about why critical thinking is important—it's really connected to lifelong, self-directed (*I figured it out!*) learning.

ACTIVITY OPTION (p. 143): Play the "How Do I Know This Is True?" game. Bring in some headlines from the student or local newspaper. Put them on a PowerPoint slide or overhead, and show them to the class. Go around the room and have students fill in the following: I know this is true because _____. Any student can say "NOT" and then explain why it is not true. If it is true, and no one challenges, students just keep adding to why it's true.

ACTIVITY OPTION (p. 143): For homework, ask students to find two web sites on the same topic, one really credible web site and one that is suspect. Students can choose their own topic or you can assign one. For example, if a student is interested in anorexia, she might find the National Institute of Mental Health has a good site, and someone with a personal homepage does not. The important part is that students have to defend their reasoning.

ACTIVITY OPTION (p. 147): See if you can get your hands on a video of this *Monty Python* sketch for the class to watch or Google it and watch it online. After viewing it, divide the class into two groups to discuss the difference between an argument as defined in this chapter and a contradiction.

ACTIVITY OPTION (p. 150): This is another opportunity to take an article from the newspaper and look for arguments that support a fact (or not). Bring a short newspaper article to class (short and current is best, and something that will engage students). Follow the pyramid in Figure 5.3 to explore the reasoning. The class can work as a whole, or in small teams. This activity could also be used for homework.

ACTIVITY OPTION (p. 154): Alcohol on college campuses is a hot topic. Use this opportunity to talk about this issue and how it pertains to your campus. Brainstorm a list of questions that students would want to know about alcohol use and abuse on campus. Divide students into groups of two to three and give them a specific question from the list they just generated. Tell them to find the answer and bring it to class next week. Make sure that they tell you the source, and why they thought it was credible.

ACTIVITY OPTION (p. 159): Have the class fill in their names on a rough chart you draw on the board or create a PowerPoint slide or transparency of Figure 5.4 to indicate where they fit. You should do it first to model how you make decisions based on your personality type and decision-making style. Discuss your commonalities and differences as decision-makers and give some real examples to make the concepts more concrete to students.

ACTIVITY OPTION (p. 161): Ask students to respond to either one or both of the questions from this "Insight → Action" exercise. Consider using them as a homework assignment that can be e-mailed to you and one other class member. Before you respond to the student, have class members give each other feedback. Ask students to list the most significant things they learned from reading their classmate's reflection. Was their partner's response different from their own? Why or why not? Give examples. After you read the responses, give feedback to the students.

ACTIVITY OPTION (p. 166): Bring a pillow to class! Write some common first-year student statements on cards (roommate or family concerns are good ones) and ask students to come up in pairs and use the Pillow Method to address the problem.

ACTIVITY OPTION (p. 168): Have students develop a three- to five-slide PowerPoint presentation for the class describing a technique in this chapter for analyzing arguments, becoming more creative, exploring different decision-making styles, applying the Pillow Method (with examples), or any activity in the chapter that helped them to understand this chapter. (Students can work in teams and you can assign topics if you wish.)

9. What homework might I assign?

Because there are many exercises in the chapter, any one of them could be used for a homework activity.

Journal Entries
One: One of the topics in this chapter is metacognition—thinking about thinking.
Have students write a one page journal entry, describing the three elements of metacognition and how improving their metacognitive skills could make them a better learner.

Two: Ask your students to find a news item that is interesting to them and examine it from at least two opposing viewpoints. Then, ask them to describe their own opinion on the subject. Be aware that this could lead to a sensitive situation as your students may be hesitant to examine their own ideas.

Three: Use the Insight → Action prompts as journal or blog assignments.

10. What have I learned in teaching this chapter that I will incorporate next time?

_____

_____

_____

_____

_____

_____

CHAPTER 6: ENGAGING, LISTENING, AND NOTE-TAKING IN CLASS

1. Why is this chapter important?

You can't open a college success book without seeing a whole chapter devoted to being involved in class, paying attention, and taking notes. In fact, if you "Google" note-taking, you'll find thousands of hits, along with books completely dedicated to the subject. So why do so many students still struggle with taking notes when so many resources are available?

Note-taking is actually a complicated process. You must listen, write, and decide what's important at the same time. Students often don't know how to focus on the main ideas and what signals to look for in the text or from their instructors that say "This is important!" When you come right down to it, most students are never told how to *attend* class—not just show up, but participate in the learning process. Being engaged in class is an essential component to college success. While it is important for students to be *physically* present in class, it is even more important for them to be *mentally* present.

Students also have probably never thought about the fact that the way an instructor teaches may or may not be a good fit for the way they learn. They may simply report that they dislike Professor X or they find Professor Y to be boring. Many students never think about the relationship between how their teacher teaches, how they learn, and how to take effective notes either when reading a text or listening to a class presentation. By empowering students with the knowledge of how to learn optimally, they can easily translate their instructor's teaching style into their own learning style. This enables students to take control of their own learning both inside and outside the classroom.

Think back: Can you ever remember anyone telling you that when you go to class you really have to train yourself to pay attention? Maybe for a few students it feels natural to go into the classroom, sit in the front, tune out everything else that is going on, ask questions to stay engaged, and take good notes. However, that's not the case for most students. Students may have to be reminded that listening effectively requires learning about the process and then practicing the skills. Some really important tips are to sit in the front of the room, ask questions, and practice good note-taking, but also skimming the material before class is a key strategy for being prepared to focus. It sets the stage for knowing what the professor is going to discuss. Encourage students to get to class early, and stay late (to foster relationships or ask further clarifying questions). Remind your students that it is important to be physically and mentally prepared before class begins. Often instructors give an outline of the day's session at the beginning of class, and at the end, they tend to summarize. So it is vital for students to tune in right away.

It's really important that students make the connection that some of their successes or failures in school may be connected to the way they learn and the fit with the instructor. Students can't control the way an instructor teaches; they can only control what they do about it. However, many students excuse their lack of learning by criticizing the way their instructors teach. Emphasize that it is always the students' job to adapt to their instructor's teaching, *not* the instructor's job to customize their teaching to each student's learning preference.

2. What are this chapter's learning objectives?

- ➤ How to get engaged in class
- ➤ How to listen with focus
- ➤ How to vary listening styles according to lecture styles
- ➤ How to ask questions in class
- ➤ How to take good notes
- ➤ How to use notes to achieve the best results

3. How should I launch this chapter?

This chapter (like the subject of every chapter of *FOCUS!)* is vital to students' college success. Anecdotally, many instructors report that today's students appear to take fewer notes—perhaps because they find it too taxing, perhaps because they are largely kinesthetic learners, or perhaps because they've never learned how to do it effectively. Here are some suggestions you might try to launch this chapter.

- **Ask students to take a few minutes to think about an instructor whose lectures they find easy to understand.** Because awareness is a really important part of this chapter, ask students to spend a lot of time this week observing their professors and identifying those whose lecture styles they can easily understand and those whose styles are more difficult for them. This may even help them develop a habit of tuning in to professor's styles. Of course, the level of interest a student has in the course material will figure in, but at some fundamental level, students need to discover what works best for them and learn to develop "coping strategies." For example, if students are extraverts who enjoy lively discussion, but that is not the style of the professor, they might ask a classmate to discuss the lecture over lunch. You may have to encourage your students to try many different classroom strategies. By asking your students to become hyperaware of their professors' teaching methods, they will begin to see what adjustments they need to make in order to learn more effectively. Discuss the insights your students gained this week as a class, because there will be some common characteristics that students will describe about the ideal/clear professor. However, there will be variations on what your students prefer, based on their VARK preferences and their SuccessTypes Learning Style Indicator results.

- **Do a mini lecture and ask students to take notes.** Before you go too far into the chapter, do a mini lecture, perhaps about study skills or maybe just something fun with a lot of facts. Ask students to take notes. Pepper your lecture with words like advantages, important, causes, findings, purpose, reason, and conclusions. Use numbering such as first, second, third. After about ten minutes, ask students to compare notes with the student next to them, and notice the differences, if any, in their notes. This should lead into a discussion about how people may take notes differently, but also highlight the fact that signal words are used to help emphasize points. A similar "formal" exercise like this appears in the chapter (Exercise 6.3, p. 197) and later here, "Note-Taking 4-M" ("Forum").

- **Remember that ESL Students may require additional attention from you.** Make sure you also go over the listening tips for students who are not native speakers of English. You may have to reserve some time on the side for extra work with these students. It can be a sensitive situation if they are only one or two in the class. Instead of singling out your international students in class, invite them to your office or to meet you in the school cafeteria for lunch. Tell them that it's important to you that all of your students have the best opportunity to learn in your class, and ask these students if they have questions. If they don't have any questions at this point in the term, reiterate your willingness to help if the need arises. It's important that you respect the boundaries of your international students. Some may not require additional help, while others may simply be shy about asking for it. Often, they can be highly motivated students.

- **Going beyond the book.** As was mentioned earlier, there are literally thousands of resources available for students to learn the skills of engagement, listening, and note-taking. The missing link for many is connecting those skills to something that is meaningful and timely. Have your students find out if there are note-taking or study skills workshops offered on your campus. If so, find out the times and require students to go. If it is a workshop showing students how to take notes from a text, make sure students use a reading from a text book in a course they are currently taking. In fact, whatever activities you use in this chapter, require students to use real live material that they apply to courses they are currently taking.

4. How should I use the *FOCUS* Challenge Case?

Lindsey seems to be an engaged student—at least she wants to be—and she has a supportive family who is interested in her academic success. She has encountered a situation in her computer science class that unless she changes soon, she is doomed to fail. Not only is the material foreign to her, but the teaching style of the instructor, lecturing, is difficult for her to process, and English is his second language. Lindsey has also made some assumptions about the instructor, namely that he has too many students in the class to spend time with each one, so she dare not approach him. She can't drop the class (it is too late), and she needs the class for her financial aid. Lindsey needs help.

Be aware that this situation is common among first-year students. Often they are faced with instructors who have little teaching experience, are not native English speakers, or seem unavailable to students. Ask your students to reflect on suggestions they might give Lindsey's instructor, if they could. After they identify ways her instructor could be more engaging in class, ask them how Lindsey could become more engaged. Remind students that it is Lindsey's responsibility (and theirs, as well) to become engaged in the classroom, not her instructor's job to be more engaging (although many conscientious faculty work continually on developing new and better teaching skills). After this exercise, take a few minutes with the class to discuss one or two things Lindsey can do to make the situation better. Ask them if they would follow the advice they give Lindsey themselves. If they wouldn't, ask them why.

5. What important features does this chapter include?

Again, you will see some of the really important recurring features in this book. While you and your students are becoming very familiar with these features, now would be a good time to change things up a bit. One way to do this is to ask students to complete their favorite feature. Have them present their feature to the class and explain what criteria they used in their selection.

Readiness and Reality Checks

As mentioned in earlier chapters, it's important for students to think about *what they don't know about* what they are about to learn to help them *FOCUS* on learning new things. However, this chapter can be a bit tricky for students. Many students *think* they know how to take notes and listen in class. But what might be missing are the techniques of doing *both* well at the same time. It will be interesting for students to check their "reality" with their readiness for this chapter. Start class off with the following activity: enlarge the Readiness and Reality Checks and paste them on butcher block paper, which you tape to the wall. When students arrive, give them sticky notes. Ask them to anonymously rate each item, then place all of their sticky notes on the butcher block paper (or simply put their marks on the butcher block paper itself). Look for patterns in the class. This could be a fun way to integrate the concept of being prepared for class in a non-threatening environment.

Challenge → Reaction → Insight → Action prompts

There are many different Challenge → Reaction → Insight → Action prompts in this chapter. A few key ones include asking students what "engagement" means. This is a term that is used so frequently in higher education, but not everyone knows what it means. One way to come to a group definition of "engagement" is to pass out 3 x 5 index cards to your class asking them to define it. Have students look for common definitions and ask the class to create a master definition. If your class misses a key component of engagement, provide it in the master definition. For students to look for their own levels of engagement, a clear understanding of what it means as well as understanding the "rules of engagement" are important. Listening "hard" is another key term, as well as helping students understand their strengths and weaknesses related to note-taking and exposing them to a variety of options.

Your Type Is Showing

This feature provides a good opportunity for students to take a hard look at how their professors teach. Launch this feature by having students "stay alert" to all of their professors throughout the week and how they run classes. Is a particular instructor a "rapid-fire" lecturer, a "slow-go" one, an "all-over-the-map" lecturer, a "content-intensive" type, a "review-the-text" guru, a "go-beyond-the-text" type, or an "active-learning" one. Then ask your students to hypothesize about which personality type their professors might be exhibiting based on their lecture style!

If ever there was a time when students could really see the connection between the way that they learn and how it impacts their learning, this is the chapter when it may come together. The way extraverts want a class to be conducted is different from the way introverts want the class to be run. Sensors versus iNtuitors prefer a different kind of structure in the classroom. Thinkers want to skip the rapport part, while feelers may think that a professor is mean or aloof. And judgers just go crazy if a professor is not structured and organized. Remember what is written this chapter "the responsibility for effective communication lies with the listener, not the speaker." Students must learn to find ways to make it work for them and not expect the professor to change. On the other hand, as an instructor, this chapter may cause you to think about how you teach. Have you varied your format and approach enough so that you are tapping into everyone's style and preference?

Control Your Learning: Your Toughest Class

Students need to understand that while they may not be in the drivers' seat; they do have some control over how much they learn. A good back seat driver lets the driver know when it's dangerous or they are not comfortable while not insulting the driver. Students should be assertive enough to explain to a teacher when they do not understand without offending him or her. If they can understand exactly why they are having trouble, they have a better chance of explaining this to the instructor, or simply change what they need to do to optimize their learning. The Lecture Style Analysis Sheet is a great way for students to zero in on exactly what is happening in each of their classes and provide some needed insight.

Self-Assessments

In Exercise 6.2 there is a self-assessment that asks students to respond to questions about how well they listen in a variety of circumstances. At the end of the assessment the students add up their scores and can see where their scores fall within three ranges that differentiate among excellent, good, and listeners who need to change. This is a great opportunity for some peer teaching. Ask your excellent listeners to "teach" the class. They may identify certain behaviors for their peers that enable them to listen "hard." In addition, the Insight → Action prompt that immediately follows this assessment helps students to reflect on what part their behavior plays in how well they are attending. This prompt could also provide the foundation for a discussion on listening skills.

Cultivate Your Curiosity: Quiet Your Mind!

This "Cultivate Your Curiosity" mini-article helps students to focus on how to quiet their mind to enable them to focus better. They are asked to think about where to focus their attention, how to effectively spend their free time, how worry less and do more, how to forgive and forget if something is interfering with their learning, and how to "be present"— giving their all to what they are doing.

FOCUS on Careers

The career focus in the chapter is journalism and we meet *Newsweek* journalist, Karen Springen. Ms. Springen explains why excellent listening and note-taking skills are important to her profession. A fun way to emphasize these skills for your students is to pair them up. Ask each student to 'interview' his/her partner, then give a mini-press release to the class about the interview. Were they able to remember vital facts from their notes or did they release unreliable information? Ask students to identify Ms. Springen's personality type, based on her interview in the book. Does she fit the most common psychological type for her career? At this point, it is a good idea to remind students not to get "stuck" thinking they should not be in a profession just because it does not suit their personality type. Karen

Springen's advice is sound: get a little practice (in this case she suggests the school newspaper) to see if you are suited to a particular career.

6. Which in-text exercises should I use?

There are three exercises built into this chapter. Each is unique and a very engaging for students. Connect these activities, if you can, to courses students are taking and real-life situations for them.

EXERCISE 6.1 ONE WAY VERSUS TWO WAY LISTENING

Why do this activity?
This is a great activity to prove to students why it's important to ask questions in class. In Lindsey's case, she was hesitant to ask questions for fear of looking as if she didn't know what was going on. This activity shows students that asking questions clarifies information and in the process you are imprinting and remembering more than if you were passively listening.

What are the challenges and what can you expect?
Students should really enjoy this activity and laugh a lot when the drawings don't look at all like the one that the student lecturer is trying to describe. One challenge is that this can be time consuming if students have drawings that are very complicated and a time limit is not assigned. Sample drawings you can use for this activity are provided in the Additional Resources section at the end of this manual.

How much time will it take?
25-30 minutes

How should I debrief?
Have students see the chart with the rounds as well as the elapsed time, what they thought was correct, and what actually was. In some way the chart will "debrief" for the class, but you should ask for a few students to recap what they learned by doing the activity.

EXERCISE 6.2 HOW WELL DO YOU LISTEN?

Why do this activity?
There are a number of reasons why this is a good activity for students. Students may never have even thought about how they listen. Here, they can quickly identify areas where they need improvement. They also get immediate feedback on areas where they excel. In addition, it reinforces for students that they have a great amount of control over their own success in college. This activity requires students to respond to questions and results in a score that differentiates excellent listeners, good listeners, and listeners who need to improve their skills.

What are the challenges and what can you expect?
The only real challenge will be that students may not want to admit to the some of the things that they don't do. If their scores are low, they may be embarrassed to admit it. You have to create a

---

climate where students can readily admit what they need to improve upon. Providing an enlarged copy of the diagnostic could help here. Again, pass out sticky notes to your class. Ask them to anonymously place their answers on the butcher block paper. Pay special attention as your students use their sticky notes. This will allow you to identify students who have low scores without alerting their peers.

How much time will it take?
15-20 minutes

How should I debrief?
A good way to debrief is to have students line up on a continuum. Ask those on the lower end why they think they are not good listeners, and then ask for someone on the high end to give that person one specific tip that works for them. Continue to do this with all students. Another option is to have students send you an e-mail about what they discovered about their listening skills.

EXERCISE 6.3 NOTE-TAKING 4-M ("FORUM")

Why do this activity?
Effective note-taking is critical to college success. Allowing students to compare their notes with others can only help students to see where they might need to improve. Consider letting students try this technique for a real test in your class. Let pairs of students work together for the "best possible" notes to use in a real situation.

What are the challenges and what can you expect?
You will find that some students take copious notes because they don't know how to distinguish between essential and non-essential material.. If two or three students with the same style are put together, they won't learn very much from each other. These students may think quantity is better than quality. Try grouping students based on their types, or level of skill they have demonstrated in some other note-taking activity. Students should answer the "M" questions: what do students find that matches in their notes, what missing, what does the lecture mean (the main points), and then measure how much they learned by using a "Visible Quiz." (Sample letters you can use to make "Visible Quiz" cards are included in the Additional Resources section of this manual.)

How much time will it take?
10-15 minutes

How should I debrief?
You have a few options here. First, you might create a few sets of notes. Purposefully create some good and some bad examples. Or think about saving notes from the semester before to save you from creating your own, but make sure it's the same lecture. Ask students to identify which are more helpful notes. Why? Which "M's" played a part in the good or weak notes? Remember quantity does not necessarily mean quality.

EXERCISE 6.4 VARK ACTIVITY

Why do this activity?
This activity is designed to help students make connections between their preferred VARK learning modality and an actual assignment. Taking good notes really does involve all of the modalities so think about assigning students to do something that they would not normally choose—this might be the time to develop a skill a little more rather than use their preference.

What are the challenges and what can I expect?
There are no real challenges in this activity except if students do an activity that is not a preference for them. The point to try and get across to students is that they may have to adjust their style for an instructor who does not teach to their style so hopefully students will see that they can be effective note takers, even when not using their optimal approach.

How much time will it take?
30-40 minutes

How should I debrief?
Because you have the option of having students e-mail you results, give a presentation, post experiences online, or do a class chat, there are a variety of ways to debrief. Since students may have come up with some great ideas, think of a way that all students could have benefit of the examples. While everyone may not be posting something, consider collecting and electronically posting the different examples.

7. Which additional exercises might enrich students' learning?

Taking Notes the Colorful Way
Class activity
Materials needed: Three different colors of magic markers, an article from the newspaper (choose something current and interesting)
Time: 30-50 minutes, depending on the size of the group
Goal: To help students identify the main parts of a story
Place students in small groups of 2-3. Give each student colored markers and the story. Have one additional copy of the story for the group. Have each student read the article and individually using three different colors; mark the headings, main ideas and details of the story. Next, students in the group compare colors and work together to produce one colored coded story that they all agree on. (If you don't want to use colors, students can circle some parts, underline others and star the last).

<u>**Listening with a Purpose**</u> (Staley, C. (2003) *50 Ways to Leave Your Lecture* (p.112))
Class activity
Materials needed: none
Time: lecture plus 20-40 minutes
Goal: To help students listen attentively to lectures and respond to course material

Team	Role	Assignment - After the lecture is finished
1	Questioners	Ask two questions about the material.
2	Nay-Sayers	Comment on two points with which the group disagrees.
3	Yea-Sayers	Comment on two points with which the group agrees.
4	Explainers	Give two specific examples that explain the lecture.

Before the lecture, give the teams their assignments. After the lecture, allow the teams to confer. Proceed from group to group, asking each team to do what you have requested. After all teams have finished, discuss listening skills with the entire group. (Variation: additional roles many be created for variety or to demonstrate a particular principle.)

<u>**Web Connections—Finding Help Online**</u>
Out of class activity
Materials needed: A computer
Time: 30-50 minutes
Goal: To help students identify sources online that will help them learn to be better note takers
Have students search and find at least five different web addresses for note-taking. List the web addresses and have students choose the best source and explain why. Collect the top choices for students (they can send you their choices electronically) and create an online note-taking supplement for the class.

8. What other activities can I incorporate to make the chapter my own?

We all tend to have our biases on our favorite way to attend, be engaged and take notes. Share your story with the class. You might further put your own spin on this chapter, depending on how your class is organized. If you are lucky enough to be teaching this class as part of a learning community, you will have multiple opportunities to use real class information to try our some of the note-taking techniques.

Included here, all in one place, are Activity Options taken from the Annotated Instructor's Edition.

ACTIVITY OPTION (p. 172): Use a "think-pair-share" approach to this activity. First, have students answer the "What Do *You* Think?" on their own, and then pair up with the student next to them. Pairs of students must agree on the top two mistakes that Lindsey is making, as well as the top two things that she must immediately do. Each pair of students reports to the class and a master list is made. Finally, ask students if there is something that they think is really critical that is not on the list. It is possible that one or two students may key in to some really important underlying issues that Lindsey needs to address.

ACTIVITY OPTION (p. 176): In addition to being cheated out of learning, the issue with interrupting class is really about a student's right to learn. When one student disrupts the class, they have robbed others of their right to learn and in a sense stolen their money. Sometimes students won't speak up about others who are unruly, but you can be sure that you have students in class who are upset if their learning is frequently disrupted. You might even ask students how they would feel if someone was constantly talking to their neighbor. To test this out, before class, ask two students to stage talking in class and then debrief. How did classmates feel about the disruption?

ACTIVITY OPTION (p. 177): Divide the class into two groups. Ask students to discuss as a group the "Insight → Action" activity. Next, ask students to develop rules of engagement for the class. Compare lists and come up with a set of rules that the whole class can live by.

ACTIVITY OPTION (p. 179): Assign students to listen to the same lecture. You may have some on campus that you can download for the class in podcast format, or ask students to attend the same lecture. Have students watch for gestures and speech patterns to figure out what were the most important points. Have students return to class to report what they thought was most important. As an alternative, you can give a lecture or videotape someone to do this as an in-class activity.

ACTIVITY OPTION (p. 183): For homework, have students observe their other classes for a week and come to class briefly describing the type of lecturers they have. They must include one example that illustrates the type. As a class compare the types and strategize about how students can successfully adapt to the style.

ACTIVITY OPTION (p. 189): This is a great opportunity to get students to line up based on their scores, ranging from low on one side of the room to high on the other. First, remind students that it's okay if they are not yet good listeners. The goal of this activity is to learn from each other. What can students who are not aural learners on the VARK do to compensate or translate into a learning preference they do have?

ACTIVITY OPTION (p. 198): As a culminating activity for this chapter, have each student present to the class one of the VARK activity options (their choice). In addition to presenting the activity, have students explain why they chose a particular activity, how it's a good match for their VARK learning style preference(s) and personality profile, and what they learned about themselves while doing the activity.

9. What homework might I assign?

Give students lecture notes that you have prepared and have them use one of the note-taking techniques described in the chapter to take notes. Tell students that they must write the notes on one side of a 3 by 5 index card that they can use later for an in class quiz.
The goal is to help students see the value in taking concise notes.

Journal Entries

One: Have students write a one page journal entry, or send you an e-mail describing a note-taking strategy that works best for them and why. Tell students that it does not have to be exactly like the approaches suggested, but would be even better with a combination of strategies that works best for them.

Two: Have students write a one page journal entry, or send you an e-mail reflecting on a situation where they felt there was a disconnect between them and their instructor. Did they do anything about it? If so, what? What was the result of doing or not doing anything? If they could do things differently now, what would they do?

Three: Use the Insight → Action prompts as journal or blog assignments.

10. What have I learned in teaching this chapter that I will incorporate next time?

CHAPTER 7: DEVELOPING YOUR MEMORY

1. Why is this chapter important?

In the last chapter we talked about the fact that you can't open a college success book without seeing sections, chapters, and whole books on how to be involved in class, pay attention and take notes. The same can be said for learning how to successfully develop memory skills. No matter what and how they study in college, students will be required to memorize and recall information. While some people just seem to be naturally good at it, others are not. But, the good news is that students can learn to make the most of their memories.

While we often talk about memory-enhancing techniques, most students have never been taught them, specifically. If you survey your class, most likely students have done a ton of studying, but most would be hard pressed to tell you exactly what technique they use, other than simple strategies like re-reading or highlighting. Sometimes students will say, "I can't understand why I did so badly on my literature exam; I re-read the short stories six times!" (But how much did they process and commit to memory?) Or "I wore out my yellow highlighter studying for my calculus test!" If you check their textbooks, nearly all of every page is highlighted because they don't know what's important. When studying for a calculus test, re-reading isn't a good way to master the material; working problems sets until you understand the principles and processes is. So, what are some of the techniques this chapter suggests that can actually work wonders?

First, in this chapter students will learn some of the basic research and information about memory. Memory and cognition are actually complex research topics, but this chapter makes this information accessible to students, and then focuses on practical strategies for students to try. They will learn about the Three R's of Remembering: Record, Retain and Retrieve. The image of a digital camera is used to help students visualize the camera and how it works to remember these terms. Once students have mastered this, they go on to learn about the twenty different ways to master their memory. The broad categories that students learn about include how to make information stick, how to make it meaningful, how to make it mnemonic, how to manipulate it, and how to make material funny. Students should be encouraged to try each of the techniques and find a few that really work for them. Later in this chapter when students review the "Your Type Is Showing" feature see if students can connect their favorite techniques with their personality tendency. They will learn about how memory fails us (The Seven Sins of Memory: How the Mind Forgets and Remembers) and also about the impact of drugs on memory.

2. What are this chapter's learning objectives?

> Why memory is a process, not a thing
> How memory works like a digital camera
> How to improve memory using twenty different techniques
> How memory can fail you
> How drugs affect memory

3. How should I launch this chapter?

Think about launching this chapter by asking students how they memorize information for a test. Ask students to start to list the different ways they approach material and list them on the board. When there are no more examples coming from the class, ask students to see if these techniques cluster together in any way. You might begin to see examples of mnemonic devices, silly sentences, chunking, manipulating materials or other ways that go together. Help students to label these groups of techniques, and let students know that you are going to learn more about each of these approaches.

- **Ask students to take a few minutes to think of a time when they went into a test feeling prepared.** Why? What did they do to prepare and how did they do it? Ask students to describe how they felt? Confident? In control? Relaxed? Now ask students to explain what they did. Did they work alone? Did they work with a group of friends who quizzed each other? What specific techniques did they use?

- **Ask students to recount a time when they went into a test unprepared, because they didn't study enough, or were just not sure they were prepared.** It's generally clear to students when they know that the reason they did not feel prepared going into a test was because they simply did not study enough. What is harder to pinpoint is the feeling of uncertainty. Sometimes students do study a lot, but they are just not studying in an efficient way. Some of the study techniques in this chapter should help. For example, the "Cultivate Your Curiosity" mini-article, Act on Your Memory! contains some excellent strategies used by actors to memorize their lines.

- **Going beyond the book.** Studying and remembering information is really a multi-part process. First, you have to be studying what is really important. Students can do a bang-up job of remembering a list of facts or times and dates, but if it's really not important for the test, it is not going to help. Facts and dates may not be all that important on an essay test. Do they really comprehend the information they're memorizing? It's important to know what needs to be learned, and what a test will be like. Will there be multiple choice questions? Will the test include essay questions? Encourage students to ask their professors about suggestions that they may have on how to approach the material for the test. Does the professor have any sample tests that can be looked over? Do they know any students who had the professor the previous semester? The more one knows about how they will be tested, the more focused their study techniques can become.

4. How should I use the *FOCUS* Challenge Case?

Kevin is like a growing number of students who are now in college. These students are either returning to college to finish a degree they started a long time ago or older students who have always longed to get a degree and are just starting. Maybe they are in a job with no future, or one that they don't enjoy. Many of the jobs that individuals held twenty years ago did not require a college degree, but now they require at least a bachelor's level diploma. Students like Kevin, bright and capable, find themselves at a crossroads in their lives. Do I give up my full time job and security to go back to school? When you think about it, at forty with longevity predictions well into one's 80's, Kevin has many years to do something he loves. But, Kevin begins to question his ability. It's clearly not as if he isn't trying. He needs to work smarter, not harder. Have the class discuss one or two things Kevin can do to be more effective studying. What advice would they give him?

5. What important features does this chapter include?

Again, you will see some of the really important recurring themes in this book. By now you are familiar with these. A few points will be discussed about each.

Readiness and Reality Checks
By the time students are in college, they have had more than their share of opportunities for remembering things. Most likely they have not thought very much about what they have done, or how they have studied. They just know that they have been faced with many memorization challenges—for many students strict memorization was what exams consisted of. The Readiness Check may be eye-opening for some students. And because many students either don't find high school challenging or bypass opportunities to learn at their best in that environment, they may assume they have this topic nailed. Of course, it will be interesting for students to check their Reality Check results at the end of this chapter.

Challenge → Reaction → Insight → Action prompts
There are many different Challenge → Reaction → Insight → Action prompts in this chapter. The very first Challenge → Reaction "What do you remember?" is a great early chapter activity. What can students articulate about that early nursery rhyme or song that allows them to still remember? Have them perform a poem they remember or a childhood song they recall, just for fun. Was it the words, the music, or the dance that they did? Another really important Challenge → Reaction is the "Subjective Memory Test." This subjective self-assessment has two sections, one (A) for general memory tasks and another (B) for academic memory tasks. If students are beginning to find the C → R prompts to be repetitive or intrusive, remind them to make a game of them to see what they really know. One of the purposes of the learning system is to encourage students who respond to a challenge with "Oh, that's easy" to discover when reacting to the challenge that their reaction consists of "Uh…" because knowing and articulating these responses is more challenging than it appears.

Your Type Is Showing
No question about it, there is a relationship between psychological type and memory. Sensors for example, are drawn to details. They may be the students who do well with memorizing facts and dates. INtuitors, on the other hand, might do well on essay exams, as they prefer big-picture thinking. Even the way that students approach memory aids most likely vary depending on their type. Judgers might organize information in very structured way, while perceivers, might develop very creative ways to retrieve information. In the text, there is a chart where students are asked to predict ways in which their type might indicate ways in

which they use their memory. This is a great activity to discuss in class and is one of the "Teachable Moments" listed in the Annotated Instructor's Edition of the book.

Control Your Learning: Your Toughest Class

In this activity, towards the end of the chapter, students are asked to think about their toughest class. What kind of information are they asked to remember for that class? Do they have to remember information from complex readings, formulas, lectures? Students are asked to provide five examples for each memory principle by trying to "make the material stick, make it meaningful, make use of mnemonic devices, manipulate the material to help learn it, and to make it funny." For their toughest class, have they been successful so far? Do they think they might do things differently? This might be a great class discussion for students to share techniques especially if students are taking similar classes. Students may be surprised to find that many different techniques can work for the same material. You might ask students to copy this page of the book (p. 222) and hand in their responses so that you are aware of their answers. You may even want to report the range of responses back to the class.

Self-Assessments

The only assessment for this chapter is a Challenge → Reaction prompt entitled the "Subjective Memory Test." This subjective self-assessment has two sections, one (A) for general memory tasks and another (B) for academic memory tasks. Students are asked if their scores for parts A and B differ, and if their scores dropped as they went down the list (since the list gets harder and harder). A later Insight → Action prompt helps students to reflect on this challenge.

Cultivating Your Curiosity: Act on Your Memory!

Most likely, students in your class watch their fair share of television and movies. They may well be interested in how actors and actresses learn their lines. It's not just about saying their lines or simply learning them, but successful actors and actresses learn their lines by techniques such as chunking, setting goals (how I will deliver the lines?), moving around while learning, and concentrating on the meaning of the words. Hopefully, the curiosity surrounding the success of their favorite stars will motivate students to study their approach. You might want to start this discussion off by asking students how they learn song lyrics without even trying? Is repetition at work? Do they associate particular songs with important events attached to them, like first dates?

FOCUS on Careers

The career focus in this chapter is acting. We meet DeLanna Studi, an actress. Has anyone in the class considered a career as an actor or actress? While an E/I, N, F, P, is the most common psychological type for this profession could other types be successful in this profession? Of course they could! But, it might be interesting to discuss why the E, N, F, P/J might be the most common type. What about the job outlook for this career and job stability? What impact does this profession have on one's other goals in life? This in an exciting career for those suited to it, but it may not be for everyone. It is interesting though that Studi says that "acting is 85% work and 15% talent." Ask students if they know any students on campus who are taking theater classes or have starred in campus performances. Ask them to find out what techniques these student actors use.

6. Which in-text exercises should I use?

There are two exercises built into this chapter. Each is unique and a very engaging for students. Connect these activities, if you can, to real life courses and situations for the students. Included here are descriptions of why they have been included, how much time each one will probably take, and how you might debrief each one.

EXERCISE 7.1 TEST YOUR MEMORY

Why do this activity?
This is a great activity to help students to see that there are varieties of memory techniques that one can use to study the same list of words.

What are the challenges and what can you expect?
There are really not many challenges for this activity. The list of words is not too long, and, in fact, it can be a good confidence builder for students who never thought they were very good at memorizing information. Students will be able to see that a few simple techniques can really improve one's ability to remember information.

How much time will it take?
This activity should take about 30 minutes, depending on how much time you wish to devote to debriefing.

How should I debrief?
One of the really valuable parts of this activity is for students to see that there is more than one way to approach remembering information. Students should share their techniques with the class. See if there are a few common approaches to learning this material. List the different approaches. Have students indicate their learning type to see if there is any connection between types and approaches to learning the lists.

EXERCISE 7.2 VARK ACTIVITY

Why do this activity?
This activity is designed to help students make connections between their preferred VARK learning modality and an actual assignment. This activity is really helpful for students to try a way of remembering something based on the way they learn best.

What are the challenges and what can I expect?
There are no big challenges in this activity. You might suggest that students try more than one technique for this activity so that students become familiar with a variety of ways to learn information.

How much time will it take?
This activity can be done outside of class: the only time it takes is the actual debriefing in class, so you can take whatever time you need. Or, you can choose to respond to students individually in an e-mail or directly on their assignment.

How should I debrief? Have each student present to the class one of the above activity options (their choice). In addition to presenting the activity, have students explain why they chose a particular activity, how it's a good match for their VARK learning preferences, and SuccessTypes, and what they learned about themselves while doing the activity.

7. Which additional exercises might enrich students' learning?

I Want To Be an Artist
Class activity
Materials needed: Newsprint, markers, and a list of 20 words (randomly chosen from a newspaper)
Time: 30-50 minutes, depending on the size of the group
Goal: To help students create a visual to remember information
Place student in small groups of 3-4. Give each student colored markers and paper. Groups should develop a picture (visual) that helps them to remember all of the words in Exercise 7.1.

Silly Sentences
Class activity
Materials needed: the same 20 words used in the activity above (or 20 others is you wish), newsprint, and markers
Time: 20-40 minutes
Goal: To help students create a visual to remember information
Students should work in groups (maybe in the same groups as in the activity above), to learn the list of words by coming up with some silly sentences to help them remember the lists. Have groups share their sentences with the class and have class members decide on which sentence would most help them remember the words.

Compare and Contrast
Out of class activity
Materials needed: A prepared lecture on the pros and cons of studying in groups or studying alone (or some similar lecture)
Time: 30-50 minutes
Goal: To help students differentiate and remember similar information
Deliver a short lecture to the class on the positives and negatives of studying in groups versus studying alone. As a class, develop a chart that helps students compare and contrast material presented. After the chart is completed, have students put the charts away. Give a quiz asking students to list the pros and cons. (You may decide if the quiz counts.) When students are finished completing the quiz, ask them to describe how they remembered the information.

8. What other activities can I incorporate to make the chapter my own?

If your students are part of a learning community, taking courses that are linked, check with the other instructors to see if there is any content that they suggest students learn for the next test. Use a number of the techniques suggested in this chapter to learn the material. If you are teaching older, non-traditional students you might ask them if there is something at work that they need to learn. Are they taking a certification exam? As much as possible, make learning the suggested approaches in this chapter personal by using real-life, right-now material.

Included here, all in one place, are Activity Options taken from the Annotated Instructor's Edition.

ACTIVITY OPTION (p. 202): Students should take a few minutes to share their responses to "What Do *You* Think" questions. Ask students to work in small groups and assign one or two questions to each group, then have them report to the class. If you have older, nontraditional students in the class, you might ask them to lead the groups.

ACTIVITY OPTION (p. 204): This is a wonderful opportunity to get students in groups to disclose their different responses to Part A and Part B. In small groups, have them determine two to three reasons why they did better on one part (most likely it will be Part A). Have students stay in groups to look at Part B and decide which top three things they have trouble with. You can teach this chapter with the class working in teams to make sure that all students learn effective strategies for developing their memories.

ACTIVITY OPTION (p. 206): Since students have probably done this activity in preparation for class, consider doing a visual activity in class. Put a variety of items out on your desk (about ten), and leave them there for two minutes. Put them back in a bag and then ask students to write down as many as they can. If you are using related objects, like the things from your briefcase, students are more likely to remember them, as opposed to unrelated items. You might even try two sets of items to make this point and then guide students to the conclusion that categorizing, relating, and grouping things can help them remember.

ACTIVITY OPTION (p. 210): For the next class, have students bring in a list of terms they need to memorize for another class. Often first-year students are taking biology or history, or even math formulas can work for this exercise. Have students present their challenges and, in small groups or as a whole class, brainstorm ways to chunk or categorize the information.

ACTIVITY OPTION (p. 217): Using the same list that students brought in to memorize for another class—or if they didn't do this before, have them bring in a list now—ask students to use a strategy from "Cultivate Your Curiosity" to learn the list. For example, if they choose goal setting and moving, they might set a goal such as learning all of the major battles of Civil War in American History while moving around the room to demonstrate the locations where the battles were fought.

ACTIVITY OPTION (p. 219): Break the class into four groups and have them memorize all of the presidents of the United States or some other common list. (You might have to fill in the gaps for a few students.) Assign one group to use the spelling approach, another the locate, another the link or narrate, and the final group the peg system. Give groups about fifteen minutes to learn their lists, and then report back to the group the strategies they used and how successful they were.

ACTIVITY OPTION (p. 222): Have students send you an e-mail summarizing this "Control Your Learning" activity. This reflective activity that will not only help students identify some major points that you want to stress, but it's an opportunity for you to give individuals suggestions for their toughest classes.

ACTIVITY OPTION (p. 223): Have students quickly come up with a mnemonic sentence to remember the seven memory faults. Give them five minutes to do so, and then have a few students volunteer to read their sentences to the class.

ACTIVITY OPTION (p. 227): Have each student present to the class one of the activity options in Exercise 7.2 (their choice). In addition to presenting the activity, have students explain why they chose a particular activity, how it's a good match for their VARK preferred modality, and what they learned about themselves while doing the activity.

ACTIVITY OPTION (p. 228): To conclude this chapter, students should communicate the most important memorization method they learned about in this chapter. Ask students to e-mail one classmate, or you, a short description of which strategy they selected and why. Put this all into one document and send it to the entire class as a list of best practices for students.

9. What homework might I assign?

Ask students to turn in study techniques for a test or quiz they will take. The goal here is to help students apply some of the techniques they have learned in this chapter to information they are currently learning.

Journal Entries
One: Have students write a one page journal entry, or send you an e-mail reflecting on a the most valuable technique they learned in this chapter. Do they think they can use it in all types of memorization? If so, why and if not, why not.

Two: Use the Insight $\rightarrow$ Action prompts as journal or blog assignments.

10. What have I learned in teaching this chapter that I will incorporate next time?

_____

_____

_____

_____

_____

_____

_____

_____

_____

CHAPTER 8: READING AND STUDYING

1. Why is this chapter important?

It goes without saying that reading and studying in college are critical to student success. You might think that students have been doing this all of their lives, so why should this be a problem? After all, these students have made it to college so they must have been doing some things effectively all along, right?

Consider things like this as you teach this chapter. First of all, many of today's students do read, some don't very much, but research indicates that half or fewer say they don't enjoy reading, and few read for pleasure. Some have never been taught how to read effectively, how and what to highlight or take notes when they are reading. In addition to students using their own approach to reading and studying which may work part of the time, students may begin to wonder why they have to learn when they already know how to do so. The question is: Will the study habits they've used in the past be sufficient for the rigor of college courses? Often the answer to that question is no.

While most students have done plenty of reading prior to college, they may not have been taught read strategies since sixth grade. In addition, don't be surprised to find that a fair number of students have never read an entire book—not even a novel. Non-readers are probably not going to tell you this because they are embarrassed, so you might even comment that this is a fact because of movies, television, and the Internet. Hopefully, students will see that there are times when the media that they have used before to get by, may not work anymore. Let students know that in this chapter they will learn techniques that will serve them for a lifetime, and that it's not too late to become a successful reader.

Students will not only learn how to distinguish between the different kinds of reading, they will learn about the right ways to read, how to take notes when reading and specific techniques like SQ3R (study, questions, read, recite ,and review). They will also learn about a concept called metacognititon. Metacognition is thinking about how one thinks and learning about how one learns. This concept is not about how someone else thinks or learns but how one might think about their own thinking and learning. Students will learn what they do efficiently, and what they may need to improve. Students will learn techniques for taking notes such as writing in the margin and how *not to* make the entire page bright yellow when highlighting. In addition to learning some of these specific approaches, students will understand why they are taking the courses that they do when they learn about a concept called integrated learning.

Integrated learning helps students see how disciplines connect. For example, students may wonder why they are required to take a course in ethics: "I am a business major, why would I need a course in ethics?" Or "I am chemistry major and I am going to be working in a lab by myself. Why would I need a course in ethics?" This chapter will help students understand the connections between and among disciplines. When they study something that has meaning and fits into and approach that says, "yeah, I need to know this," learning will be enhanced.

2. What are this chapter's learning objectives?

> ➤ Why reading is important
> ➤ How to engage in focused reading
> ➤ How to tackle reading assignments as an ESL student
> ➤ What metacognition is and how it can help students
> ➤ How to become an intentional learner
> ➤ Why learning is greater than the sum of its parts

3. How should I launch this chapter?

Consider launching this chapter by asking students for a show of hands in response to the question "Who thinks of themselves as an efficient reader?" Quickly ask students to explain what they do. Then, ask for a show of hands for those who feel they are masters at studying. You will probably find a number of the same students raise their hands because of the strong connection between reading efficiently and studying. But don't be surprised if you find that there are fewer students who believe they are masters of studying. Why? Some students may enjoy reading novels and see that as "being a good reader," but the proof for reading and studying effectively are measured by the tests they take, and their grades on tests may not be as high as they'd like..

- **Ask students to take a few minutes to describe reading something they really enjoyed and why.** Help students to label the different kinds of reading that they do: flipping through a magazine and reading directions for uploading music for their iPod, is very different from reading a text book. Help students realize that the way they approach reading the material that they will then have to study further is connected to how efficiently they will remember information for a test.

- **Ask students to describe a time when they felt that they studied efficiently.** What time of the day was it? Where were they? What were they wearing? Were they listening to music at the same time? How long did they study? Did they take breaks? How did they know they were studying efficiently? Did they feel that they studied efficiently because they got a good grade on a test or quiz, or because they felt as if they really understood the material? Ask students to share their experiences with each other. Do you find any common characteristics in the class?

- **Going beyond the book.** If you are teaching this course as part of a learning community of linked classes (for example, first-year seminar, introduction to psychology, male-female communication, and freshman composition) hopefully you will have access to the readings and books that all of the students in your class will be reading at the same time. (*Hint*: if you have any way that you can convince someone to connect your student success courses with another course, do it! Even these small linked courses become communities of learners, or learning communities, and without doing things much differently, research shows that learning is enhanced.) If your campus uses a common reading—a novel that brings in critical social issues, for example—for all entering students use this book or even parts of it to apply reading and studying strategies. You might even consider choosing one of the current best sellers and form a book club to discuss the common reading once a week over coffee or lunch. This social connection to reading may be just what non-readers, like Katie from the *FOCUS* Challenge Case, can benefit from.

4. How should I use the *FOCUS* Challenge Case?

Katie Alexander is probably a student that an instructor would enjoy having in class. She is energetic and outgoing. It's not until the first test or quiz that you begin to wonder why Katie didn't do well. Is it because she isn't smart? Mostly likely it's because Katie doesn't know how to approach the material. She is overwhelmed. She depended on watching movies for the core literature books she had to read in high school and can't do that anymore. She wants to do well, but she is drowning. Have the class discuss one or two things Katie can do to be more effective at reading and studying. What advice would they give her? Students like Katie are fairly common among today's students. They are often kinesthetic learners and sensors who want structured, detailed material they can grab hold of. Abstract information doesn't sink in, and coupled with poor reading skills, the combination can be debilitating. Katie may benefit from working with a reading tutor, one-on-one, a specialist who can teach her specific strategies that will work for her. Or she may need to take a developmental reading class before she goes much further in her academic career. But inarguably, reading well will be essential to her college success.

5. What important features does this chapter include?

The recurring themes in the book can guide how you approach this chapter. Because students should be familiar with these you might find out which features they like the most and tailor your class to what they like. Think about asking the class to break into small groups comprised of those who like the same feature. Can they lead a discussion on part of the feature they like the most?

Readiness and Reality Checks
For this Readiness Check, check to see how students responded. Most likely students will report that they do think reading and studying will affect their college success. What might be of interest is to see how much control students think they have over reading and studying. Students may just see themselves as "good or poor" readers and studiers, based on past experience. What they might not realize is that everyone will benefit from learning the techniques in this chapter, no matter where they start in terms of their skills. As always, it will be interesting for students to check their reality with their readiness for focusing on this chapter.

Challenge → Reaction → Insight → Action prompts
The Challenge → Reaction → Insight → Action prompts in this chapter are very thought-provoking and will help students with metacognition. Challenge → Reactions such as "Are there right ways to read?" should help students to think about *how* they read. Is their

approach a good one? Later on in the chapter an Insight → Action prompt asks students to take a hard look at their own reading skills. They are asked to think about feedback they have received over the years as well as identifying their own strengths and weaknesses. Another really important Challenge → Reaction is entitled "Your Study Habits." Using this prompt, students are asked to read ten statements about study habits and rate themselves. The Challenge → Reaction → Insight → Action prompts in this chapter provide opportunities for self examination and reflection about reading and studying. Some students are overconfident about their reading and studying skills. Some, on the other end of the continuum, are terrified that their skills won't measure up. And some are content to hope for the best. It's important to use the C → R and I → A prompts to "sell" the chapter to all types of individual student's orientations toward the content.

Your Type Is Showing

In this chapter there is a very clear description about the different psychological types and how each type approaches reading and studying. Students are asked to respond to questions about why psychosocial type might be connected to reading and studying. They are asked to read short descriptions of types and how individuals who have this type learn. Just follow what is suggested in the text, including the discussion questions. How you debrief, however, can vary. You can have students write an essay about the connection between type and how they learn and send it to you, or you can have a class discussion. However, what is really valuable is for students to see which students have their same or different type, and what they do to help them focus. What you don't want to happen is for students to read that the Sensing-iNtution and Judging-Perceiving scales relate most to college success and worry that they may have the "wrong" type. However, the descriptions in the text are intentionally written to be even-handed and point out potential pros and cons of all types.

Control Your Learning: Your Toughest Class

In this section students are asked to control their learning and think about their toughest class. They are asked to look back over the section of this chapter on reading and honestly assess the extent to which they believe reading is part of what they find challenging about this class. Students are asked a series of questions about how they approach reading in the class and what they do, specifically. They are asked if they honestly plan on changing the way they have previous read and if they will use some of the new techniques that they have learned from this chapter. This is probably not an assignment that you want students to share with you or others. If they don't plan on using new techniques, will they tell you that? They probably won't. What is important for students to realize is that they ultimately have control of this learning. The amount of work (effective work) they put in, will most likely relate to what they will get out of this course.

Self-Assessments

There are two exercises in this chapter that are self-assessments. The first is Exercise 8.1 where students read an article and check the time it takes them to read as well as their comprehension rate. (This exercise is explained later on in this Instructor's Resource Manual.) Students often assume that speed readers are the best readers. The chapter makes the point in several places that fluency and comprehension are just as, if not more, important than speed.

The second self-assessment is a Challenge → Reaction prompt on study habits and asks students to check off issues such as boredom, fatigue, surroundings, etc., that might present reading challenges. Because reading has become an issue of national concern with more people engaging in alternative activities like movies and the Internet, the chapter points out that reading is a skill we must not lose as a culture and why.

Cultivating Your Curiosity: Reading When English Is Your Second Language

This article is of value to both native speakers of English and those who's first language is another. English is not the easiest language to learn. The readings in this part of the chapter contain suggestions for ESL students, but are fun and interesting to everyone. You might choose to meet separately with your ESL students to talk further about this mini-article, as well as encourage empathy in native English speakers by pointing out how challenging it might be for them to attend college in Korea or Russia or some other country with a language very different from English.

FOCUS on Careers

The career focus in this chapter is teaching. In this chapter, we meet Barbara Swaby, a literacy expert. You probably do much of what a number of students in the class who are considering becoming teachers will do. The most common psychological type (for teachers of reading, as noted in the "Create a Career Outlook") is E/I, S, F, J. Other types could be successful in this profession but you might want to take a minute to brainstorm what challenges an iNtuitive, thinker, or perceiver might have if they decide to follow this route. What about the job outlook for this career and job stability? Fortunately, the outlook is good. What other benefits are there to this job? You might be able to help students learn about the benefits and fulfillment of teaching as a career by sharing your thoughts.

6. Which in-text exercises should I use?

There are five exercises built into this chapter. Included here are descriptions of why they appear in this chapter, how much time each one will probably take, and how you might debrief them. Each activity addresses a particular skill that students can develop.

EXERCISE 8.1 WHAT IS YOUR READING RATE

Why do this activity?
In this activity students read an article in the text and time how long it takes them to read the article. At the end, the average time it takes a college student to read this (between four and six minutes) is revealed. There are comprehension questions at the end. Some students may see the activity as a challenge, and play "beat the clock." But they may find the comprehension questions are hard or impossible to answer when they have finished. Use this activity to lead into a discussion of the qualities of a good reader.

What are the challenges and what can you expect?
You may not know that you have students in the class who are really struggling with reading. If they have an identified learning disability, they may or may not have told you. If students took

---

longer than six minutes to read the article, they could well be enrolled in a developmental reading class or they may need extra help. This could be a very sensitive subject, so treat it carefully. It's even possible for students to make it through their previous levels of education and actually be technically illiterate. If all your students are below average readers, emphasize that that's why they're in college—to improve their skills—and that you'll work with them or help them find resources as best you can. Remember the aphorism introduced in Chapter 3: HELP is not a four-letter word!

How much time will it take?
This activity should take about 15 minutes depending on how much time you debrief.

How should I debrief?
Students are told to go back and check their answers and whether or not they are reading right. Ask students to e-mail you their times and if they got everything correct. Encourage any student who is having difficulty to let you know. Do they need extra time for reading? Would they like an assessment of their reading skills? Would they like some extra help with reading? Connect these students to the right campus resources.

EXERCISE 8.2 A PRESS CONFERENCE WITH AN AUTHOR

Why do this activity?
This activity is designed to get students to read "deeper" into the chapter. By developing a mock interview with the author they are questioning the choice of material and activities as opposed to just taking them at face value. It's also a fun activity that involves the whole class. Prior to this in class activity, you might assign students to bring in one question they might want to ask the author. Collect them and just give them to interviewer. You might even consider setting up a class conference call with the author or selecting the best questions to e-mail her.

What are the challenges and what can you expect?
You should not have any challenges with this activity. You might want to collect and screen the questions before you give them to the interviewer so that you eliminate duplications or questions that are not relevant.

How much time will it take?
This activity should take about 30 minutes depending on how much time you debrief.

How should I debrief?
Because the point of this is to get students to think "deeper" as opposed to surface learning, you might simply tell them that this was the point of the activity. Ask students if they felt they were thinking at a different level or remembering more using "behind the scenes" questioning. Would they ever use this technique? Why or why not?

EXERCISE 8.3 MARGINAL NOTES

Why do this activity?
In this activity students are asked to go back though the section on reading in this chapter. If they used a highlighter or underlined words, they are to make notes on a separate piece of paper or on sticky notes they attach, or write in the margins why they chose to mark these particular items.

What are the challenges and what can you expect?
One of the biggest challenges is that sometimes students mark entire paragraphs. Hopefully when students they try to explain why they did this, it will make sense to them that this technique is not highly effective.

How much time will it take?
This activity should take about 30 -40 minutes depending on how much time you debrief.

How should I debrief?
What you probably want to know is what students learned about themselves during this activity. The metacognitive activity will help them take a look at their technique and self-assess as to whether or not it's effective. If you can find an example of a student who is an effective "highlighter" or "under-liner," ask him or her to share the examples with the class. You can also show them your copy of this section of the text and what you've marked as important and why as a model.

EXERCISE 8.4 YOU ARE WHAT YOU READ

Why do this activity?
This is a fun way for students to explore some reading that fits what they enjoy, and use the Internet to find some books to read with their classmates. Students are to go to a major book company site and choose six books they may be interested in and use PowerPoint or a word document to copy and past in the "thumbnails" of the books.

What are the challenges and what can you expect?
Students should enjoy doing this activity. Be sure that you ask students to share their choices with each other. Students who are non-readers may get hooked on a book that someone else recommends when they see the thumbnail and hear about the book.

How much time will it take?
This activity homework activity should take about an hour. Depending on how you expect students to share their work with others the class time will vary. You may have them paste their thumbnails and perhaps a critique of each book into a PowerPoint slideshow or print out a similar color document they create.

How should I debrief?
If you choose to share book selections in class you might want to see if there are similarities in the class. Also you might want to find out if everyone even knew about thumbnails and online reviews. How do people learn about good books? Do they go to the best seller list? Do they depend on a friend's recommendation?

EXERCISE 8.5 VARK ACTIVITY

Why do this activity?
This activity is designed to help students make connections between their preferred VARK learning modality and something they learned in the chapter. This activity is really helpful for students to try a way of remembering something based on the way they learn best.

What are the challenges and what can I expect?
There are no real challenges in this activity. You might suggest that students present this VARK activity results to the class so that they learn from each other about how much time they spend on reading, what studying aloud can do, asking and writing down the what and why questions, and copying notes in a variety of ways.

How much time will it take?
This activity can be done outside of class: the only time it takes is the actual debriefing in class and you can take whatever time you need especially if you have students present to the class. If they do present, you can spend up to a full period doing this.

How should I debrief?
If students present to the class, have them explain why they chose a particular activity and what they learned about themselves while doing the activity

7. Which additional exercises might enrich students' learning?

Crossword Race (from Staley, C. (2003) page 95.)
Class activity
Materials needed: A crossword puzzle that you create, using terms from the text, generated at http://puzzlemaker.school.discovery.com/CrissCrossSetupFrom.html
Time: 30 minutes or so, depending on the size of the group
Goal: To motivate students to read the text, learn course material ,and work collaboratively
Generate a puzzle using course content at the above web site or another one you find. You may allow students to work on the solution in pairs or small groups, perhaps as a timed competition.

Marking Your Mark
Homework and class activity
Materials needed: Four highlighters, any article of 4-5 pages of interest and relevance to the class (You provide copies for each student along with four extra copies)
Time: 30 minutes
Goal: To help students learn how to highlight important information in a reading
For homework, assign students the article you have chosen and ask them to read it, highlight what they think is important and then make a summary of the reading in outline form, only using the words that they highlighted. When students return to the next class, put them into four groups. Tell students to choose the best outline in the group and decide why they chose that particular one. As a group, have students highlight a blank copy that you provide. In class,

compare the four highlighted articles. Are their similarities or differences? Discuss what students learned doing this activity.

<u>Words of Success</u>
Homework and class activity
Materials needed: The local newspaper and a quiz
Time: 30-50 minutes
Goal: To help students choose the main points of readings and develop study cards
Assign students to read one section of the newspaper as a class assignment. For example, you might choose to assign the local news, world news, sports, entertainment, or the home and garden section. If the section is long, assign a set number of pages. Allow students to write down 20 words in any way that they want (in a mapping format, clustered together, etc.) and bring the words to the next class in preparation for a quiz. Give them a quiz on the reading with some specific facts that they must recall. Did students choose many of the same words? Is there any connection between the words that students chose and how well they did on the test?

8. What other activities can I incorporate to make the chapter my own?

If your students are in a learning community with linked classes, check with the other instructors to see if there is any reading material that you could use to when teaching students about reading and studying techniques. If not and students are in a variety of different courses, ask students to bring in or do their homework assignments on material that will serve a purpose for them. Improved reading and study techniques may well translate into great grades

Included here, all in one place, are Activity Options taken from the Annotated Instructor's Edition.

ACTIVITY OPTION (p. 231): Take a few moments to discuss students' individual responses to the "What Do *You* Think" questions. You might ask students to work in small groups and come up with the three most important things a student like Katie should do and have each group report to the class.

ACTIVITY OPTION (p. 233): Consider meeting your students in the cafeteria for lunch every few weeks to discuss a book. If your campus has a Common Book program (where all entering students read the same book), you could dissect chapters together over lunch. Or, choose any book that students want to read and read it together. Think about something small—a book that might be appealing to "reluctant readers."

ACTIVITY OPTION (p. 236): Although it's not a good idea to publicize individual reading rates and comprehension scores, students may still be curious about what constitutes fast or slow reading. Ask them to write down their times and the number of questions they answered correctly and submit them anonymously. Ask them to identify which question(s) they answered incorrectly. Collect these items are report back to the class. Students can make their own comparisons. Remind students to send you an e-mail or see you if they have some questions about their own reading.

ACTIVITY OPTION (p. 238): As a class, choose the top five from the list of fifteen common reading issues listed. Which can be changed? Get a discussion going with the goal that each issue can be improved. It is about one's own control and attitude about the reading challenge.

ACTIVITY OPTION (p. 240): This activity can be assigned for homework or done in class. Give students a two- or three-page article or current newspaper story to read. Tell them to read the article only once, writing their comments, questions, and reactions as suggested in this chapter. Have students pair up and show each other what they highlighted and what kinds of notes they put in the margins. Was their approach different from their partner's? If so, what differed and why? Have them share their responses with the class.

ACTIVITY OPTION (p. 242): Even simple, everyday reading requires cultural literacy. Ask students to bring a cartoon or joke to class that requires cultural literacy to understand. The amount of information out there increases exponentially every day, especially with the advent of the Internet, so one can't know everything. But the more one reads the more likely one is to be culturally literate.

ACTIVITY OPTION (p. 242): Consider bringing in an article or a chapter from another textbook (or even try this technique with the next chapter in this book). Have students write a one-paragraph summary of the article or chapter after using SQ3R. Remind them that one way of skimming is to look at the headings in the chapter or the topic (first or second) sentence of a paragraph.

ACTIVITY OPTION (p. 242): This "*FOCUS* on Careers" is a perfect piece to use for taking notes and having students summarize the main points the author is trying to make. Students could do this for homework, and share with the class how they wrote in the margins, how long it took them to read, and what strategies they used to stay focused.

ACTIVITY OPTION (p. 254): Hand out topics on index cards to groups of students (3 to 4 in a group). Topics can be most anything, but examples might be things like stem cell research, global warming, or immigration. Give students five minutes to list all the disciplines they would have to study to fully understand the topic.

ACTIVITY OPTION (p. 258): This is a good opportunity for reflection. Ask students to summarize their responses to the Reality Check and send it to you via e-mail. Tell students that they must also include references to both their VARK and MBTI types. Ask them to give at least two examples of when they were aware of how their types either helped or hindered their reading and studying.

9. What homework might I assign?

Ask students to show you how they highlighted their text for an upcoming test in another class by bringing the textbook for that class to your class. Take quick look to see if they highlighted too little or too much, and if they captured the main points. Remind students that it's best to highlight the second time they do the reading.

Journal Entries

One: Have students write a one page journal entry, or send you an e-mail describing a reading that was very difficult for them this past week. If they read nothing that was difficult, ask them to describe something they read, and explain the strategy they used to read it and comprehend it.

Two: Have students write a one page journal entry, or send you an e-mail describing one of their other classes this week. Explain what the class was about and identify how many disciplines are directly or indirectly related to the information they were learning.

Three: Use the Insight → Action prompts as journal or blog assignments.

10. What have I learned in teaching this chapter that I will incorporate next time?

_____

_____

_____

_____

_____

_____

_____

_____

_____

_____

_____

_____

_____

_____

_____

_____

_____

_____

_____

_____

_____

_____

_____

CHAPTER 9: TAKING TESTS

1. Why is this chapter important?

Wouldn't it be great if students could go through college without ever having to take a test? Think of all the hours you'd save by not having to grade stacks of exams? But test taking in college is a necessary evil, and some students appear to be better at it than others. There is hope, though. In this chapter students will learn about how to control test anxiety; what do to before, during, and after a test; as well as why it is important to avoid a growing concern among faculty nationally—cheating! If students follow the wealth of advice provided in this chapter, their attitudes toward tests may change for the better, and so may their performance.

Test anxiety can stem from many different sources. A fear of failure or a drive toward perfectionism can immobilize some students. They may feel pressure to maintain a scholarship or not disappoint someone. But one of the main reasons that students' anxiety mounts is because they simply don't prepare enough or prepare carefully enough. However, there are always ways to help students overcome the stress surrounding exams, and for these students, this is one of the most beneficial components of this chapter.

It's not surprising that the better you prepare for a test, the less anxiety you will have, generally speaking. Careful planning and knowing what will be covered on a test are keys to success. Clearly, some personality types like to approach tests methodically in this fashion. Other students appear not to know what to do, so they do nothing or very little. According to the text, the MBTI scale that shows the biggest differences on test-taking is the Sensing-iNtuition scale: iNtuitives can jump to conclusions and make careless mistakes, while Sensors don't trust their intuition and go over and over questions, second-guessing themselves. The more students know about their learning style and behaviors, and the more they use this knowledge when preparing for and taking tests, the more successful they will be. This chapter is key for student success. And, the more you can help students apply what they are learning in the chapter to tests they are taking now in all their courses, the better.

2. What are this chapter's learning objectives?

➢ Why students should change their thinking about tests
➢ What to do before, during, and after a test
➢ Why cramming doesn't always work
➢ What "test anxiety" is and what to do about it
➢ How to take different kinds of tests differently
➢ How cheating can hurt a student's chances for success

3. How should I launch this chapter?

One of the best ways to launch this chapter is to connect it to students' current lives. Chances are, they have just finished test, or could be taking one very soon in one class or another. Start with a show of hands. How many students have taken at least one test so far this term? Two? Three or more? How many students would like to do better on the next test they take? Probably lots of hands will fly into the air. Assure students that if they make use of at least some of the techniques in this chapter, they will.

- **Line students up on a continuum with students who feel they always do well on tests at one end and those who feel they do not on the other end.** Have students think about their typical approach to test-taking—in high school, on standardized tests, or in their current courses, for example. Ask them to place themselves on either end of an imaginary continuum with one wall representing "Always do well" and the opposite wall representing "Always do more poorly than I'd hoped." Generally, you will find students spread across the continuum with most wanting to improve. Ask students why they placed themselves where they did. What are they doing right or wrong? Ask what they think they need to do to move themselves along the continuum in a positive direction..

- **Line students up on a continuum with students who study the night before a test (cram) on one end and those who begin to prepare at least a week in advance (or continually during the term) on the other end.** Ask students to share their experiences with each other. Are there common characteristics among students at both ends or in the middle? Are there ever times when cramming works? In fact, you might find some very successful students who wait unit the last minute to prepare. Have a discussion on why this might not work all of the time. Can anyone in the class share a last-minute cramming horror story?

- **Going beyond the book.** Like most study skill techniques, there are literally thousands of resources available for individuals to learn test taking skills. Are there workshops on your campus? If so, see if you can time it so your class goes to one in preparation for a test or quiz you are giving. If you check with the workshop leader you might even ask them to come to your class. If the presenter can't come to your class, find out the times and require students to go. Whatever activities you use in this chapter, or beyond the book, make sure students apply them to tests in courses they're currently taking.

4. How should I use the *FOCUS* Challenge Case?

There might be a Joe Cloud sitting in your class right now, and you may not even know it. Students like Joe from both large and small high schools may have been very successful prior to college. Joe is from an underrepresented population, and "all eyes are upon him," paying all his college expenses and watching his academic progress from afar. In his case, the performance pressure mounts until it reaches a dangerous level. His coping mechanisms have begun to fail. While some students may realize that they are struggling in a class and get help, others, like Joe, will just continue to do what they are doing, falling further behind, or simply stop attending a particular class Perhaps they are too timid, or disclosing failure is not culturally acceptable, for example. Joe was beginning to experience panic attacks brought on by mounting anxiety. The more he tried to catch up in the class, the more ineffective he became. Have the class discuss one or two things Joe could have done before things got out of control. What advice would they have given him? As you read this *FOCUS* Challenge Case, you cannot help but feel for Joe. Many of your students will empathize with him because they themselves are in similar situations or they have friends who are. What's important about debriefing this *FOCUS* Challenge Case is to bring up the subject of actual intervention. Without individual help from his instructor, the Counseling Center, the Office of Multicultural Affairs or some similar office on his campus, Joe may be doomed. He is in danger of becoming a retention statistic and returning home feeling himself to be a failure.

5. What important features does this chapter include?

If you assigned different students to different groups to prepare and discuss specific features of the chapter for Chapter 8, change the assigned features for this chapter. If you haven't done this, try it this time. Ask students to work in small groups to present the features outlined here.

Readiness and Reality Checks
Most likely students will report that they do think test taking will affect their college success. What might be of interest is to see how much control students think they have over test taking. Students may just see themselves as "good or poor" test takers. What they might not realize is that everyone will benefit from the techniques in this chapter, no matter where they start in terms of their skills.

Challenge → Reaction → Insight → Action prompts
All the Challenge → Reaction → Insight → Action prompts in this chapter are worthwhile because they ask students to examine their own behaviors. Depending on how much time you have for the chapter, you can do them all as a group, or assign different students difference ones. Challenge → Reactions such as "Preparing for tests" are great for everyone to do. "To Cram or Not to Cram" may be for specific students, as some would not dream about cramming for a test. These students may just report out to the class. Is their approach a good one? Later on in the chapter the Challenge → Reaction "Your Exam Strategies" is one that the entire class would benefit from as is "Taking Objective Tests." Use these prompts to have students decide which of their current strategies work and which need improvement, and then commit to trying new strategies and noting the results.

Your Type Is Showing
Previously the idea of connecting type with the way students take a test was briefly discussed. The chapter indicated that there is a very clear connection between the different psychological types and test taking. In the "Your Type Is Showing" feature students are asked to respond to questions about how they respond to test questions and why psychological type might be connected to test taking. They are asked to describe how their results apply to themselves. How you debrief can vary. You can have students write an essay about the connection between type and the impact on test taking, or you can simply have a

class discussion. Students are typically very interested in the "Your Type Is Showing" features because they are fascinated by self-exploration at this stage of their development.

Control Your Learning: Your Toughest Class

In this section students are asked to control their learning and think about their toughest class. They are asked to identify a key challenge they face as it related to the chapter and to develop a step by step action plan with how to deal with it. There is a very specific example that Joe Cloud, the *FOCUS* Challenge Case student in the chapter, could develop. Make sure that you ask students to share their step-by-step plans with each other. Are there common approaches? There should be. What are they? Some of the key indicators will be things like making sure they understand exactly what is on the test or to reread some of the sections in this text. See what comes up in your class as common themes.

Self-Assessments

There are no formal assessments in this chapter; however much of the chapter is written such that students are constantly asked to assess what they do before, during, and after tests by placing a + ("Yes, I do this") or a ✓ ("I really should do this more") before each suggestion. There is one self-assessment that is in the form of a Challenge → Reaction: "Do *You* have test Anxiety?" Students fill out the survey and come up with a score. Students are asked to add up their scores and to see if their scores are in a healthy range. If not, there are some descriptions that follow including four different but related components of test anxiety.

Cultivating Your Curiosity: *Reduce* Math Anxiety and *Increase* Your Test Scores!

This is of value to both A+ math students and to those who struggle. Since 85% of college students in introductory math classes have some level of anxiety, the 15% of students who don't can share some tips. One of the fundamental tips for addressing anxiety is practice makes perfect. The more students do math and are successful, the easier and less stressful it becomes. This is a hard concept to sell to a student who already is fearful of math, but students have to believe that if they prepare for a test, their anxiety will be lower, and their confidence will be higher. The most fascinating aspect of this article is the research indicating that those with the highest levels of ability are often the students who are most susceptible to math anxiety because they use their spare working memory to worry, resulting in "choking," rather than using it productively to get results.

FOCUS on Careers

In this chapter, we meet Beth Robinson, Executive Director, PSAT/NMSQT Program and College Planning Services, The College Board. She answers questions about the qualities of good test questions and why students might "choke" on exams. There are probably not many, if any, students in the class who even realize that there are real people who create test questions for standardized tests. They've probably never thought about it. The career outlook for a manager of a non-profit organization is something that they may have thought about either, especially those who are considering a business major. Many psychological types can be drawn into the non-profit sector. The importance of including this profession is getting students to think broadly about career options, and this one may not have been on their radar screens at all.

6. Which in-text exercises should I use?

One activity is built into this chapter. Here is the description of this VARK activity.

EXERCISE 9.1 VARK ACTIVITY

Why do this activity?
As are all of the VARK activities, this activity is designed to help students make connections between their preferred VARK learning modality and something they learned in the chapter. Again, this activity is very helpful as students vary ways to use their preference(s) as the chapters continue.

What are the challenges and what can I expect?
There are no real challenges in this activity. You might suggest that students present their VARK Activity results to the class so that they learn from each other about how they prepare and study for tests as well as how to deal with test anxiety.

How much time will it take?
This activity should be done outside of class; the only time it takes is the actual debriefing in class. For example, you may wish to conduct an in-class discussion, an on-line chat, or ask for an e-mail summary.

How should I debrief?
If students present to the class, have them explain why they chose a particular activity and what they learned about themselves while doing the activity

---

7. Which additional exercises might enrich students' learning?

Absolutely Right!
Class activity
Materials needed: A list of words (included here)
Time: 30 minutes, depending on the size of the group
Goal: To help students understand how certain words can be clues to the answers on tests
Give students the following lists of words (scramble them up) and see if they can group them into two categories. One category is _absolutes_ that make a statement most always false. They can be positive or negative. The second category is _maybes_. When something is described using these terms, most likely it's true. See if students can describe what is similar for the words that they place in either group.

Absolutes

always	never	entirely	everyone	everybody
without a doubt	only	absolutely	100%	all
largest	biggest	smartest	no one	never
worst	least	every	no one	nobody

Maybes

sometimes	usually	a few	average	more
larger than	smarter than	frequently	better	most
occasionally	may	might	typically	commonly

Follow the Directions

Homework and Class activity

Materials needed: Any article of 4-5 pages of interest and relevance to the class

Time: 30 minutes

Goal: To help students learn how to respond to a specific question about an assignment or for essay questions

For homework, assign students the article you have chosen and ask them to read it. Give students one of the following words included here and ask them to write a short essay question about this article using the verb they were given. Ask students to answer the question and bring it to class. Share questions and discuss what students learned doing this activity.

compare	contrast	defend	define
explain	evaluate	hypothesize	identify
illustrate	justify	list	relate
summarize	outline	clarify	analyze

Grabbing for Success

Class activity

Materials needed: Two paper bags and strips of paper

Time: 30-50 minutes

Goal: To help students to identify test taking strategies

Assign students into two teams. Teams are to take 15 minutes to develop 15 true or false questions about this chapter. Each team places their questions into a different paper bag. Students on team A have to respond to questions that team B has prepared for them and vice versa. The instructor, you, have the right to throw out a question (Yes, there are bad questions!). The winning team gets candy or bonus points.

8. What other activities can I incorporate to make the chapter my own?

FOCUS encourages students to tie information from the chapters to themselves personally and to real life, just- in-time activities. Consider having students make a list of the tests or quizzes that are coming up for them, and ask them to assign themselves specific study techniques, of their choice, for their tests. It's important for students to reflect on the activity so that they learn what works best for them and that improved test taking techniques will translate into better grades.

Included here, all in one place, are Activity Options taken from the Annotated Instructor's Edition.

ACTIVITY OPTION (p. 261): Since students may not want to reveal their answers to number 5, you can use a variation of Angelo and Cross's One-Minute Paper to help debrief this case study. Ask students to take out a piece of paper (or you can provide index cards) and answer two questions anonymously: What is Joe's biggest challenge, and what is the one thing you would suggest that Joe do? Collect them, and report the results to the class.

ACTIVITY OPTION (p. 262): Generate a discussion with students about their level of interest in this chapter's material. Some students may believe that they are already good at taking tests. Some may have test anxiety and want to avoid the material. But if they don't care and are not good at test-taking, they are in big trouble. Ask students to jot down, anonymously, why they are or aren't interested in this chapter. Gather the responses and get a discussion going.

ACTIVITY OPTION (p. 264): Put students in groups of three for about five minutes to discuss their best ideas about how to prepare for tests. After five minutes, come together as a class, and go around the room and ask each student to explain one technique. Students cannot repeat techniques. What may come out of the discussion is that different techniques work for different students, but that particular themes emerge that hold true for everyone.

ACTIVITY OPTION (p. 267): Consider assigning pairs of students to one of the sixteen activities listed in this section and ask them to role-play the situation, either as described or if this suggestion isn't followed. One student could be assigned to act out going into the open-book test unprepared (number 15). The second student could become his "inner voice" and describe what is happening and what would happen if he followed this bullet's advice.

ACTIVITY OPTION (p. 267): Copy the A+ student tips and cut them into strips of paper. Hand one to each student in the class. Go around the class and ask each student to say why their tip would or would not work for them.

ACTIVITY OPTION (p. 269): Ask students to reflect on how their personality type on this one dimension affects their test-taking and to send their reflections by e-mail answering the question "Do these research results apply to you and how?"

ACTIVITY OPTION (p. 272): Break up students into four groups and ask each group to focus on the cognitive, emotional, behavioral, or physiological aspect of test anxiety. Ask the groups to come up with five suggestions on how to deal with this area of anxiety.

ACTIVITY OPTION (p. 278): The answers to the seven interview questions are packed with good information about testing. Pair up students and give them ten minutes to identify the three most important points, in their opinion, that Beth Robinson makes and why. Student pairs can then report back to the class.

ACTIVITY OPTION (p. 280): Consider bringing in a multiple-choice test you create with some tricky responses and have the class, as a group, go through some of the strategies listed.

ACTIVITY OPTION (p. 284): Have students make a four-slide PowerPoint presentation to share their step-by-step plan for their most challenging class. Make sure that students identify which class they are talking about and what makes it challenging.

ACTIVITY OPTION (p. 288): For the final activity in the chapter, have students design a one-page tip sheet that contains suggestions for taking different types of tests that have personal relevance for them and e-mail it to you. Put all the tip sheets into one document and send it to the entire class.

9. What homework might I assign?

Because you want to be sure that students connect the techniques and approaches they are learning in this chapter to real tests and quizzes, make sure that their journal entries ask them to reflect about what they have learned, what they hope to gain, and what they have already applied to taking tests.

Journal Entries
One: Have students write a one page journal entry, or send you an e-mail describing a recent test or quiz they took. What did they do to prepare (give specifics) and did they believe that it helped? Why or why not? Would they do anything differently next time? If so, what? What grade did they get on this test or quiz and were they satisfied. Why or why not?

Two: Have students write a two page journal entry, or send you an e-mail describing what finals they will be taking. They should identify each class, and then describe the test that will be given. (If they don't know the format, see if they can ask their instructor. Tell them to inform the instructor that they need to know this information for a class assignment.) Have students make a time line that includes specific dates, and what they will do to prepare.

Three: Use the Insight → Action prompts as journal or blog assignments.

10. What have I learned in teaching this chapter that I will incorporate next time?

_____

_____

_____

_____

_____

_____

_____

_____

_____

_____

_____

_____

_____

CHAPTER 10: WRITING AND SPEAKING

1. Why is this chapter important?

We all know that effective communication skills are some for the most desired outcomes of a college education. There is virtually no occupation that does not require writing and presentation skills in one form or another. Therefore, it's not surprising that the general education programs at most institutions require students to develop competence in these areas throughout their education. Many schools have "Writing across the Curriculum" and "Speaking across the Curriculum" initiatives in place in which students work on their communication skills in all of their classes. This chapter focuses on developing a foundation for the development of these skills in a first-year experience course. Students will learn about the how the writing process works, and how to build a better paper with a key section about what constitutes plagiarism. They will also learn about public speaking, a significant fear for many students, and how to overcome it. The chapter also includes a unique section on how to put together a top-notch PowerPoint presentation, and students will learn how personality type impacts the way they write and present.

Most beginning college students don't think about the writing process. If they had strong preparation in high school they are fortunate, but believe it or not, many entering college students have never before been required to write more than a few paragraphs. Students will learn about prewriting and what is involved, as well as the actual writing and rewriting stages. They will be exposed to some first-year writing traps that are called "and then" writing, "all about" writing, and "data dump" writing with actual examples to critique. The Seven "C's' of writing described in this chapter provide a useful step-by-step approach to thinking about how they write. You can bet that most of your students have never thought about this. The section on writing ends with a discussion of plagiarism. The Internet has made finding information so easy that sometimes students don't even realize that they are stealing someone else's words or ideas. A first-year seminar is the ideal place to learn about plagiarism , before they unintentionally (or intentionally) violate your institution's academic ethics code. Many colleges have very strict rules about plagiarism that could lead to dismissal.

Were you surprised to learn that public speaking is the number one fear of Americans? For those who are highly fearful, standing in front of a group can generate sheer terror! Students learn about "10 Ways to Oust Anxiety" and you, too, may find some tips helpful—especially the section on PowerPoint.

2. What are this chapter's learning objectives?

- ➢ How writing works as a process: prewriting, writing, and rewriting
- ➢ How to avoid the three common writing traps of first-year students
- ➢ How to build a better paper via the seven "C's"
- ➢ How to avoid intentional and unintentional plagiarism
- ➢ Why speaking skills are valuable

➢ How to overcome a fear of public speaking
➢ How to craft a winning presentation
➢ How to use PowerPoint as a visual aid
➢ How personality traits relate to speaking and writing preferences

3. How should I launch this chapter?

As you may have done with other chapters, try to get a sense of your students' preexisting perceptions of writing and speaking by asking for a show of hands. Do students consider themselves to be strong writers? If so, quickly ask students to explain what they do well and why they perceive this as one of their strengths. Now, ask for a show of hands of those who feel they are strong public speakers. Most likely you will find some students who raise their hand for one of these skill sets or the other. You may not find too many students who are confident about both speaking and writing. What's really important is that students realize that they are not alone if they feel they need development in these areas. Sometimes students just don't realize that many other people struggle with writing and that the apparently "oh, so confident" speaker who sits next to them has the same fear of standing in front of a group, but has learned good coping mechanisms. That's not to say that misery loves company, but it is comforting to know that you are not alone.

- **Ask students to take a few minutes to describe their first writing experiences.** Take a few minutes to go around the room to have students share what they remember about their earliest writing projects. Were they on big lined paper, where they learned to shape their letters and write their name? Was it a story they wrote about a made-up character or their first book report? Sometimes these very first experiences are very powerful memories that are extremely positive or very negative. However, most young children enjoy writing stories and don't suffer from "writer's block." But don't be surprised if a student explains a primary, middle, or high school situation in which they worked very hard but did not get a good grade. Did it have an impact on how they think of themselves as writers now?

- **Ask students to describe a dynamic speaker they know or have heard.** Who is this individual? When did they hear them speak? What was dynamic about their speaking style? Generate a list of the characteristics of dynamic speakers. What are some common characteristics that they all share?

- **Going beyond the book**. You can be sure that there are many, many resources for students beyond this book. Most every college has a writing center or an oral communication center or workshops on improving speaking and writing skills. There are countless online resources for writing, presenting, and developing PowerPoint presentations. You can also encourage students to find one or two links and share them with the class.

4. How should I use the *FOCUS* Challenge Case?

Regardless of the type of institution at which you teach, you probably have students like Darnell Williams in your class. Darnell put very little effort into high school and skated by. The only aspect of high school he enjoyed was playing football. Now he is "trying college out" by taking only two classes. He has followed general advice he's heard about the importance of communication skills in college, so he decided to tackle two required courses. He wants to do well (note that he spent three hours writing his essay and rewrote it four times), but he is not particularly interested in his composition and public speaking classes, and because he isn't engaged is his classes, he could be at risk for dropping out. He begins to blame his high school writing teacher for not doing a better job for preparing him for college. Darnell needs to accept that fact that he has to take control of his learning, regardless of what happened in the past. Darnell probably also has some degree of communication apprehension, which he will have to overcome by getting extra help. Let's hope he will.

Use this *FOCUS* Challenge Case not only to ask your students to discuss the "What Do *You* Think?" questions but to point out issues like how important it is for students to engage in their classes, even if they don't find the content particularly compelling, or how high school standards may differ from college standards, or how important it is to invest effort to do your best, even if coursework is challenging. At the end of the chapter, discuss the "*Now* What Do You Think?" section with your students to see if their original perceptions have changed. The story offers an array of issues with which your students will relate.

5. What important features does this chapter include?

The recurring themes in the book can guide how you approach this chapter. As in the previous chapters consider dividing the class into smaller groups or pairs and assign students to features that are of interest to them.

Readiness and Reality Checks

How do students respond to this Readiness Check? There is no doubt about it; students will report that they do think writing and speaking will affect their college success. But it may be the case that some of your students think they have very little control over their ability to become a better writer or speaker. Think about dividing the class into two groups by asking students to separate on the item "How much control do you expect to have?" In these two groups, ask students to discuss how they can change? Do those who have higher scores on the control question have a different attitude than those who do not? Come together as a class and discuss the fact, that with the right attitude, skill development and practice, they will become stronger in these skills. As always, at the end of the chapter have students check their Reality Check with their original Readiness Check for the material in this chapter.

Challenge → Reaction → Insight → Action prompts

This chapter is full of excellent Challenge → Reaction → Insight → Action prompts. Challenge → Reactions, for example, ask students about their perceptions of the writing process, about the common weaknesses of first-year students' writing, about the "Seven C's" of good writing, about whether speech anxiety is a problem for them (PRPSA), about the "Seven P's" of crafting a winning presentation, and about whether a passage from a hypothetical student's paper is plagiarized. As usual, the Insight → Action prompts ask students to apply material to themselves, prompting reflection and change. Use the C → R prompts as discussion generators and the I → A prompts as journal suggestions or online postings to which individual students respond.

Your Type Is Showing

Have you ever thought about the relationship between personality type to writing and speaking? In this "Your Type Is Showing" students are asked to respond to questions about which type might be connected to a fear of communicating (introverts, sensors, and feelers). Students also read short descriptions of types and how individuals with this type tend to approach writing. Knowing your type is not simply a way to justify behavior ("Oh, now I know why I'm afraid of public speaking" or "Yup, that's me—I just pick really broad topics to write about, and I can never focus" (perceivers)). Instead, understanding type is a way to help students understand how they operate and what they need to do to use their strengths and develop their weaknesses.

Control Your Learning: Your Toughest Class

Students are asked to think about their toughest class and control their learning. They are asked to think about the speaking or writing assignments in this class (or if, for example, their toughest class is a math course, to choose another class). What is the assignment and what are they required to do? Often, students will identify a 10-20 page research paper that they have to do as their toughest challenge. The shear number of pages is enough to send some students into the "I can't do this mode." For those who fear presentations, some students may be counting the days to when they have to stand up and speak, getting more anxious by the hour. Students are asked to develop a step-by-step plan based on what they have learned in this chapter and e-mail you (or the instructor of their challenging class) the plan they choose. This self-exploration is key to changing behavior. Make sure you follow up later in the class to have students reflect on whether they are using the plan they developed, if it worked—why or why not—and what adjustments, if any, they would make for the future. You might even consider *requiring* students to make a plan, follow it, and then respond to what happened, rather than leaving the implementation of the plan to choice.

Self-Assessments

Many of the Challenge → Reaction → Insight → Action prompts in this chapter are basically self-assessments. For example, students are asked about how they write, and whether or not they believe they have speech anxiety using these prompts. James McCroskey's "Personal Report of Public Speaking Anxiety," a well-known research instrument, is used as a Challenge → Reaction in this chapter.

Cultivating Your Curiosity: Relieve Stress the "Write" Way

In this chapter of *FOCUS* Cultivating Your Curiosity: Relieve Stress the "Write" Way! helps students to understand that writing can be really therapeutic. Research studies are discussed that indicate how writing has a positive impact on physical and psychological health. Students are asked to write about something that is troubling them and consider keeping a journal.

FOCUS on Careers

The career focus in this chapter is on careers that require strong communication skills. In this chapter, we meet Lauren Ward Larsen, a nationally know speaker on blood donation who represents Johnson & Johnson and speaks to thousands of potential blood donors each year. She points out that even as a "professional" she still gets nervous about presenting and gives tips on what she does to calm herself. She also identifies some of her worst nightmares as a presenter, and what she does to anticipate these problems. When she is asked "What makes speakers dynamic?" her response is a simple one: "knowing that I can make a difference. To me, a dynamic speaker is one who understands her audience enough to touch their hearts with her words." Students also learn about the career of marketing, Ward's former (and in a sense, current) profession. The most common psychological types for this field are ESTJ, ENTJ, or ENTP. Notice, the strong E and T needed for this field. Marketing professionals need to be creative, show initiative, understand and use technology and have strong communication skills. What about the job outlook for this career and job stability? Fortunately, the outlook is good, but there is fierce competition for entry level jobs.

6. Which in-text exercises should I use?

Three exercises are built into this chapter. Included here are descriptions of why they have appear in the text, how much time each one will probably take, and how you might debrief them. Each activity addresses a particular skill that students can develop.

EXERCISE 10.1 DEARLY DEPARTED

Why do this activity?
In this activity students are given a choice to write or present about a famous historical figure with whom they have something in common. For example, if a female student wants to be a pilot, she might consider choosing someone like Amelia Earhart. This activity should help students learn about the journey people take on their way to their dreams.

What are the challenges and what can you expect?
There should not be many challenges for this activity, since students are given an option on how to present the information, either by either speaking or writing. They also get to choose who they want to learn about in an area of interest to them.

How much time will it take?

Most of the work for this activity should be done out of class. Depending on how many students elect to speak, rather than write, or if you decide to let those who write also read their obituaries in class, your time will vary. Or the activity could be done entirely through e-mail, however discussing many interesting historical figures would be missed.

How should I debrief?

Again, this depends on how you choose for students to present, either to you individually or to the class. Regardless of the method, it's important that students get timely feedback on their projects. Consider using a rubric for self and peer assessment too. Develop a rubric as a class, prior to students doing this activity so that everyone understands what is expected of them and they can judge themselves and others on the agreed upon criteria.

EXERCISE 10.2 WHAT MAKES SPEAKERS DYNAMIC? PET PEEVES! (by Staley, C., 2003, p. 138.)

Why do this activity?

Ask individual student volunteers to give a 30-second speech on a pet peeve or something that really makes them angry. As they speak, they should hit the side of the lectern or the desk at the front of the room with the rolled-up newspaper you've provided from time to time for emphasis. This activity helps students to become comfortable presenting in front of the class, for a short period of time, presenting something that they feel passionate about.

What are the challenges and what can you expect?

One challenge may be that students become a little too animated with this activity. Warn students not to offend others with their language or damage the lectern, if you think these things could become issues.

How much time will it take?

This activity should take about 20-30 minutes depending on the size of the class.

How should I debrief?

It's important for students to discuss how they felt about presenting, especially those with communication apprehension. Also, ask students to identify some of the characteristics they observed in presenters who were dynamic. What are the characteristics and behaviors that make speakers dynamic?

EXERCISE 10.3 VARK ACTIVITY

Why do this activity?

This activity is designed to help students make connections between their preferred VARK learning modality and something they learned in the chapter. The activity suggests that visual learners storyboard a PowerPoint presentation, for example.

What are the challenges and what can I expect?

There are no real challenges in this activity. You might suggest that students present this VARK activity results to the class so that they learn from each other.

> **How much time will it take?**
> This activity can be done outside of class: the only time it takes is the actual debriefing in class and you can take whatever time you need if you have students present their results in class.
>
> **How should I debrief?**
> If students present to the class, have them explain why they chose a particular activity and what they learned about themselves while doing the activity.

7. Which additional exercises might enrich students' learning?

What's in an A? (by Staley, C. (2003), pp.132-136.)
Class activity
Materials needed: Several student papers (with names removed) from previous terms (to focus on writing) and videotapes of past students speeches (to focus on speaking), and copies of the criteria sheets (blank or filled in) that follow
Time: Approximately one hour
Goal: To help students identify the criteria by which speaking and writing assignments are graded and thereby strive for peak performance
View the videos in class and have students respond via the criteria sheets or discuss the already completed criteria sheets. The exercise may be done separately for speaking and writing, or you many focus on both skills during one extended session. If you begin with speaking ask students to help you create general criteria upon which grades for student speeches are based, for example

Dynamism Contest (based on Staley, C. (1999), p. 8-60.)
Class activity
Materials needed: Bring to class a list of sample topics (for example, "the best thing about college…," "the worst thing about college," etc.)
Time: 45 minutes to an hour
Goal: To help students identify the characteristics of dynamic speakers
This activity occurs in "rounds" with two students volunteering for each "round. When given the "ready, set, go" command, you will announce a topic and the two speakers will begin speaking for one minute, both at the same time. Each speaker's goal should be to capture the attention of the class by doing anything possible to accomplish this. At the end of the round, the two speakers should turn away from the other students while the class votes on who "won" the round by capturing more attention. After all the speakers have finished, as a class generate a list of behaviors that makes speakers dynamic.

8. What other activities can I incorporate to make the chapter my own?

Depending on how your class is structured—in a community college with a stand alone course, or in a linked learning community course—you have a variety of ways that you can make this chapter your own. Stand alone courses are the most challenging, especially when students in your class are not taking similar courses. But, the skills in this chapter are universal. One thing you might try is to identify a few common experiences students might have and use this as a springboard for a writing and presentation activity. For example, is there a speaker or event on campus that everyone can attend?

Included here, all in one place, are Activity Options taken from the Annotated Instructor's Edition.

ACTIVITY OPTION (p. 291): Have students write a letter from Darnell to a younger sibling incorporating the four points listed in "What Do *You* Think?" This letter can be used in other activities in this chapter when writing skills are explored.

ACTIVITY OPTION (p. 293): Divide the class into small groups and give each group one or two of the "Challenge → Reaction" questions to discuss. After five minutes, have one member of the group report to the entire class. You may be surprised at how confused many students are about writing.

ACTIVITY OPTION (p. 296): Often, students need help writing a good, clear thesis statement and need opportunities to practice. Give students a scenario about some controversial, current topic. Ask them to take a stand and bring a thesis statement to class. Encourage students to look online or in a writer's handbook for suggestions on how to write a good thesis. Have students bring their thesis statements to the next class and they can critique each other's.

ACTIVITY OPTION (p. 297): Show your students some online examples of visual organizers for writing or provide handouts that explain visual techniques to help them become better writers. There are many visual organizing tools online or your writing center will have examples such as outlining, mapping, and brainstorming activities. Use one of the visual organizers to help students, as a class, structure an essay about why it's important to go to class.

ACTIVITY OPTION (p. 300): Consider having students respond to this "Insight → Action" by sending you an e-mail or writing a one-page essay about this using the first person. This essay could be brought to class, and students could give feedback to each other.

ACTIVITY OPTION (p. 307): Allow students to choose either a writing assignment or a presentation. Those who decide to write must share it with the class for feedback. Those who decide to present must present in class and get feedback. In addition to the assignment, students must include how their learning style connects to the reason they chose a particular option.

ACTVITY OPTION (p. 310): Have students find your institution's policy on plagiarism and bring it to the next class. What are the consequences of plagiarizing? If students are dismissed from the college can they ever return? Does it vary by instructor? Students should understand this policy in depth.

ACTIVITY OPTION (p. 313): Have students line up on a continuum with those who are nervous about presenting at one end and those who are not at the other. Have students trade perceptions of speech anxiety and what can be done to overcome it.

ACTIVITY OPTION (p. 315): Have students watch a presentation on television or provide a speech for students to watch and ask them to identify the seven P's.

ACTIVITY OPTION (p. 321): For the final in-class activity, students should develop a PowerPoint presentation on some aspect of writing and speaking. Assign students or groups of students to parts of this chapter such as "Avoid These Three Writing Traps," "Build a Better Paper: The Seven C's," "Ten Ways to Oust Anxiety," and so on. Use the five suggestions in the chapter about PowerPointless presentations as the criteria for assessing the presentation. Students can assess each other.

9. What homework might I assign?

Students can do a two- to three-page paper on famous orators in history. If you prefer, focus on the best political speeches in the past decade, for example. In addition to this paper, students should complete journal entries. Encourage students to reflect on both their writing and presentation skills in this week's entries.

Journal Entries

One: Have students write a one-page journal entry, or send you an e-mail describing a writing assignment that was very difficult for them in the past few weeks. If they didn't have a particularly challenging writing assignment within that time frame, ask them to describe any fairly major writing assignment they completed and explain the strategy they used to write.

Two: Have students write a one-page journal entry, or send you an e-mail describing an interesting speech or presentation they saw this week. What was it? Who gave the presentation and what made it interesting and dynamic?

Three: Use the Insight → Action prompts as journal or blog assignments.

10. What have I learned in teaching this chapter that I will incorporate next time?

_____

_____

_____

_____

_____

_____

_____

_____

_____

_____

_____

CHAPTER 11: BUILDING RELATIONSHIPS, VALUING DIVERSITY

1. Why is this chapter important?

Students will most likely be especially interested in this chapter. They will want to know more about something of key importance in their lives—their relationships with others. *You* might not even have thought much about the importance of relationships and their effects on college success. Some of the fundamental research on college persistence indicates that students must make both academic progress and connections to the institution and others to stay in college and succeed. The skills students will learn about in this chapter are about managing their emotions and getting along with others. So this chapter is not about academic skills like studying or reading, per se, but instead about the non-cognitive skills that affect college success. These non-cognitive skills that make up one's emotional intelligence (including knowing yourself, working well with others, handling stress, having empathy for other's situations, and being optimistic), for example, often have *more* impact on students' persistence and dream fulfillment than academic skills. Of course, some students come to college for the wrong reasons, such as their parents' insistence or the fact that they had nothing else that they could think of to do after high school. But, if you believe that basically we all want to do well in life and fulfill our dreams, then failing in college and not meeting your own and other's expectations can have a far-reaching impact on self regard. And low self-regard can have a variety of effects. For example, it may impact the way we deal with conflict.

In this chapter, students will explore communication conflict and love in relationships. When students are asked to think about how they do this, not only will they be exploring the way that they deal with conflict, but how their personality type plays into their communication style. For example, strong thinking types may not know that their logical, matter of fact way of breaking off a relationship might have a devastating effect on someone else.

In addition to learning about love and relationships and communication, this chapter flows from an emphasis on emotional intelligence into a powerful discussion of diversity. If you don't really know yourself and how and why you act and think the way you do, you may not be able to understand someone else's perspective. For example, if a student in your class was raised to believe that individuals with particular backgrounds are less able than others, and that they don't understand why they think that way, diversity may be an illusive concept. An inability to understand yourself, and to be flexible and open-minded can be a barrier to appreciating diversity. The good news is that emotional intelligence can be taught and enhanced, and improvement will lead to more success in relationships, and greater appreciation for the diversity that surrounds us.

2. What are this chapter's learning objectives?

- ➢ What emotional intelligence is
- ➢ How EI relates to leadership
- ➢ Whether EI can be improved
- ➢ How scientists define romantic love
- ➢ How communication is at the center of romantic relationships
- ➢ How to improve communication with people you care about
- ➢ How people manage conflict in five basic ways
- ➢ What constitutes a "danger signal" in a relationship
- ➢ Why diversity makes a difference
- ➢ Why service-learning is valuable
- ➢ Why global learning is important

3. How should I launch this chapter?

This chapter is easy to launch because of students' natural curiosity about the content. Students are generally intrigued by the notion of emotional intelligence; many have never thought or heard about it before. And most students are either in a romantic relationship now, just ending one, or in the market for one, so chances are you won't need to do much to get students to rally around the beginning sections of the chapter. Note that the chapter starts with a more personal focus and moves to a broader focus on diversity. Research indicates that many of today's college students believe (inaccurately) that diversity is an issue we have "solved" as a society, or they have wearied from the emphasis on diversity in K-12, just as they have become tired of other academic emphases. Use the chapter's flow to your advantage since as academics, we know that both these subjects are of the utmost importance.

- **Use the *FOCUS* Challenge Case as a starting point to open up the chapter.** Because self awareness is really central to this chapter, students need to be taking a good hard look at how they react in various situations and why. But, identifying that they may not be responding in appropriate ways is not always easy. It's much easier to criticize someone else's behavior than it is to be self-critical. Use Kia as a way to open up dialogue. There may be students in your class who are doing something similar to sabotage their own success.

- **Ask students to identify ways in which some of the dimensions of emotional intelligence (EI) are connected to college success.** A variation of this activity could be to give students index cards with each of the EI skills written on them. Have students form groups and think about some behavior a student might display that works against being emotionally intelligent. See http://www.reuvenbaron.org/bar-on-model/essay.php?i=3 for a complete list of the five scales and fifteen subscales of emotional intelligence.

- **Going beyond the book**. Have students try a "Google" search using the words "college success and stress management" or "college success and adaptability." In fact, see if the class can generate a list of college success factors linked with vocabulary and concepts from the chapter and do some additional searching. You will see that there are many ways in which both you and your students can go beyond what is in this chapter. For students who are considering psychology as a major, you might suggest that they begin to explore the whole notion of emotional intelligence. For students who are considering communication studies as a major, the area of conflict management is filled with ways in which students will be able to see what they are learning and how it connects to majors and careers, as well as self development. For students who are particularly intrigued by diversity, they may be interested in finding campus groups that explore this topic.

4. How should I use the *FOCUS* Challenge Case?

Kia Washington is a student who is at very high risk for dropping out. She begins her college career in a very stressful way. Because of a mishap, she doesn't have on-campus housing available to her, she is not sure about her classes, and she is strapped for money. Although she had some stressful years at home before she even left for college, she managed to do very well academically in high school. She had her ideal boyfriend named Quentin and preferred only being with him. With Quentin off to another college, and so many things going wrong, Kia is feeling lonely and isolated. She is not in a good place and sees her life as a "soap opera." Ask students to discuss the "What Do *You* Think?" questions, and during the discussion give them an opportunity, perhaps before they even know much about emotional intelligence, to point out the evidence that Kia's IQ is probably much higher than her EQ. Ask them how Kia may be sabotaging herself and her college success. While it's possible to view the case as melodramatic, it is based on real first-year students with these exact issues, as are all the *FOCUS* Challenge Cases.

5. What important features does this chapter include?

Continue to use the recurring themes in this book. The Challenge → Reaction → Insight → Action prompts are especially helpful to encourage students to think about how they might respond and what they would do in the all important aspects of relationships.

Readiness and Reality Checks
In this chapter, the Readiness Check responses for students could be somewhat different than in other chapters. As mentioned earlier, cognitive factors such as studying and test taking are concepts that students have heard about before. When it comes to learning about emotional intelligence, however, students may not know much about it, and they will be motivated to learn more. The comparisons between the Readiness and Reality Checks always provide a good opportunity for self—and group—reflection and class discussion.

Challenge → Reaction → Insight → Action prompts

In addition to the Readiness and Reality Checks, the Challenge → Reaction → Insight → Action prompts in this chapter not only provide self-assessments, but can and should be used to spark class discussion. There are three different Challenge → Reaction opportunities including one that asks students if they are involved in a relationship and how they might respond manage conflict as well as their views on diversity. Insight → Action prompts related to improving emotional intelligence, collaborative ways of managing conflict and communicating effectively and students perceptions about diversity are also excellent opportunities for students to make suggestions on what they should do to make positive change.

Your Type Is Showing

The "Your Type Is Showing" feature in this chapter works well as a role play between two students. Then the rest of the class should guess which of the four type scales is best represented by each partner and why they chose the type that they did. While there are no right and wrong types, in and of themselves, there are combinations of personality types that make communicating in relationships more challenging. This is a great activity to perform and discuss in class.

Control Your Learning: Your Toughest Class

In this "Control Your Learning" activity, students are reminded that they can't control how others respond, but they can control how they behave, which in turn will impact how others might respond. This particular activity instructs students to think about how they can communicate with an instructor in their most challenging class. What's really important in this activity is that students are asked to focus on themselves and what they may be doing that might adversely affect their relationship with the instructor, as opposed to what the instructor is doing. They are asked to identify what they can do differently, what the instructor might expect, and what they can change to improve the situation with their instructor, all of which ultimately impacts learning.

Self-Assessments

This chapter has no formal assessments but a number of Challenge → Reaction prompts are self-report surveys. These surveys are about how one might respond in emotionally charged situations, insights into quality relationships and students own views about diversity. All of these self-assessments can be used in reflective writing activities and class discussions.

Cultivate Your Curiosity: Build Relationships, One Drop at a Time

In this chapter of *FOCUS*, curiosity is addressed early in the chapter when students read about building relationships "one drop at a time." They read a summary of the best-selling book, *How Full Is Your Bucket?*, and identify the analogy of adding or subtracting liquid from a bucket depending on how they respond either positively (adding to), or negatively (subtracting from) the bucket.

FOCUS on Careers

In this chapter, we meet Linda Holtzman, a college professor and diversity trainer. Today the corporate world places a high emphasis on teamwork, collaboration, and communication skills. Students should be asking themselves is this a career for me and "what is the most common psychological type for this profession? Does it match my psychological type? While there is variety in many aspects of the type, extroverts dominate the field as they are working with people much of the time. Who in the class would be happy in this job? Why or why not.

6. Which in-text exercises should I use?

Three exercises are built into this chapter. As you have done in other chapters, have students connect these activities to real life situations. The descriptions of the activities follow, including how much time each one will probably take, and how you might debrief them.

EXERCISE 11.2 WHAT'S THE DIFFERENCE?

Why do this activity?
It's important to do this activity to show students that while some aspects of how diverse or similar we are to others are important, there are ways in which we have no idea how alike we are. At first students develop lists of all the ways that they differ from the partner they choose. When you call "time's up," students share their lists with each other.

What are the challenges and what can you expect?
There should be no challenges for this activity. Often students begin to find commonalities between each other, perhaps that they haven't even known about throughout the course.

How much time will it take?
This activity should take 20-30 minutes.

How should I debrief?
One of the best ways to debrief is to go around the room and ask each pair to individually list one thing that was the same as their partner and one that was different and that surprised them. Keep a list on the board of these surprising moments.

EXERCISE 12.2 CIRCLES OF AWARENESS

Why do this activity?
There are a number of reasons why this is a good activity for students. Students will find classmates who are similar and even more important classmates who are different. Students may never have been given the opportunity to discuss with others what it means to be different and how by doing so, a new-found awareness may emerge.

What are the challenges and what can you expect?
While it is something that can be moderated and wouldn't happen with most groups, it is possible that there are some students who are not comfortable with differences. Keep in mind the black and white dualistic kinds of thinking that first-year students may have.

How much time will it take?
This activity should take 20-30 minutes.

How should I debrief?
One way of debriefing is to ask students to go around the room and ask them to fill in the blank "When I talked with a student who was different than me I learned_____."

EXERCISE 12.3 VARK ACTIVITY

Why do this activity?
This activity is designed to help students make connections between their preferred VARK learning modality and an actual assignment. At this point in the semester if you notice that multimodal students are tending to choose one type of activity consistently, consider assigning them a preferred VARK modality that they have not yet done.

What are the challenges and what can I expect?
There are no real challenges in this activity except that if you do assign modalities, some students will miss the opportunity to choose for themselves.

How much time will it take?
VARK Activities are typically done outside of class and reported on in class. Time will vary, based on the size of your group and reporting formats.

How should I debrief?
You may debrief however you wish, based on the specific learning outcomes you wish to reinforce.

---

7. Which additional exercises might enrich students' learning?

An Emotionally Intelligent Friend
Class activity
Materials needed: Kia's Washington's *FOCUS* Challenge Case
Time: 30-50 minutes, depending on the size of the group
Goal: To help students identify the main parts of a story
Place student into five groups that correspond with the five components of emotional intelligence: intrapersonal (self awareness), interpersonal (relating to others), stress management, adaptability, and general mood. In these small groups, ask students to identify whether Kia displays strong emotional intelligence in the area they are assigned. If not, ask students to identify why Kia does not, giving a specific example of her behavior. Also, if they were her emotionally intelligent friend, what advice would they give her to improve? Share group responses with the class.

The Stars Don't Always Shine
Class activity
Materials needed: article from a recent People's Magazine
Time: lecture plus 30-40 minutes
Goal: To help students analyze the behavior of others in terms of emotional intelligence (EI) skills and conflict management

Make copies of a recent *People* magazine article about a Hollywood star who displays inappropriate behavior. Ask students to read this for homework, and come prepared to discuss the EI competencies and conflict management style of the star. To be sure that the students come prepared, tell students they must describe at least three of the five EI competencies using examples, and identify one of the five conflict management styles described in this chapter.

8. What other activities can I incorporate to make the chapter my own?

Depending on the composition of your class, you could approach this chapter a little differently. If you have mostly traditional students, you can follow the *FOCUS* Challenge Case that highlights Kia, but if you have nontraditional students or a mix of both, you might ask older students to write a case study that makes sense for them. In addition, if your class is very diverse, take full advantage of this if students are willing to share their perceptions of being part of an underrepresented population.

Included here, all in one place, are Activity Options taken from the Annotated Instructor's Edition.

ACTIVITY OPTION (p. 325): Ask students to respond to these questions on their own, and then pair up and compare their responses with those of the student next to them. Do they think her relationship with Quentin will survive? Why or why not, and what should she do? Choose one student from each pair to report to the class.

ACTIVITY OPTION (p. 326): This is a great opportunity to use the "Visible Quiz" activity by Staley (2003). Make a set of four cards using a different color cardstock for each letter (a, b, c, d) for each student. Ask students to give their answers to the "Challenge → Reaction" questions by holding up their chosen card for each question. This activity provides you with immediate information on individual student's opinions and generates class discussion.

ACTIVITY OPTION (p. 330): Ask students to work in small groups to describe behaviors of successful college students (i.e., studying ahead of time, being realistic about what you can and can't do, going to class, etc.) and see how these behaviors might fit into the five scales of emotional intelligence.

ACTIVITY OPTION (p. 330): For homework, divide the class into three groups and assign each group the term *resilience, hardiness,* or *learned optimism.* Each group must come to the next class prepared to describe how their term connects to success in college. Students must define the term and provide examples or role plays that relate their term to college success.

ACTIVITY OPTION (p. 332): Each of the five scales of EI has subscales. Students can find these online (http://www.eiconsortium.org/measures/eqi.html). For example, stress management is comprised of two subscales: stress tolerance and impulse control. As a class, identify the two most challenging scales for students and identify the subscales that make up these scales. How do these connect with success in college?

ACTIVITY OPTION (p. 333): In groups, ask students to develop the top five characteristics of an ideal partner and rank them in order of importance. Ask students to develop this same list for what they might be looking for when they're in their seventies. Are the two lists the same? Do rankings change? Is what they chose as top characteristics in their college years the same as what they predict they would choose later in life? Discuss this as a class.

ACTIVITY OPTION (p. 337): Divide the class into six groups and give each group a card with one of the examples: trapper, blamer, mindreader, gunnysacker, hit and run fighter, or Benedict Arnold. Groups should not show each other their card. Have two to three students from each group volunteer to role-play their example, while the other groups guess which "crazymaking" behavior they are portraying.

ACTIVITY OPTION (p. 341): This is a great opportunity to divide the class into five groups and give each group a scene to play out while other groups guess the types. Discuss with the class what these couples could do to ease the conflict in their relationships.

ACTIVITY OPTION (p. 341): Ask students to respond to this "Insight → Action" activity by answering one or more of the questions using an essay format. Students should send their essay to you as an attachment to an e-mail message. It's an opportunity for you to make a personal connection with them.

ACTIVITY OPTION (p. 347): If you are comfortable with this activity, create a "Human Continuum" (Staley, 2003) as a way to launch a discussion about diversity in class. Create an imaginary line along the front of the room, for example, and label each opposite pole. You can use descriptors such as majority/minority, 100 percent American/foreign, and so on. Then ask students to place themselves along the line. You may be surprised at how students place themselves on this continuum. For example, students who are light-skinned may place themselves closer to a label for students of color than someone who has darker skin. Often, how we identify ourselves is by using internal, rather than external, indicators. Defining the meanings the two poles held for students can lead to a rich discussion.

ACTIVITY OPTION (p. 353): As was suggested early in this chapter, consider using this "Insight → Action" activity as a prompt for an essay. You can use all questions, or some, or even add a question to have students answer. Students can share the essay with each other for peer feedback, or hand it in or e-mail it to you.

ACTIVITY OPTION (p. 353): The VARK activity is a great way for students to choose an aspect of the chapter that had meaning for them and present it to the class. Ask students to make four PowerPoint slides for their presentation. Students can also respond to both the *"Now* What Do You Think?" activity and the Reality Check by sending you an e-mail with their results, or by comparing their results in class with a partner.

ACTIVITY OPTION (p. 354): For the final activity have students design a PowerPoint presentation (four slides) in groups on either the role of emotional intelligence, love, or conflict in the lives of college students and their success. Presentations should include a definition, describe possible challenges concerning the issue, its impact on college success, and suggestions on how to manage the challenge.

9. What homework might I assign?

Ask all students to observe a current popular television show and describe the conflict management style of the main character. Describe this in class. The goal is to help students be able to recognize conflict management styles.

Journal Entries

One: Have students write a one-page journal entry, or send you an e-mail describing one EI skill they think that they want to improve. Students must identify why they think they need to develop the skill using an example, and what they will do to improve it.

Two: Have students write a one-page journal entry, or send you an e-mail reflecting on a time when they showed good conflict management skills and a time when they did not. Ask students to label each of these styles using the five examples in the chapter. For the negative example, ask students to describe what they wish they had done.

Three: Use the Insight → Action prompts as journal or blog assignments.

10. What have I learned in teaching this chapter that I will incorporate next time?

_____

_____

_____

_____

_____

_____

_____

_____

_____

_____

_____

_____

_____

_____

_____

_____

_____

CHAPTER 12: CHOOSING A COLLEGE MAJOR AND A CAREER

1. Why is this chapter important?

Did you think, even for a minute, about the title of this chapter when you first read it? How about the addition of the word career? Do you think first-year students know much about how to build a career? Typically, students think about majors and jobs, and loosely use the word career. In this chapter students will not only be asked about what major they might choose and what jobs are associated with that major, but they are introduced to information about how to build a career related to a particular field. Students are encouraged to think about how the disciplines connect and how taking a course in one area connects to another. For many students things just don't connect. "Why should I have to take a course in interpersonal communication if I am going to work as a computer programmer?" a student might ask, for example. This chapter will help students to self-assess, dig deeper, and look at connections between who they are, what they want to do in life, and which courses they will take. What better way to begin to find closure in the course than to tie things all together.

Understanding how things connect is a central theme in this chapter. When students first read about majors and careers, they are not thinking about courses and connections. The "College in a Box" concept is very concrete and visual for students and will spark a great debate on how the disciplines connect. This concept of how they connect is done so well in "The Circle of Learning" diagram that you don't want to overlook the opportunity to discuss it in class. Also, two fundamental questions that seem so simple, but really help focus students are addressed: "What do people study in college?" and "Why do people study these things?" The whats and the whys lead to four quadrants of understanding that can help students get college out of the box and into the concept of a connected, circular chain of learning. Once the connections make sense to students, it's a lot easier to look at why they should stick it out in their most challenging, but sometimes least interesting classes, how personality type connects to majors and careers, and what really is involved in developing a career.

Careers just don't happen. Careers are developed over time. All too often college students want to jump out of the gate and earn the same amount of money that has taken their parents years of accomplishment and diligence to reach. As you read in the text, Mel Levine says that many young adults are not finding a good fit between who they are and what they are doing, so in his words they see themselves going nowhere. His observations may sound ominous, but all the more reason for students to volunteer, do internships, and gain experience. Make sure that students take these opportunities seriously. Having experience doing something can either confirm that this is what students want to do or have them experience an "ah-ha" moment when they realize that this job is not for them. In fact, this entire chapter can be an "ah-ha" moment for students when things finally begin to fall into place and their college experience starts making sense.

2. What are this chapter's learning objectives?

- ➢ Why "College in a Box" isn't an accurate view of coursework
- ➢ How the disciplines connect in the Circle of Learning
- ➢ How to build an Academic Map
- ➢ How to choose a major and a career
- ➢ How to focus on the "I's"
- ➢ What a "SWOT" analysis is
- ➢ How to "SCAN" your skills
- ➢ Why majors and careers aren't the same thing
- ➢ How to consider academic anatomy
- ➢ How to launch a career
- ➢ How internships, co-ops, and service learning can give students experience

3. How should I launch this chapter?

Several, if not many, of your students may be thinking along the same lines as Ethan by now. Somehow, many students think things will quickly and naturally fall into place when they get to college, even during their first term. They expect to be drawn into a discipline, have clear insight into the "right" career for them, and when that doesn't happen, they begin to doubt themselves and their decision to attend college in the first place. Many, like Ethan, will drop out. Some will return, but perhaps only after their lives are even more complex, with a family, for example. What the "Ethans" we work with need to take to heart is Tolkien's quotation at the beginning of this chapter, "All who wander are not lost." Some wandering is to be expected when it comes to making choices that will affect the rest of your life. Think back: did you know when you were 18 or 19 that you'd have taken the career path you've taken? Here are some ideas for launching this chapter.

- **Use the *FOCUS* Challenge Case as a starting point to open up the chapter.** This *FOCUS* Challenge Case is a terrific one to open up the chapter. Significant research indicates that when students know what they really want to do and get into a major that is a good fit for them, the likelihood of graduating is fairly high. On the other hand, some students may just be following in mom or dad's footsteps or pursuing a major that they think will lead to a job that really pays well. Students need to discuss that while Ethan's parents may have "enabled" him and without even realizing it, made things even more difficult for him. It's not uncommon to be in a searching mode in your first or first several terms. Use Ethan as an example of someone who is unclear and perhaps even impatient about figuring it all out—and talk about what "figuring it all out" means during your first term of college. Is it even possible?

- **Ask students to pair up and share with each other what they think they will major in.** Students enjoy both talking about what they do and don't know about their majors. It's kind of freeing to talk with someone who is not judging the rights and wrongs of the major. For some students it might be the first time that they even talked about it. Come together as a class and share what you have learned. The bottom line is that you want students to really do some self exploration in this chapter and to be open-minded about what it is they really want to do with their lives.

- **Going beyond the book.** There are more resources available than you can imagine when it comes to choosing majors and careers. First, you might begin exploring your own campus. Depending on the size of your institution, there might be a fully staffed career center with individuals who help with résumé writing and career searching or just one or two individuals who help in this area. Regardless, it's a place to begin and you want to be sure students know where it is and what resources it offers. One additional source that is a must for this chapter is www.careerbuilder.com. Not only can students look at jobs in a particular area, but they can look at upcoming local career fairs and the job outlook on this comprehensive web site.

4. How should I use the *FOCUS* Challenge Case?

As mentioned earlier, Ethan Cole is not a rare student. In fact, if you think about it, twenty to twenty-five years ago, students like Ethan would not even be considering college. Dyslexics rarely went on to college, and ADD or ADHD were not diagnosed frequently. If truth be told, there are still professors teaching who are simply not interested in hearing about the "whys" of students' learning challenges. Either students make it, or they are out! If students like Ethan who struggle a bit and haven't discovered how to focus their passion meet up with a professor with this perspective, they can become totally discouraged and drop out without much deliberation. This *FOCUS* Challenge Case is filled with opportunities for discussion and the questions in "What Do *You* Think?" are a good lead-in. Consider using this section as a jumping off point.

5. What important features does this chapter include?

Of course, by now you and your students have literally memorized the "habit-forming" (hopefully!) features of the text. You may split up the features, so that some students who enjoy the Readiness Checks and Reality Checks focus on those, while others who really think "Your Type Is Showing" is the most interesting may discuss that feature. Let them follow their interests and lead the class. The Challenge → Reaction and Insight → Action prompts are especially helpful to encourage students to think about how they might respond and how they connect to careers and majors. This chapter, overall, contains some of the most unique, innovative. and individually helpful material in the text.

Readiness and Reality Checks
Students should be fairly responsive when filling out the Readiness Check. Students are interested in what they are planning to major in. And, interest in questions, such as how much they think this chapter will affect their career, should be very high. In fact, what might happen is that the comparisons between the Readiness Check and the Reality Check might point out that students are particularly interested in this chapter because of its practical value and their own insecurity about making what they may see as the "wrong" decision.

Challenge → Reaction → Insight → Action prompts

The Challenge → Reaction → Insight → Action prompts continue to be good opportunities for class discussions, student reflective papers, or class activities. There are eight different Challenge → Reaction → Insight → Action opportunities in the chapter. The Circle of Learning diagram provides both Challenge → Reaction and Insight → Action prompts. Three additional Challenge → Reaction prompts related to careers, and Insight → Action prompts related to careers and academic anatomy are extremely student-centered.

Your Type Is Showing

Students will really take notice of this section as they look at how certain personality types relate to certain majors and careers. While many examples of careers and related types appear throughout the entire text in "Create a Career Outlook" features, this chapter contains an excellent summary. In addition, in Figure 12.12 students can see how the two middle letters of the four connect to career choices. For example, both the ST and NT types tend to be successful in law enforcement, only the NF tends to orient towards the arts. While these are not cut and dry categorizations and many successful musicians and artists are not NFs, there are certain aspects of these types that are better suited towards these fields. You will find that students really enjoy this section of the chapter. Seeing the types in this format clarifies the relationship between types and career choices.

Control Your Learning: Your Toughest Class

In this "Control Your Learning" activity, students are asked to identify whether or not their toughest course is a general education course or one in their intended major. If it's a general education class, they list the ways this course can help them in their career or help them become a truly well-educated person. Often students complain about general education courses and report having little interest in their content. "What does a course on art appreciation have to do with my future? I'm not going to be an artist. I'm not planning to visit art galleries every weekend." Talk with your students about how that course or any other they bring up will help them live fuller, richer lives. If the course is in their intended major, they respond to why it is so challenging. Are they keeping up with the work? Finally, students are told to send the instructor of this class an e-mail, indicating what they are trying to do to improve in the course, giving specific examples. If a particular course comes up as many students' toughest class frequently in your class discussions, you may wish to alert your colleague to the possibility of a student e-mailing them, so that they are given advance warning. Or you may wish to have your students e-mail their "Control Your Learning" plans to you.

Self-Assessments

This chapter has no formal assessments, but it does contain a number of Challenge → Reaction prompts that are self-reported surveys. These surveys are about what students would value in a career , the "SCAN Your Skills" prompt where they self-report on which skills they might need in the 21st century, a SWOT analysis of their own skills, and a Career Values Auction. All of these self-assessments can be used in reflective writing activities and class discussions.

Cultivate Your Curiosity: Focus Your "I's"

In this chapter of *FOCUS*, "Cultivate Your Curiosity" provides a number of examples and thought-provoking bits of information about what students need in order to transition into the workforce after college. The need to focus on four "I's" are described: inner direction, interpretation, instrumentation, and interactions (the Four "I's" of career-life readiness).

FOCUS on Careers

The career focus in this chapter is on recruiters and other types of HR professionals. In this chapter, we meet Tanya Sexton, associate partner in the Lucas Group, who was formerly an accountant and now recruits in the field of accounting and finance. She matches up employees who are searching for jobs with companies who are searching for employees by looking for the best fit. In fact, in the chapter, she describes herself as a "fitness expert." Human Resources is an attractive career field—the people side of business—and as the chapter points out, competition for entry level positions is stiff.

6. Which in-text exercises should I use?

There are four exercises built into this chapter. Have students connect these activities to real life situations especially their own majors and careers. Included here are reasons why you should do these, the challenges to expect, and how to debrief the exercises.

EXERCISE 12.1 THINK TANK

Why do this activity?
It's important to do this activity to show students the fundamental concepts behind how information is related. Students will learn about the abstract concept of an academic map, by applying the information to a brainstorming activity about one of three possible new products. They are asked to select a product, design it, and indicate all the academic disciplines that they would have to know at least something about in order to create their product.

What are the challenges and what can you expect?
One challenge you might have is that groups of students may want the same task. Decide ahead of time if you want more than one group doing the same challenge, or that you will divide the class into three groups ahead of time, and simply have students draw which activity they will be required to do. Students seem to enjoy responding to a task and coming up with a basic concept for their product. The activity of coming up with an academic map and the disciplines involved may be a bit of a challenge, but most groups will be able to do this well, and the activity will help the section on academic maps make more sense. It's possible that students may overlook a discipline or two, so make sure that they identify all of the possible areas they need to know something about in order to create their product.

How much time will it take?
This activity could take up to 45 minutes, if students are totally engaged and each group presents its results.

How should I debrief?

Students will really enjoy sharing their products and their design. Give them opportunity to do this in class, but be sure you go over which of the disciplines are involved in creating the product as well as reviewing their academic maps. Remember to have each team draw its academic map on the whiteboard

---

EXERCISE 12.2 GROUP RÉSUMÉ

Why do this activity?

There are a number of reasons why this is a good activity for students. By doing a group résumé students will be able to see the "collective wisdom" of the group. Throughout *FOCUS*, the importance of interpersonal skills and working collaboratively has been stressed in the text itself and the online "Team Career Activities." Not only does this group activity help students to see all the academic expertise in the class, it also provides an opportunity for students to think of skills that they've never even thought of when one of the group members lists it.

What are the challenges and what can you expect?

There really are no challenges for this activity, expect for the fact that you may want to limit students to about 15 minutes or so to do the actual task since you do want to give students the opportunity to present their group résumés to the class.

How much time will it take?

As stated above, you might want to limit students to 15 minutes.

How should I debrief?

Students are instructed to hang their newsprint on the walls to create a gallery and present their group résumés to the class. Students enjoy this aspect of the activity so make sure you leave time at the end of the class to do this.

EXERCISE 12.3 GET A JOB

Why do this activity?

This is really a terrific activity for students to identify the kinds of skills that college students need to develop to be marketable in the 21st century. In addition, it helps students to see that they actually have a job in college—being a college student! The job may not pay well, in fact you have to pay for it, but students will see that their job in college really is to think and to learn.

What are the challenges and what can you expect?

There really are no challenges for this activity. When working in groups students fairly quickly come up with the job description of a college student.

How much time will it take?

This activity could take up to half an hour of in-class time.

How should I debrief?
After sharing job descriptions with the group, consider asking students to send you an e-mail, or write a brief essay if they think they are better qualified to apply for this *job* now than they were at the beginning of the semester. Make sure they tell you why or why not.

EXERCISE 12.4 VARK ACTIVITY

Why do this activity?
This activity is designed to help students make connections between their preferred VARK learning modality and an actual assignment. This section of the previous chapter suggests that if you've noticed that multimodal students are tending to choose one type of modality consistently to consider assigning something different. For this chapter, you may wish to solicit suggests from the group about how to vary the activity.

What are the challenges and what can I expect?
There are no real challenges in this activity, but again, consider asking students to choose a modality that is not one of their preferences and note the results.

How much time will it take?
This activity is done outside of class, and you ask students to report to you via e-mail, it needn't take class time on a weekly basis. If you ask them to present their results (all Visuals to report, all Aurals to report, etc.) so you see how individuals perceived the activity differently), it could take up to half an hour.

How should I debrief?
How you choose to structure this activity will influence how you debrief it. If students chose a style that was not a strong preference for them, make sure they describe what was comfortable for them and what was not when doing this.

---

7. Which additional exercises might enrich students' learning?

How to Build a Student for the 21st Century
Home work activity
Materials needed: Students must find and print the *Time* article "How to Bring Our Schools Out of the 20th Century from the December 18th, 2006 edition
Time: Full class time (at least one hour)
Goal: To help students identify the need to understand multiple disciplines to be successful in the 21st century
Divide the class into two groups. Assign all students to read this article. One group has to come to class to discuss the interdisciplinary aspects needed to create MySpace and the other group does that same describing YouTube. In addition, ask each student to identify two things that surprised them about this article and why.

Building Resources
Class activity
Materials needed: The Internet and an LCD projector
Time: Homework assignment, plus 30-40 minutes in class
Goal: To help students build a repertoire of web sites for careers resources

For homework, ask students to identify four to five web sites other than www.careerbuilder.com or www.monster.com. Using the web sites that they bring to class, assess the effectiveness of each. Why is this source good? What features does the web site provide? What evidence do they have that this is a credible site? If they find a job on a web site, what is the next thing they should do? Ask them to choose a job that they find online, and go to the company's web site. What about the web site might make them believe this it is credible (the last time it was updated, check the address to see if this is a valid company). What might a student check on before they go on an interview for a job that is posted without a web site listed or one that they can't check out prior to going for an interview? (Never go alone!)

8. What other activities can I incorporate to make the chapter my own?

If you have mostly traditional students in your class, there will be much exploring and discussing majors and careers from a learning perspective. If some or all of your students are nontraditional students or a mix of both, you might ask older students to contribute their own career experiences. Why did they come back to school? Do they want to change careers? Why or why not? Is the career they are currently in well suited to their personality type? In you don't have nontraditional students in the class, ask the students to e-mail a family member and ask them about how they chose their career and if they had it to do over, if they would be in the same job.

Included here, all in one place, are Activity Options taken from the Annotated Instructor's Edition.

ACTIVITY OPTION (p. 357): Students should take a few minutes to share their responses to the "What Do *You* Think?" questions. Divide the class into four groups and give each group a question to discuss. After 5 to 10 minutes, ask one member of each group to present their response to the class.

ACTIVITY OPTION (p. 361): In Figure 12.1 students saw a typical schedule. Have students list their own schedules in a similar format and then place their courses on the Circle of Learning. Can they describe connections between two or more of the classes they're taking this term?

ACTIVITY OPTION (p. 363): Have students break into groups to answer these two key questions. As each group writes its brief response to the two questions on the board, ask students to identify themes across groups' responses.

ACTIVITY OPTION (p. 365): Ask students to place their general education courses or core requirements in the four quadrants: Natural Science, Humanities, Engineering, and Social Sciences. Discuss students' rationales for their placement decisions.

ACTIVITY OPTION (p. 370): Ask students to interview a person who is very successful in a career. What does the person do, what specific jobs has the person held previously, and for how long? Students can do this as an outside assignment and bring their findings to class. Were there many instant success stories? Probably not.

ACTIVITY OPTION (p. 370): The ten questions here can be turned into a project. First, find out which majors most students are interested in. Group students together and have each group interview for one major. Make sure that all majors of interest in the class are covered. In the same groups, have students develop a fact sheet about the major to be presented in class and distributed to all students.

ACTIVITY OPTION (p. 371): After students complete the "Challenge → Reaction" activity, ask them to fill in the blanks in the following sentence and bring it to the next class: Based on what I discovered about myself in doing this activity, three career choices for me are
_____, _____, and _____, because
_____.

ACTIVITY OPTION (p. 377): Assign students a real or fictitious possible job opportunity (perhaps on campus or in the surrounding area) to research, and ask them to come to class prepared for a mock interview. Time permitting, let as many students participate in the mock interview as possible. The rest of the class should decide who they would hire and why.

ACTIVITY OPTION (p. 378): Students can write a two-page essay on this "Challenge →Reaction" activity. In their essays, not only will you be able to see if students are connecting some of the major points in this chapter, but you will be able to assess their writing. Encourage students to make use of campus resources if they need help in writing.

ACTIVITY OPTION (p. 381): This is a great opportunity to have students first think about these questions, and then compare their responses with a partner's. Students can report back to the entire class on their answer to question 4.

ACTIVITY OPTION (p. 385): Find some examples of bad résumés. Check with your career center for examples. Give groups of students the same four or five résumés and ask them to rate the résumés on a scale of 1 to 10 with 10 representing best and to be prepared to justify their ratings.

ACTIVITY OPTION (p. 387): For the final activity in the chapter, ask students to design a five-slide PowerPoint presentation. Students must include a possible choice of major; a specific career within the major, including predictions about the availability of the job and salary information; and how this choice of major and career connects to information in the "Your Type Is Showing" box.

9. What homework might I assign?

Assign all students in the class to choose a career, either their intended or another, and list the top six general studies classes they should take for this major and why. Students should come back to the next class prepared to discuss this. The goal is to help students understand the many connections between and among general studies courses and careers.

Journal Entries
One: Have students write a one-page journal entry or send you an e-mail describing whether this chapter made them change their mind about what major and career they will pursue or if they are still going to follow the same one they had originally decided upon. If students are still undecided they should write about that. In all cases, students must explain and give examples of what they learned in this chapter and how it influenced where they stand now.

Two: Have students write a one-page journal entry or send you an e-mail reflecting on a time when they were in a class in which they saw no purpose to something they were studying. Ask students how they might see this course fitting into the Circle of Learning concept., now that they have read this chapter.

Three: Use the Insight → Action prompts as journal or blog assignments.

10. What have I learned in teaching this chapter that I will incorporate next time?

_____
_____
_____
_____
_____
_____
_____
_____
_____
_____
_____
_____
_____
_____
_____
_____
_____
_____
_____
_____

CHAPTER 13: WORKING TOWARD WELLNESS

1. Why is this chapter important?

As you begin the last chapter of this text, you might be wondering why this all-important chapter is at the end. Hopefully you have used some of the "Chapter Crossover" suggestions in the Annotated Instructor's Edition and touched on this chapter on an "as needed" basis. The problem with any first-year seminar course is that everything is important, and all of it should be learned right away! Of course, wellness is a concept that is embedded in all we do. In fact, just as was the case in Chapter 11, it's the non-cognitive aspects of emotional intelligence and wellness, for example, that most often cause an academically capable student to leave college. In this final chapter of *FOCUS*, students learn about the importance of physical, mental, and spiritual health. They learn how to recognize that stress, poor nutrition, lack of exercise, not enough sleep, alcohol and drugs, and sex can impact college success.

We all have stress in our lives. Most everyone has had times in their life when they may be eating too much or too little, or not exercising or sleeping enough. Some people struggle with alcohol and drugs and casual sex. This chapter incorporates five suggestions that can help address negative wellness behaviors. While these five suggestions are listed under how one can deal with stress, the same suggestions can apply to most anything. First and foremost, students need to understand and believe that what they are doing is negatively impacting their lives enough that they want to change it. If they think a "party hardy" mentality is not impacting their grades, or if they realize it and don't want to change, the likelihood of improvement is nil. In fact, one of the reasons that this chapter may have an impact on students now as opposed to earlier in the semester is that now they are ready to listen. Some students, unfortunately, must experience some of the negatives of poor wellness choices to be convinced that they need to change if they want to stay in college. The suggestions are simple, but powerful. First, change the situation—you don't have to party every night, you don't have to stay awake until 4 A.M. most nights, so do something about it. Second, change your reaction—remember that the only real thing in life we can change is our reaction to situations. We can't control everything, but we can control how we respond to life's challenges. Keep up is the next suggestion—keep up what is working right whether it is going to class every day, eating breakfast, or sleeping enough. The next suggestion is to improve problem solving skills. Individuals who see no way out, or no way to change become stuck in negative patterns.

Sometimes the fact that a person cannot change is related to real physical or psychological reasons. Anxiety, extreme stress, and types and levels of depression often must be treated by a physician or counselor. Make sure that students do not see seeking this kind of help as a sign of weakness, but just as a diabetic needs insulin, sometimes medication and intervention are needed for us to live full lives. Often drug and alcohol abuse and inappropriate sexual behavior are an indication that real change must take place or a downward spiral will continue. Whether there are traditional first-year college students in your class or adults working full-time with families, the message that must come through loud and clear is that people can change and improve all the important wellness aspects of their lives. It's up to them, but heading students in the right direction is key.

2. What are this chapter's learning objectives?

- ➢ How wellness is defined
- ➢ Who is responsible for wellness
- ➢ The importance of physical, mental, and spiritual health
- ➢ How to assess wellness choices by creating a Wellness Wheel
- ➢ How to deal with six aspects of wellness that affect first-year students: stress, nutrition, exercise, sleep, alcohol and drugs, and sex
- ➢ How to create a wellness plan that will impact college success

3. How should I launch this chapter?

Wellness may be a strange-sounding concept to some first-year students, who typically think of wellness as the opposite of illness. "Of course, I'm well. I haven't had a cold for ages!" The best way to launch the chapter may be with by asking students to define wellness.

- • **Use the Wellness Survey, coupled with the *FOCUS* Challenge Case, as a way to open the chapter.** At the beginning of this chapter, students are asked to take a Wellness Survey. You can begin your discussion of the chapter by asking students to discuss how Anthony's Wellness Survey might have looked. By using Anthony as the focus of discussion students can talk about issues that may be too personal to reveal. It's a lot easier to talk about someone else than oneself on some of these sensitive topics. Do a think/pair/share activity. Ask students to think about the one thing they would advise Anthony to do. Students then pair up, and decide of the two suggestions, which is better and report it to the class. Students should be very specific such as "no more going out during the week" or "go to math class every day." The class has to decide which one thing will have the most impact on changing Anthony's downward spiral and why.

- • **Use the Wellness Survey as a way to open up discussion.** The Wellness Survey includes six sections related to stress, nutrition, exercise, sleep, alcohol and drugs, and sex. Think about dividing the class into six groups and have each group identify two items that seem most directly related to college success within their assigned category of the survey. For example, in the first section on stress, perhaps the group thinks that items 1 ("I control my stress level") and 5 ("I learn from poor wellness choices I make and change my behavior") most impact college success. Groups should be able to defend their choices. In addition, ask students to recommend what they would suggest to a student who was having difficulty in their area. Make certain the discussion remains general, so that students don't feel threatened by a perceived need to disclose personal information.

- • **Going beyond the book.** There are many resources you might use that your students will benefit from. This chapter is one where you will find big differences on where students are in regards to wellness, depending on their age. Traditional college age students will be looking at wellness issues through a lens that is different from a student who may be returning to school while working and raising a family. Triggers for stress may be very different, but the results and subsequent stress indicators may be similar. It's important to direct students to on campus resources, and to let students know that regardless of their age or situation, campus resources can benefit them all. Additionally, since the highlighted career in this chapter is a physician, consider inviting a doctor or the head of the Student Health Clinic on campus to class as a guest speaker.

4. How should I use the *FOCUS* Challenge Case?

Anthony Lopez is all too typical of many traditional college students. Anthony wants to do well, but he has gotten himself off to a bad start by setting up patterns of behavior that will be difficult to change. He hasn't been going to math class regularly, his eating and sleeping habits are poor, and he is partying way too much. His buddies now think of him as a "regular" and throw parties in his room. He has been engaging in unplanned sex, which is likely to trip him up physically or psychologically in the future. Rather than setting boundaries and making good choices by thinking about repercussions down the road, Anthony now finds himself in the uncomfortable position of trying to "go backwards" and requesting that others change along with him (no more parties in his room, no more unprotected, casual sex, etc.). The Minor in Possession (MIP) charge is something that will definitely require a phone call home, if the police or campus security haven't already called home for him first. Anthony needs some really quick, practical advice.

Students may find it easy to criticize Anthony, but chances are they, or some friend of theirs, is in a very similar position. The morale of the *FOCUS* Challenge Case may well be the wisdom of thinking ahead, rather than simply living for the moment. If you have non-traditional students in your class, you may wish to ask for their take on the story if, for example, Anthony was their son. Or ask them how the story would read differently if Anthony were a non-traditional student.

5. What important features does this chapter include?

The Challenge → Reaction → Insight → Action prompts in this chapter can provide in-depth reflection and bring closure to the course. This chapter is "all about them"—students themselves, not academic skills or specific non-cognitive issues like emotional intelligence (although there is certainly crossover between this chapter and Chapter 11).

Readiness and Reality Checks
Students should be really interested and ready to learn more about wellness. It is possible that this chapter will be a "just-in-time" teaching and learning moment. At the same time, students may think they know everything there is to know about this chapter and be surprised to learn something new. The Readiness Check and Reality Check provide a good comparison point for students and this comparison could also serve as a discussion prompt for a final reflective assignment.

Challenge → Reaction → Insight → Action prompts

There are many Challenge → Reaction prompts in this chapter asking students what they already know about wellness issues, and a variety of Insight → Action opportunities that provide multiple ways to help students explore their own wellness. Sometimes students believe they "know it all" simply because they took a health or sex education class in high school. Yet many myths hang on. Some students, for example, may still think that drinking alcohol will keep you warm in a blizzard, when in fact, that may be the worst thing you can do. In this chapter, students are asked to keep track of their exercise and sleep patterns so that they can identify patterns that they might not have been aware of.

Your Type Is Showing

Have you ever thought about the connection between type and exercise? Your students may not have. For the first time students might have figured out why they did or did not stick with an exercise routine. For example, for strong extroverts, exercising with a friend is the motivation they may need. These same people may have given up on the solitary walk long ago. Group students with similar types and see if they enjoy the same kinds of exercise. Most likely they will. Or have them decide on new activities they'd like to take up, perhaps with their friends in your class.

Control Your Learning: Your Toughest Class

In this "Control Your Learning" activity, students are asked to identify whether or not wellness issues are affecting their success in the class. For example, students are asked to consider if sleep or lack thereof is impacting how they do in this class. Is it an early class and they just can't get up? Are they always tired and this is a class that requires a lot of focused attention? Students are to circle which of the ten statements are impacting their success in their toughest class and then to develop a plan on how to improve. In the Annotated Instructor's Edition, it is suggested that you let a peer leader, if you have one, conduct this class without you. Doing so may lead to some really honest dialogue on what is going on in class.

Self-Assessments

This chapter's primary assessment is the Wellness Survey and resulting Wellness Wheel. In addition, there are two surveys about how one might respond to wellness related issues. When students look at their Wellness Wheels, the areas that are closest to the hub of the wheel are those requiring serious examination and change.

Cultivate Your Curiosity: Crazy for Fast Food?

In this chapter of *FOCUS*, "Cultivate Your Curiosity" is a really sobering look at fast food and its impact on health. The 2004 Academy-Award nominated documentary *Super Size Me* outlines the journey of thirty-three year old Morgan Spurlock. For three months, Spurlock only ate at McDonald's, stopped exercising, and led a sedentary lifestyle. The consequences were astounding.

FOCUS on Careers

The career focus in this chapter is on occupations in the medical arena. In this chapter, we meet John Travis, a physician who is also a wellness pioneer. Students also learn about the job of a physician. The outlook for this job is good, even though there is a large influx of physicians from foreign countries. Many American physicians are specializing in a particular area of medicine which is more lucrative than being a general practice physician. Notice that John Travis believes that studying traditional medicine by working toward a medical degree is not the best route to a career in wellness. His M.D., Masters degree in Public Health, and many years of experience have given him a unique perspective. The "Create a Career Outlook" focuses on a physician who specializes in keeping people well instead of helping them recover from illness.

6. Which in-text exercises should I use?

There are five exercises built into this chapter and other self-assessments that appear as Challenge → Reaction or Insight → Action prompts. All of the activities in this chapter are practical ways to help think about their own wellness. Below are reasons why you should do these, the challenges to expect, and how to debrief them.

EXERCISE 13.1 WELLNESS SURVEY

Why do this activity?
This activity introduces students to six components of wellness (stress, nutrition, exercise, sleep, alcohol and drugs, and sex). In addition to possibly expanding students understanding of wellness, they can take stock of their own wellness strengths and challenges.

What are the challenges and what can you expect?
If students are really honest about filling out this survey, they may not be willing to share their results. If you do require them to report their results either to you or to the class, you may not get truthful answers. It's best not to put them on the spot.

How much time will it take?
The time required will vary, based on how you elect to conduct the activity.

How should I debrief?
Let this be a self reflection activity where students don't have to report their results. Or, if you have student leaders (peer leaders) for the class, you might have them lead a discussion, but they too should not expect students to report results. Students may be willing to discuss sleep or nutrition, but don't expect students to be forthcoming on alcohol, drugs or sex. Instead, you might require them to select a single area for improvement to report on or e-mail you about. Or you may simply let them use their results as stimuli for self-reflection.

EXERCISE 13.2 VARK ACTIVITY

Why do this activity?
This activity is designed to help students make connections between their preferred VARK learning modality and an actual assignment. For this final chapter students should complete the activity using their preferred modality.

What are the challenges and what can you expect?

There are no real challenges in this activity, but since this is the last chapter and if time permits, consider asking students to choose more than one style.

How much time will it take?

The time required will vary, depending on how you choose to conduct the activity.

How should I debrief?

Students can present to the class or as the instructions suggest, give a report, send the results to you via e-mail, post them online, or contribute to a class chat. Again, since this is the last chapter be sure that students report what they did to either you or the class as a whole.

EXERCISE 13.3 WORKPLACE STRESS SURVEY

Why do this activity?

This activity is designed to help students understand stressors that exist in the workplace. Many students believe that the stress levels in their lives will reach their peak in college with the demands of studying and assignments. However, the workplace has a full array of stress factors of its own and with income demands and family obligations (such as those that nontraditional students face), stress can easily go up rather than down after college. It's important for students to put things in perspective.

What are the challenges and what can you expect?

If you have a class of both traditional and nontraditional students, you may see them get into a "Who's got it worse?" debate—younger students who have to ask their parents for money or work at no-brainer jobs to pay tuition or older students who try to focus on school, the mortgage, the kids, the boss, and try to keep it all together despite feeling "splintered"? You should also be sensitive to the differences between these two groups, particularly if younger students are attending college "all expenses paid" by their parents and older students are struggling with multiple obligations.

How much time will it take?

Expect to spend 20 or so minutes on this activity.

How should I debrief?

Students can present to the class or as the instructions suggest, give a report, send the results to you via e-mail, post them online, or contribute to a class chat. Again, since this is the last chapter make sure that students report to either you or the class what they did.

EXERCISE 13.4 "HOW DO I LOVE THEE? LET ME COUNT THE WAYS"

Why do this activity?

You have probably heard of the freshman fifteen. When first year college students are away from home and regular balanced meals are a thing of the past due to fast food, drinking calorie-laden alcohol, and often developing generally bad eating habits, they are susceptible to weight gain. This activity has students take a hard look at their favorite foods, and the calories consumed when they are eating it.

What are the challenges and what can you expect?
There really are no challenges for this activity unless they have serious weight issues to which they are sensitive. Typically, students may be curious to find out just how many calories they are consuming when they eat their favorite foods.

How much time will it take?
This activity should take no longer than 10 minutes to discuss in class.

How should I debrief?
This is a really good activity for the whole class. Just ask students to go around the room, tell what they favorite food is and how many calories they consumed when they ate it. Were they surprised? Remind students that they can still have their favorites, but they might want to monitor the frequency and amount, unless of course it's something really healthy like carrot sticks!

EXERCISE 13.5 WHICH DINNER WOULD YOU ORDER?

Why do this activity?
This activity is designed to help students understand that some things they may see as smart eating choices may not be. The exercise notes that portion size, preparation method, and brand/restaurant can impact calories, but using an online calorie-counter the taco salad and the vegetarian option are less desirable options than the meat and potatoes option. The activity is not designed to discourage vegetarians or deny students the fun of the occasional splurge. Instead, the exercise is intended to show that "what you see is not always what you get."

What are the challenges and what can you expect?
There are no real challenges in this activity. Students will enjoy it.

How much time will it take?
This exercise should only take 10 minutes or so of class time.

How should I debrief?
Simply go around the room and gather students original guesses and their insights after consulting the calorie-counter reports.

---

7. Which additional exercises might enrich students' learning?

A Wellness (and Not So Wellness) Collage
Class activity
Materials needed: Old Magazine, glue, and poster board
Time: 50 minutes
Goal: To help students see how the media shapes our wellness habits
Divide the class into two groups. Using old magazines, have students cut out advertisements, phrases, and photos to make a collage about wellness. One group will develop a collage that shows all the positive images of wellness, while the other will develop a collage using negative images.

Revisiting the Envelope

Home work activity and in class discussion

Materials needed: envelope and letter that students gave you at the beginning of the course

Time: Full class time (at least one hour)

Goal: To help students see if the predictions they made about their first semester in college came true or not

In the very first class, students wrote a letter to themselves answering some important questions. Students described who they were and what they wanted to be. They described what motivated them, what they valued, as well as identified dreams and goals. In addition, they were to respond to the phrase "If it is to be, it is up to me" and discuss whether or not they thought this phrase described them. Did they think they would make smart choices, set realistic goals, be able to monitor themselves, and create their own future? Students placed this letter in a sealed envelope and gave it to you. Now you will return the envelope to the student and these original predictions can become the basis of their final class 2-3 page writing assignment. Students should turn in their work, but come prepared to share their experience with the class.

My Gift to You

Class activity

Materials needed: None

Time: 50 minutes

Goal: To thank each other for a gift that they have given you

Go around the room and ask students to tell the student next to them (everyone will have a turn to give and receive) some gift that they gave them. For example, a student might say "You really made me think about drinking too much" or "Thank you for helping me see that I needed to spend more time on my English essays." Or another might say "Thank you for sharing your tip about how to study. That really sank in, and I used that technique." All students should feel appreciated by something that they might not have realized they did. They gave a gift. Let everyone hear all of the gifts.

8. What other activities can I incorporate to make the chapter my own?

The classroom dynamics and exactly what is discussed in this chapter may vary widely, depending on the age of your students. If you have a mix of students in the class, you might see if some of your non-traditional students would like to lead discussions. They may not want to be put on the spot, so ask them privately, but consider finding ways to engage these students. These very same students may have real needs in other areas so it's not as if they could be excused from the class. Just keep in mind that student needs may vary. In fact, regardless of the age of your students, think about asking students anonymously what topics they would like to spend the most time on, and adjust the class accordingly.

Included here, all in one place, are Activity Options taken from the Annotated Instructor's Edition.

ACTIVITY OPTION (p. 400): Break up the class into three or four groups and have them respond to the five questions in the "Challenge → Reaction." Ask students to come up with a number of responses to each question. Some students may not want to reveal their real responses, but hearing members of the group discuss the issues might encourage those who need help to get it.

ACTIVITY OPTION (p. 403): Is the glass half full or half empty? Go around the room and ask students to come up with one thing that is stressful to students in college (*i.e.,* failing a test, breaking up with a significant other, a pet dying, etc.). In this activity, have one student respond to the situation with a glass-half-empty response, while another gives a glass-half-full response. For example, "I failed the test, and I don't think I can pass the course" versus "I failed the test, and I am going to talk with the instructor to see what I can do to improve." The point is that often how we respond to life's setbacks directly impacts the result.

ACTIVITY OPTION (p. 406): Ask students to make a copy of their Wellness Wheel and bring it to class, without their name on it. Collect the wheels and redistribute to the class. As a group, develop a class Wellness Wheel. What are the areas of strength in the class, and where are the areas that many students feel they need to focus on?

ACTIVITY OPTION (p. 412): It is worth asking if anyone has seen the movie *Super Size Me*. If so, did it change the way they now look at fast food? Consider hosting a movie night (with healthy snacks) and tell students to come to the next class ready to discuss it.

ACTIVITY OPTION (p. 413): Have students go online and calculate the number of calories they burned for the week. Students can use this web site: http://www.caloriecontrol.org/exercalc.html.

ACTIVITY OPTION (p. 413): Get students up and out of their chairs by doing an exercise continuum. Ask students to place themselves on the imaginary continuum with one end representing "I have increased my exercise since I have come to college" and the other end representing those who have decreased their exercise. Ask students to report how changes in exercise make them feel. For those who are exercising, ask them to share their strategies with the class.

ACTIVITY OPTION (p. 414): Ask students to make the connection between their psychological type and the way they have approached exercise in the past. What is their type and what kind of exercise do they do, if any? If they don't exercise, can they figure out why based on their type? Ask students to send you a two-paragraph essay e-mail about their analysis.

ACTIVITY OPTION (p. 415): Ask everyone who went to bed before 10:00 P.M. more than half of the days of the week last week to stand. Have these students move to the front of the room on the left. Then ask in two-hour intervals for students to form groups around the room until everyone is out of their seats. Next ask groups to come up with a number between 1 and 10 that describes how rested and alert they feel. Compare group responses.

ACTIVITY OPTION (p. 417): In addition to defining binge drinking, students should be able to describe what binge drinking can lead to. Pair students up and have them think of as many consequences of binge drinking as they can by filling in the blank: If someone binge drinks, he or she might _____. Generate a class list.

ACTIVITY OPTION (p. 422): For the final class activity, have each student come to class with a four-slide PowerPoint presentation. The slides should be titled, in order: "What I thought I would learn in this class," "What I did learn in this class," "The one thing that hit me the most," and "One thing I do now that I didn't before."

9. What homework might I assign?

Since this is the final class, consider having students write an end-of-course reflective essay and then read their essays to the class. Or for a class presentation, have each student come to class with a four-slide PowerPoint presentation. The first slide is entitled: " What I thought I would learn in this class", the second "What I did learn in this class" the third "The one thing that hit me the hardest," and the last slide "One thing I do now that I didn't before."

Journal Entries
A number of reflective final writings have already been suggested for this chapter. Students can respond to any of the Insight → Action prompts with a journal entry. Or, they may write a summary of the course and what they have learned. You might consider asking students to write a letter to next year's entering class. What words of advice would they give them?

10. What have I learned in teaching this chapter that I will incorporate next time?

FOCUS ON COLLEGE SUCCESS
TEST BANK

By Catherine Andersen

CHAPTER 1: BUILDING DREAMS, SETTING GOALS

Challenge Yourself Quiz

1. According to the text, college is a time to learn about:
    A. your motivation, values, dreams, and goals.
    B. your current motivation in college and future earning potential.
    C. your choices, time, energy and sports.
    D. your family, choices, dreams, and motivation.

2. According to the text, you cannot control everything in life, but one thing you can control is:
    A. monitoring your time and energy.
    B. making sure your roommate(s) are studying.
    C. avoiding professors who assign too much work.
    D. not feeling homesick.

3. Which is <u>not</u> listed as one of the *FOCUS* learning system's steps for learning?
    A. Accept the challenge
    B. Choose challenges that are interesting to you
    C. React to the challenge
    D. Use new knowledge to gain insights

4. Choose the appropriate order for the *FOCUS* learning system.
    A. Challenge→Reaction→Insight→Action
    B. Reaction→Challenge→Insight→Action
    C. Action→Reaction→Challenge→Insight
    D. Insight→Challenge→Reaction→Action

5. Choose the statement that is false.
    A. Values can conflict with one another.
    B. Values can serve as guideposts for making every day choices.
    C. Values are the same for individuals who share the same culture.
    D. Values can change.

LEVEL TWO

6. Which might be an instance where "instant gratification" is <u>not</u> a barrier to a student's success?
    A. Charging a round trip airline ticket for spring break in September, before knowing the schedule for exams during spring term
    B. Deciding Thursday night to leave for a ski trip the next day because you don't have any Friday classes.
    C. Purchasing an iPod that was on sale in the bookstore before buying all of your books because Podcasts are available for some of your classes.
    D. Adopting a stray dog to keep you and your roommates company.

7. The text lists eight ways to adjust your attitude. One is knowing that you have choices. Which of the following statements is an example of making an appropriate choice?
    A. You did not study for the biology midterm and failed. You decide not to stress over it, and vow to improve your study strategies for the next test.
    B. You studied for the biology midterm and failed. What was on the test was not in your notes. You are stressed and send an e-mail to your instructor asking why he didn't review for the exam in class.
    C. You did not study for the biology midterm and failed. You are stressed that you may not pass the course and decide to meet with classmates to find out if they failed too.
    D. You studied for the biology midterm and failed. You decided not to stress over it, and drop the course.

8. Which is an example of the most realistic goal?
    A. Spending the entire evening writing a twenty-five page research paper.
    B. Deciding after you received a warning from the dean at midterm that you were failing all of your courses that you will start going to class and get all "A's."
    C. Taking 22 credits in the spring to lighten your course load the next fall.
    D. Attending math tutoring at least twice a week before the midterm because math is your toughest class.

9. According to the text, "a dream is a goal without legs" means:
    A. dreams are really important and should always guide you.
    B. dreams are not as important as making money.
    C. dreams are important to relieve stress.
    D. dreams without a plan won't get you anywhere.

10. When learning something new, which of the following words is <u>not</u> a barrier?
    A. Preconceptions
    B. Assumptions
    C. Facts
    D. Biases

11. According to the author, motivation is critical to college success. Which of the following is <u>not</u> an example of intrinsic motivation?
    A. Studying because you like to learn new things.
    B. Setting high standards for your academic work.
    C. Doing well to please your family.
    D. Feeling challenged in your classes.

12. Which of the following describes the phrase "Some situations cannot be changed, but attitudes can"?
    A. Math has always been difficult for you. You changed majors because your current major requires you to take two math classes.
    B. Your teacher has an accent and it makes it hard for you to understand her. You make an appointment to see her to ask if you can get her notes.
    C. Your college roommate is a neat freak. You have a talk with her and tell her to lighten up.
    D. Your friend just bought an expensive DVD player. Inside you are jealous. He never has to work and you work every weekend.

13. This chapter stresses the importance of motivation. What do you think the following phrase means? "If you can and you don't, it means you won't" means:
    A. If you try hard enough, you will succeed.
    B. If you fail, try again.
    C. If you have the ability and don't try, you won't succeed.
    D. If you have the ability, you will succeed.

14. According to research, which is <u>not</u> a difference between a performer and a learner?
    A. When given tasks that were too difficult for them, performers felt anxious and helpless.
    B. When given tasks that were too difficult for them, learners coached themselves to try harder.
    C. When given tasks that were too difficult for them, performers felt that their weaknesses might be revealed.
    D. When given tasks that were too difficult for them, learners criticized performers.

15. Values are important in helping to make day to day choices as well as long term ones. Many values are important; select the value that is most critical to success in college.
    A. Spirituality
    B. Happiness
    C. Health
    D. Determination

Chapter 1
Answer Key

1. A
2. A
3. B
4. A
5. C
6. B
7. A
8. D
9. D
10. C
11. C
12. B
13. C
14. D
15. D

CHAPTER 2: LEARNING ABOUT LEARNING

Challenge Yourself Quiz

1. According to the text, the human brain:
   A. must use and reuse information to "hardwire it."
   B. consists of just a few neurons.
   C. does not have to be exercised.
   D. stores only new knowledge.

2. According to the text, which of the following statements is false?
   A. If you are not challenged, you may become bored.
   B. Learning does for your brain what food does for your body.
   C. Research indicates that you learn best when you are in a state of stressed alertness.
   D. Learning changes your brain.

3. Brain researchers tell us that the best state for learning has ten conditions. Which of the following is <u>not</u> a condition?
   A. You are curious about what you are learning.
   B. You are never confused.
   C. Your mind and emotions are involved.
   D. You search for personal meaning and patterns.

4. Choose the statement that is false.
   A. A healthy brain weighs about two pounds.
   B. From birth to adolescence the brain's basic circuitry is laid.
   C. People who are less educated have twice the risk of getting Alzheimer's disease in later life.
   D. It's easier to learn a language when you are older.

5. According to the VARK web site data, the most common preference for students is:
   A. aural.
   B. visual.
   C. read/ write.
   D. kinesthetic.

LEVEL TWO

6. Some students study best by recopying and summarizing their notes. Which of the VARK learning styles might these students be strong in?
   A. Aural
   B. Visual
   C. Read/Write
   D. Kinesthetic

7. According to the text, knowing your learning preferences can help you in your academic coursework. Which of the following statements is an example of a student who knows that she is a kinesthetic learner and uses this to her advantage to study for a test?
   A. She uses brightly color markers to highlight the major headings in the history text.
   B. She studies for the history midterm by asking questions and recording the answers to play back later.
   C. She memorizes the important facts by associating them with pictures.
   D. She studies for the history midterm by role playing some of the important events in history with a friend.

8. Which is not an example of a *flow* learning experience?
   A. Spending the entire evening searching on the Internet to learn more about your ancestors.
   B. Losing tack of time when reading.
   C. Skimming through the topics in the text book quickly.
   D. Spending hours on a complex math problem and finally getting it right.

9. According to the text, it is important to try to strengthen your lesser VARK learning preferences, however:
   A. it might be best to make use of your learning strengths in college and develop lesser preferences later.
   B. you must develop all learning preferences or you will never pass all of your classes.
   C. your least preferred learning style is most likely the strongest.
   D. there is no such thing as a preferred learning style.

10. Both the Myers-Briggs Type Indicator (MBTI) and the SuccessTypes Learning Style Type Indicator show learning preferences. One preference is a sensor. Which of the following jobs would most fit this type?
    A. Accountant
    B. Artist
    C. Musician
    D. Entrepreneur

LEVEL THREE

11. Which of the following scenarios describes a student who is a strong sensor and an instructor is a strong iNtuitor?
    A. You like to have a list a terms to learn and the instructor gives a specific study guide.
    B. You like to interpret what is happening and your instructor wants to stick to the facts.
    C. You prefer to have very strict directions to follow and your instructor is more open-ended and theoretical.
    D. You like to study with others, but your teacher says it's much too distracting.

12. According to Harvard psychologist, Howard Gardner, individuals can be smart in multiple ways. Of these, which of the eight intelligences is more traditionally aligned with success in college?

A. Interpersonal since it's critical to have friends in college.

B. Naturalistic, since all colleges require you take and pass a science course.

C. Linguistic, since college requires a lot of reading and writing.

D. Bodily-Kinesthetic, since you must stay physically fit to be healthy in college.

13. The phrase "translate content into your own intelligences" means:

A. if you are not good at math, avoid the sciences.

B. tutors can be very helpful when struggling with challenging courses.

C. when you are learning something, use your own learning and multiple intelligence strengths to study.

D. if you have the ability, you will succeed.

14. According to research, which is <u>not</u> a good fit between a major and career that fits your intelligence?

A. A theater major and strong logical-mathematical intelligence.

B. A fundraiser for a non-profit organization and strong interpersonal intelligence.

C. A park ranger and strong naturalistic intelligence.

D. An interior designer and strong spatial intelligence.

15. If you were to choose a statement that most accurately describes a main point of this chapter, which of the following statements would you choose?

A. You are born with a certain personality and there is nothing you can do to change it.

B. Learning is complex. You must be able to learn the way in which something is taught.

C. Everyone has different preferences and learning strengths. The key is to know what your strengths are and then use them to your best advantage.

D. If you are not linguistically inclined, it is best to consider a career that does not require a college degree.

Chapter 2
Answer Key

1. A
2. C
3. B
4. D
5. D
6. C
7. D
8. C
9. A
10. A
11. C
12. C
13. C
14. A
15. C

CHAPTER 3: MAKING USE OF RESOURCES: FINANCES, TECHNOLOGY, AND CAMPUS SUPPORT

Challenge Yourself Quiz

LEVEL ONE

1. In a national survey, nearly three-quarters of first-year students said they think it's essential to be:
    A. well-off financially.
    B. intelligent.
    C. happy.
    D. healthy.

2. Of the following, which is the most important for college students?
    A. Getting a checking account
    B. Knowing that they can rely on their parents for help
    C. Having a set allowance to spend
    D. Creating a budget

3. Which of the following make it easy for students to sink deeper and deeper into debt without even realizing it?
    A. Checks
    B. Credit cards
    C. Bank accounts
    D. Online checking accounts

4. Typically a bad credit rating stays with you for:
    A. the rest of your life.
    B. until you are married to someone with good credit.
    C. 7 Years.
    D. about 10 years.

5. If you apply, this can help you to pay for your college education?
    A. Parents
    B. Financial aid
    C. Credit card
    D. Work

6. This is defined as structured learning that takes place without a teacher at the front of a classroom?
    A. PowerPoint slides
    B. Note-taking
    C. Group work
    D. E-learning

7. It is important to remember that this is neutral and can be used constructively or destructively?
    A. Working in groups
    B. Text books
    C. The Internet
    D. Exercise

8. Maria is having trouble making her next tuition installment payment. If you looked at her credit card bill, you'd find multiple entries from fast food restaurants, spas, and online shoe stores. According to the text, one of Maria's primary problems is that she:
    A. has no budget.
    B. is out of control.
    C. doesn't distinguish between needs and wants.
    D. doesn't understand how much interest she's paying.

9. If an eating disorder develops while you're in college, you should:
    A. be strong and call on your inner resources.
    B. tell a friend who can help.
    C. don't worry about it because that will only make it worse.
    D. deek support professionals on campus.

10. You have ADHD and you are having trouble in classes what should you do?
    A. Keep it to yourself
    B. Tell your friends
    C. Go to Learning Services/Center on campus
    D. Ask to try your friend's Adderall

LEVEL THREE

11. College students with Learning Disabilities can be successful by:
    A. understanding their disability and developing strategies to help.
    B. making sure that they are medicated.
    C. studying in groups with people who have similar learning disabilities.
    D. calling the professor each night while studying.

12. Which one of these sentences is an example of the phrase "the grass is always greener"?
    A. Wishing that you will do well on the test as opposed to studying more.
    B. Thinking that someone else always has it better than you.
    C. Hoping for the best possible grades.
    D. Depending on others for the right support.

13. Which of the following situations describes a student as a "maximizer"?
    A. Spending three hours choosing a new pair of shoes from the rows and rows available at the store.
    B. Grabbing a bagel on the run to get to class on time.
    C. Limiting yourself to a choice between two different cell phone plans from the many that are available.
    D. Letting others force you to make decisions.

14. Which is preferable: "maximizing" or "satisficing"?
    A. Maximizing since you look at all the options.
    B. Satisficing since you squeeze a lot into the day.
    C. Neither are particularly valid options.
    D. It depends on what choice is being made for what purpose.

15. Which is the best example of currency as it relates to the Internet?
    A. The relative low cost of getting huge amounts of information
    B. The monthly fees for access in relation to purchasing a newspaper
    C. The availability of real time information
    D. The competitive advantage of the computer

Chapter 3
Answer Key

1. A
2. D
3. B
4. C
5. B
6. D
7. C
8. C
9. D
10. C
11. A
12. B
13. A
14. D
15. C

CHAPTER 4: MANAGING YOUR TIME AND ENERGY

Challenge Yourself Quiz

LEVEL ONE

1. According to the text, the term "time management" is somewhat misleading. Before you can manage your time, you must manage your:
   A. attention.
   B. family.
   C. day-to-day activities.
   D. course schedule.

2. When a task requires laser-like brainpower you need to:
   A. get help very quickly.
   B. stop and take a short walk before you begin.
   C. develop a single-minded focus.
   D. make a timeline for how long you need to study.

3. According to Chapter 4, not only should you be able to manage your time, but you must:
   A. manage your energy.
   B. be able to multi-task.
   C. ignore stress.
   D. relax once in a while.

4. When you come into a class angry and resentful this is called:
   A. irritability.
   B. high drama.
   C. disruption.
   D. high negative energy.

5. There are four different dimensions of energy are:
   A. Physical, Mind, Body, and Emotional.
   B. Physical, Psychological, Body, and Mind.
   C. Physical, Emotional, Psychological, and Mental.
   D. Physical, Emotional, Mental, and Spiritual.

LEVEL TWO

6. Sarah never finishes her algebra homework in time for class. According to the chapter, if she is like millions of other college students, she most likely spends too much time:
   A. social networking online.
   B. shopping.
   C. juggling sports and school work.
   D. paying attention to her looks.

7. Of the following, which is the greatest challenges most students will probably face in college and their careers?
     A. Making enough good friends
     B. Finding the time and having the ability to manage everything
     C. Having a strong work ethic
     D. Finding the financial resources needed to succeed

8. John comes to his philosophy course feeling depressed, burned out, and hopeless. He is demonstrating characteristics of:
     A. low negative energy.
     B. low positive energy.
     C. high negative energy.
     D. no energy at all.

9. According to the MBTI as it relates to time management, if you are high on the Perceiving scale:
     A. you will be judgmental of other people.
     B. people will upset you easily.
     C. you will need a judging best friend.
     D. you will have to develop your own coping strategies.

10. According to Judith Cara, when it comes to a career in public/community relations:
     A. time management is a real challenge.
     B. it's important to set the next day's schedule each night.
     C. time management skills are about as important as they are in any other career.
     D. time management is impossible.

LEVEL THREE

11. From the options below, what's the best advice you would give another student to help him stay organized?
     A. Know when your vacations are.
     B. Do all of your challenging assignments on the weekends.
     C. Schedule classes on the same day.
     D. Get yourself a planner.

12. Even if you can not control your time you can still:
     A. find time to eat.
     B. have a life.
     C. manage time.
     D. feel confident.

13. Angela is taking a full load of courses. She has a boyfriend, works 12 hours a week on campus, and studies 25 hours a week. From this description, what would you say is the major threat to her ability to succeed in college?
    A. Her social life
    B. Her course load
    C. Her professors
    D. No major threats are described

14. Which is better: alternating, outsourcing, bundling, or techflexing?
    A. It depends on the demands on your time and your lifestyle.
    B. Techflexing because technology helps save time.
    C. Outsourcing if you have the money.
    D. Alternating because it's impossible to "have it all."

15. Which of the following describes bundling?
    A. Combining activities
    B. Getting help from others on challenging tasks
    C. Alternating between different tasks
    D. Using technology as a tool to make progress

Chapter 4
Answer Key

1. A
2. C
3. A
4. D
5. D
6. A
7. B
8. B
9. D
10. A
11. D
12. C
13. D
14. A
15. A

CHAPTER 5: THINKING CRITICALLY AND CREATIVELY

Challenge Yourself Quiz

LEVEL ONE

1. We use _____ to test the soundness of arguments.
    A. logic
    B. focus
    C. concreteness
    D. process

2. Critical thinking is a particular kind of:
    A. mental thinking.
    B. focused thinking.
    C. pin-pointed thinking.
    D. open-minded thinking.

3. Good thinkers are also able to be:
    A. good questioners.
    B. good people.
    C. bad listeners.
    D. better friends.

4. Which is the first step in basic problem solving?
    A. Brainstorm the possible options
    B. Devise criteria to evaluate options
    C. Answer questions
    D. Define the problem

5. Level two of the Question Pyramid is:
    A. basic reasoning.
    B. creative thinking.
    C. complex reasoning.
    D. simple reasoning.

LEVEL TWO

6. Creative thinking requires you to:
    A. think critically.
    B. memorize a section of the text book.
    C. develop your answer by thinking about possibilities, selecting a response, and backing it up with evidence.
    D. think for yourself and come up with your own unique, creative responses.

7. The foundation upon which your problem-solving and decision-making skills rest are your:
   A. ability to use appropriate social skills.
   B. innate intellectual skills.
   C. ability to use appropriate reasoning skills.
   D. educational level.

8. Which is an example of a behavioral approach to making decisions?
   A. Someone assessing the impact their decision will have on people.
   B. Someone assessing the impact their decision will have on daily operations.
   C. Someone assessing the impact their decision will have on productivity.
   D. Someone assessing the impact their decision will have on how they will be perceived as a manager.

9. Which is an example of a person who is a non-critical thinker?
   A. Someone who is biased in the way that they approach a problem.
   B. Someone who is using past experience to understand new situations.
   C. Someone who is questioning why they might be thinking the way that they do.
   D. Someone who is trying to be as open minded as possible.

10. "Professor Courtney's so-called research…" is an example of which type of logical fallacy?
    A. False cause and effect
    B. Emotional appeal
    C. False authority
    D. Personal attack

LEVEL THREE

11. According to research, there is a strong relationships between MBTI type and decision making styles. Which of the following is true? Behavioral decision makers are most likely to be:
    A. Thinkers and Judgers.
    B. Feelers and Perceivers.
    C. Sensors and Feelers.
    D. Introverts and Perceivers.

12. If students are "thinking about their thinking" they are:
    A. not approaching learning in a productive way.
    B. evaluating the way in which they are approaching something and can make changes.
    C. probably trying to second guess their own motives for going to college.
    D. most likely day-dreaming and need to focus.

13. The CEO of a large company is interviewing recent graduates. He is only interviewing those with a Liberal Arts education. Which statement by a candidate might convince him to hire her?
   A. A Liberal Arts education has provided me with excellent knowledge of management styles.
   B. A Liberal Arts education has provided me with excellent problem solving skills.
   C. A Liberal Arts education has provided me with excellent knowledge of career planning.
   D. A Liberal Arts education has provided me with excellent skills in PowerPoint.

14. Which of the following statements is not an example of a logical fallacy?
   A. Anna is not a very reliable person. She was late for the game last week.
   B. The food in the cafeteria is loaded with fat. I am gaining way too much weight.
   C. Julia has missed so many classes. Something must be going on.
   D. If you cared about me, you would help me out on the test.

15. Which statement is the best example of someone who is trying to improve their critical thinking skills?
   A. "I really didn't know enough about that to make a good decision."
   B. "I have read many books on the subject so I know."
   C. "I clearly heard one of the candidates say that."
   D. "Global warming is a problem caused only by us."

Chapter 5
Answer Key

1. A
2. B
3. A
4. D
5. A
6. D
7. C
8. A
9. A
10. D
11. C
12. B
13. B
14. C
15. A

CHAPTER 6: ENGAGING, LISTENING, AND NOTE-TAKING IN CLASS

Challenge Yourself Quiz

1. One of the best ways to get a head start on developing good academic habits in class is to:
    A. choose your seat in class strategically.
    B. sit by your best friend so that you can talk about class material later.
    C. always e-mail the professor to remind him or who you are.
    D. take down every word from the instructor's mouth.

2. Showing up to class is:
    A. not helpful if you just physically show up and are not paying attention.
    B. critical if you don't have a friend who can take notes for you.
    C. not important if you are only graded on quizzes.
    D. only important if the instructor stresses it.

3. Listening is not as easy as we think it is. According to Chapter 6, listening is really about:
    A. good hearing.
    B. concentrating hard.
    C. energy management.
    D. overcoming noise.

4. The stages of focused listening are:
    A. paying attention, preparing, sharing, and answering.
    B. sensing, interpreting, evaluating, and responding .
    C. thinking, sensing, listening, and talking.
    D. evaluating, preparing, analyzing, and responding.

5. It is estimated that college students spend ten hours per week doing what?
    A. Drinking
    B. Studying
    C. Socializing
    D. Listening to lectures

LEVEL TWO

6. The two types of listening skills that we have are "soft" and "hard." "Soft" listening skills involve:
    A. listening to chit-chat and handling emotionally-charged situations.
    B. relaxed situations when you don't really have to listen at all.
    C. listening intently, thinking critically, and analyzing carefully what you are hearing.
    D. listening to the instructor who is most likely to give clues for the tests.

7. Professor Smith starts lecturing the moment he walks into the classroom, speaks very quickly, and rarely pauses for questions. This chapter would call him a:
    A. review-the-text lecturer.
    B. rapid-fire lecturer.
    C. go-beyond-the-text lecturer.
    D. all-over-the-map lecturer.

8. Which of the following statements is <u>not</u> true about student note-taking?
    A. Only about half of students who take notes review them.
    B. About 12% of students take verbatim notes and then do nothing with them.
    C. Students record only about 15% of the main ideas of a lecture.
    D. About 29% of students edit their notes.

9. The difference between the Cornell format for note-taking and mind maps is that:
    A. the Cornell format is for upper level courses while mind maps can be used at all levels.
    B. the Cornell format tends to use the left side of the brain's power while mind maps use both the right and left sides.
    C. mind mapping is a technique that most faculty use and they expect students to at least attempt to use it.
    D. mind mapping is the system that has been proven to be the most effective at long-term recall of information.

10. A student in your history class asks the instructor, "Which year did the Civil War begin?" This question falls into which category on the scale toward higher-order thinking?
    A. Analysis
    B. Knowledge
    C. Synthesis
    D. Evaluation

LEVEL THREE

11. A student able to understand from an instructor's lecture what would be important to study would do which of the following?
    A. Pay attention to students around you who are writing down particular parts of the lecture. If others think something is important, it must be.
    B. Meet with a group of students prior to the lecture to make sure you understand what will be discussed in class.
    C. Remember information from the text that has not been discussed in class.
    D. Remain alert to instructors signal phases such as "in conclusion," "the main reason," etc.

12. Which of the following would be the least effective way for students to learn from their class notes?
    A. Make flash cards from the notes they take after organizing them.
    B. Make a matrix of the important points and a brief summary of the points.
    C. Compare the notes with classmates and reorganize them based on both sets of information.
    D. Purchase Cliff Notes or a similar commercial product to see if they have covered everything about the subject.

13. If students are choosing to engage in class, most likely they will:
    A. find their own way to stay focused in class.
    B. use their laptops in class as a way to reinforce the lecture.
    C. come to class under all circumstances.
    D. sit next to a friend who can keep them on task.

14. For a student to be an effective listener, they must go through the four stages of focused listening: Which is the appropriate order of techniques?
    A. Sensing, Interpreting, Evaluating, and Responding
    B. Evaluating, Summarizing, Repeating, and Answering
    C. Focusing, Analyzing, Repeating, and Confirming
    D. Clarifying, Interpreting, Evaluating, and Confirming

15. If your personality type indicates that you are a strong sensor and thinker, which of the following instructor styles would you prefer?
    A. An instructor who spends a lot of time getting to know students.
    B. An instructor who is very flexible with the syllabus.
    C. An instructor who enjoys spontaneity and "teachable moments."
    D. An instructor who is organized and follows the syllabus.

Chapter 6
Answer Key

1. A
2. A
3. C
4. B
5. D
6. A
7. B
8. C
9. B
10. B
11. D
12. D
13. A
14. A
15. D

CHAPTER 7: DEVELOPING YOUR MEMORY

Challenge Yourself Quiz

1. According to the text most of us have "childhood amnesia" and our earliest memories go back to approximately:
    A. two years of age.
    B. five years of age.
    C. four and a half years of age.
    D. three and a half years of age.

2. According to the chapter, research about memory includes such factors as:
    A. culture, gender, and age.
    B. gender, age, and income level.
    C. age, income, and intelligence.
    D. culture, income, and parental communication.

3. Which of the following is not important to recognize when mastering memory techniques?
    A. Who is learning?
    B. What needs to be learned?
    C. Who you are studying with?
    D. How will learning be tested?

4. The 3 R's of Remembering are:
    A. record, review, and remember.
    B. retrieve, record, and review.
    C. record, retain, and retrieve.
    D. retrieve, remember, and record.

5. Which of the following is not one of the three parts of memory?
    A. Sensory memory
    B. Working memory (short term)
    C. Recording memory
    D. Long-term memory

LEVEL TWO

6. Which of the following is not an example of sensory memory?
    A. Hearing a car horn
    B. Seeing a lit Christmas tree
    C. Remembering the cheering at a football game
    D. Being bumped by a passing runner

7. An example of a suggestion to help with attention management is to:
    A. turn off the television while studying.
    B. multi-task so that you can get everything done.
    C. fill every spare moment with homework.
    D. study for very short amounts of time with breaks in between.

8. You don't quite remember the color of her hair or the shade of her eyes, but you do remember her phone number: 555-1234. This ability to remember a number is due to:
    A. chunking.
    B. good retrieval strategies.
    C. the fact that it's one digit off from your best friend's number.
    D. your talent for numbers.

9. Retrieving information from long term memory involves techniques. In general, which is not a particularly good approach?
    A. Organizing dates on a time line to help remember them.
    B. Categorizing the famous battles of the Civil War by location.
    C. Listing all of the vocabulary words you must learn.
    D. Grouping similar events according to some common characteristic.

10. Maintenance rehearsal helps to keep something in working memory for a short time. Elaborative rehearsal is generally more effective and involves working with the material. Which is an example of elaborative rehearsal?
    A. Repeating a phone number ten times to remember it while you look for your phone.
    B. Repeating the ingredients that you need to make a pizza on the way to the store.
    C. Repeating the list of terms you need to study over and over again until you think you know them.
    D. Making up a test using the items you need to learn.

LEVEL THREE

11. A variety of strategies for memorizing information have been described in this chapter. If a student is a strong iNtuitor, which of the following techniques might work best?
    A. Chunk information into sections.
    B. Make lists of information and rehearse it over and over.
    C. Link it to some larger picture.
    D. Make flash cards.

12. Experts on learning and the brain believe that the optimal condition for learning is relaxed alertness. Which situations might create this state?
    A. Staying up all night to cram for the test.
    B. Making flash cards and reviewing them right before a test.
    C. Making up funny rhymes to learn the science formulas for a test.
    D. Highlighting all of the important vocabulary words in a text.

13. Which is an example of effective elaborative rehearsal?
    A. A student has studied more than ten hours in the same day.
    B. A student has studied more than ten hours over four days.
    C. A student separates similar yet distinct information before studying.
    D. A student differentiates study sessions as much as possible when studying for more than one test on the same day.

14. How is it possible that students who did not drink alcohol, but were told they did, were more swayed by misleading information than those who did not drink? Which is the most plausible explanation?
    A. It is possible that there was alcohol in the drinks they were given.
    B. It is possible that students who thought they were drinking were convinced that their judgment was questionable.
    C. It is possible that students had been drinking the night before and their judgment was still impaired.
    D. It is possible that students were not serious about the task.

15. When you create an association between something to be learned and what you already know, memory is enhanced. Which is an effective way of doing this?
    A. Reading the chapter—or at least intending to—the night before the next class.
    B. Reviewing notes from your history class and visualizing a movie that you saw on television about a similar historical era.
    C. Connecting a list of errands you have to do with the stops you might make on the way home.
    D. Sitting down in a quiet area to memorize important dates.

Chapter 7
Answer Key

1. D
2. A
3. C
4. C
5. C
6. C
7. A
8. A
9. C
10. D
11. C
12. C
13. D
14. B
15. B

CHAPTER 8: READING AND STUDYING

Challenge Yourself Quiz

LEVEL ONE

1. According to the text, which is <u>not</u> one of the essential points to remember about reading?
    A. Take stock of your own reading challenges.
    B. Adjust your reading style.
    C. Converse with the author.
    D. Only read things that are interesting to you.

2. A common approach to reading and studying is the:
    A. R2D2.
    B. ACCs of R.
    C. SQ3R.
    D. SSURP.

3. When it comes to studying, the advice "Be a stickler" means:
    A. hang in there until you totally understand what you're studying.
    B. create strict rules for yourself and follow them.
    C. get your spouse or parent to enforce your study time.
    D. pay attention to details and be accurate.

4. According to the text which is <u>not</u> necessarily a good strategy for studying?
    A. Create artificial deadlines for yourself.
    B. Study earlier rather than later.
    C. Always study alone.
    D. Estimate how long it will take.

5. Which statement does <u>not</u> describe Katie Alexander?
    A. She is not used to reading much.
    B. She is oversleeping and not making it to class.
    C. She does not see how the class connects to things she needs to learn.
    D. She prefers watching movies to reading.

LEVEL TWO

6. The chapter's suggestion to "become an intention learner" includes all the following <u>except</u>:
    A. making sure you understand your assignments.
    B. focusing and studying without breaks so that you master what you're learning.
    C. scheduling yourself to be three places at once.
    D. varying your study techniques by course content.

7. Liz reads the word *metacognition* in this chapter, but still does not understand what it means. She should do all of the following <u>except</u>:
   A. look it up in a dictionary.
   B. reread that section of the chapter.
   C. e-mail her instructor, asking for another definition.
   D. ask her best friend to explain it.

8. An example in the chapter of "review, review, review" is when a student:
   A. reviews biology notes often enough to easily retain and retrieve information.
   B. goes over the information for a math test at least four times.
   C. sets up a study group for everyone to review for a test.
   D. reviews for a test at least three days before.

9. Which of the following does "learning the language" of a class mean?
   A. Study hard in foreign language class as you may need this for a study abroad trip.
   B. Learn the vocabulary of introductory courses so that advanced courses will be easier.
   C. Learning a foreign language is critical to understanding different cultures.
   D. Learning more than one language is easier in as an adult.

10. Which of the following is <u>not</u> important to being a good reader?
    A. Reading is a process; understanding is the goal.
    B. Reading requires that you occasionally back up or repeat.
    C. Reading is a race so read as fast as you can.
    D. Reading more frequently, even though it's not your favorite pastime, will help you become a better reader.

LEVEL THREE

11. The connection between personality type and reading has been described in this chapter. If a student is a strong Perceiver, which of the following statements most accurately describes their behavior?
    A. Perceivers prefer books packed with emotion.
    B. Perceivers tend to be fast readers who reach conclusions quickly.
    C. Perceivers prefer books that they can connect with their own personal stories.
    D. Perceivers enjoy reading about new and exciting places.

12. The difference between "fast food reading" and "fine dining food reading" is:
    A. reading all night to cram for a test versus buying Cliff Notes.
    B. skimming the main points of a reading assignment versus taking the time to read in depth.
    C. reading every chance you can get versus only when you have time.
    D. reading for pleasure versus reading for content.

13. Dissecting a text means:
    A. breaking up reading time into short segments.
    B. taking notes in the margins to explain something or ask questions.
    C. separating segments of a reading assignment by topic.
    D. differentiating between fact and fiction.

14. Triage is a term used by the medical profession to quickly assess a situation and treat the neediest patients first. How is the term triage used in this chapter?
    A. It is used as a strategy to help students assess where they need to put their attention when there are competing tasks.
    B. It is possible that students may need to assess their study techniques.
    C. It is possible that some students will have an easier time than others reading the same material.
    D. It is used as a strategy to assess which reading technique works for best for students.

15. Which of the following is the best technique used by successful readers?
    A. Students follow a technique prescribed by their instructor.
    B. Students follow a successful strategy that they developed themselves.
    C. Students follow a strategy that includes writing.
    D. Students follow a strategy that includes reading aloud.

Chapter 8
Answer Key

1. D
2. C
3. D
4. C
5. B
6. B
7. D
8. A
9. B
10. C
11. D
12. B
13. B
14. A
15. B

CHAPTER 9: TAKING TESTS

Challenge Yourself Quiz

LEVEL ONE

1. According to the text, the first step to test taking is:
    A. make sure you are prepared.
    B. get a good night sleep.
    C. study with a friend.
    D. check with someone who took a class from this instructor before.

2. Out of the three stages in test taking, the last stage:
    A. helps you prepare for the day of the test.
    B. helps you prepare for future exams.
    C. shows you what to study for the final exam.
    D. helps you determine how you should act during the test.

3. Which of the following is an example of "maximizing your memory"?
    A. Make sure you memorize class material the same way as a friend who is earning A's.
    B. Make it to the test on time.
    C. Make sure you eat breakfast.
    D. Make it funny.

4. According to some experts, which of the following can help your concentration?
    A. Mocha lattes
    B. A big meal
    C. Gum
    D. Cramming

5. When taking a test with a mixed format, you should make sure that you save time for the:
    A. long essay section.
    B. multiple choice section.
    C. fill-in-the-blank section.
    D. short essay section.

LEVEL TWO

6. Why is it important to study with a friend?
    A. So the study session is not boring.
    B. Teaching someone else helps you learn the material.
    C. Friends often take better notes.
    D. Comparing notes is the best way to study.

7. Cramming is a bad idea because:
   A. your teacher will think you are a bad student.
   B. you won't seem like a responsible person.
   C. cramming causes lack of sleep and increased anxiety.
   D. you won't be up to going out on the weekend.

8. During their literature midterm exam, Ryan fidgets, Ellen scolds herself for not studying harder, Aren is fearful, and Maria chokes and can't remember the answers. These four students display which of the following sets of characteristics of test anxiety discussed in the chapter?
   A. Cognitive, Emotional, Behavioral, and Physiological
   B. Panic, Physical, Emotional, and Behavioral
   C. Emotional, Physical, Cognitive, and Panic
   D. Negative, Panic, Behavioral, and Emotional

9. If the test has a mixed format, you should do which section first?
   A. Long essay questions
   B. Short essay questions
   C. Multiple choice
   D. Fill-in-the-blank

10. When taking a true/false test you should pay attention to:
   A. how many of the statements you answered false to.
   B. the pattern your answers are forming
   C. the length of the question.
   D. how the sentence is worded.

LEVEL THREE

11. Kara has extreme math anxiety to the point of throwing up before a math test. She graduated from high school with a 3.99 grade point average as valedictorian. Which of the following statements is true?
   A. Kara fits the profile of many students with math anxiety.
   B. Kara is not the kind of student who would have math anxiety.
   C. Kara should definitely drop her math course before it's too late.
   D. Kara should go into a major that does not require any classes in math.

12. When taking a test, what is an easy way to trigger your memory?
   A. Stop, put the test down, and think.
   B. Read over each question before you begin the test.
   C. Go to the last question because that usually sums up the material.
   D. Answer each question in order.

13. When reading questions, skipping words will cause you to:
    A. definitely get the answer wrong.
    B. dhow the professor that you are lazy.
    C. jump to the wrong conclusion and possibly get the question wrong.
    D. finish the test earlier than others.

14. People who change their answers when they think they are wrong:
    A. usually are correct.
    B. are wrong because initial answers are usually correct.
    C. confuse the teacher with all the marks on the test.
    D. look like they are cheating.

15. A good test question:
    A. is hard to answer.
    B. makes you smarter because it causes you to think.
    C. tests the right things.
    D. is usually answered incorrectly.

Chapter 9
Answer Key

1. A
2. B
3. D
4. C
5. A
6. B
7. C
8. A
9. C
10. D
11. A
12. B
13. C
14. A
15. C

CHAPTER 10: WRITING AND SPEAKING

Challenge Yourself Quiz

LEVEL ONE

1. Experts believe that writing anxiety is:
   A. genetic.
   B. learned.
   C. due to lack of sleep.
   D. related to ADHD.

2. Writing helps you learn to:
   A. think.
   B. develop confidence.
   C. become organized.
   D. alleviate conflict.

3. The specific argument you summarize in your paper (or speech) is called the:
   A. opening sentence.
   B. summary.
   C. thesis.
   D. topic.

4. When you sit down to write and suddenly go blank, it is called:
   A. writer's block.
   B. the tyranny of the blank page.
   C. memory loss.
   D. Both A and B

5. When you collect facts during your prewriting stage, you should organize them into:
   A. a brief summary.
   B. an outline.
   C. paragraphs.
   D. a list of facts.

LEVEL TWO

6. If you're writing a paper about traffic problems in your city and you pose possible fixes, you're probably using:
   A. a problem-solution pattern.
   B. an answer key to help confirm your hunches.
   C. apattern that can show you how to approach an issue.
   D. an example that clearly illustrates the problem

7. Zach's assignment asks him to read two Shakespeare plays: *Othello* and *King Lear*. The assignment is probably going to require using a:
    A. compare and contrast format.
    B. problem-solution format.
    C. cause and effect format.
    D. spatial format.

8. Before your writing becomes final, one of the main things you should do is:
    A. re-write it at least twice.
    B. go to a dictionary and check that all of the word choices are correct.
    C. re-read it a minimum of five times.
    D. share it with others for feedback.

9. Spell-check can let you down when:
    A. you are not exactly sure what the word means.
    B. you use the same word multiple times.
    C. you use an actual word but not the right one.
    D. you don't know how to exactly spell the word.

10. "Data Dump" writing is what happens when:
    A. you don't take the time to proofread.
    B. you write without organizing what you want to say.
    C. a group of people contributes to the same project.
    D. the professor asks you to submit an idea that comes to mind.

LEVEL THREE

11. In this chapter a number of suggestions were given to create winning presentations. Which is not an example of a suggestion?
    A. Understanding the purpose for the presentation.
    B. Taking the location of the presentation into account.
    C. Making sure that you will have a full audience.
    D. Understanding the needs of your audience.

12. Which of the following is an example of therapeutic writing?
    A. Gaining confidence about writing by submitting works to a contest.
    B. Drawing images of stressful events.
    C. Writing a journal entry about an issue that is bothering you.
    D. Using the concepts behind a good workout and applying that to writing.

13. Which is an example of "correctness" as discussed in the chapter?
    A. The student must understand his role.
    B. The teammate is considering her choices.
    C. A successful parent understands her role.
    D. Students are important players in their success.

14. "Stealing the show" with a PowerPoint presentation may happen if you:
    A. Use more than one color to integrate and differentiate the slides.
    B. Use a lot of text in the slides so that readers can fully understand concepts.
    C. Use too much animation, sound, and transitions for impact.
    D. Repeat the main ideas.

15. "If you can't shake it, fake it" in this chapter refers to:
    A. never underestimating the power of an audience to take away the jitters.
    B. the fact that the audience doesn't really know how nervous you are.
    C. pretending you're confident and it may just happen.
    D. anxiety going away after the first two minutes.

Chapter 10
Answer Key

1. B
2. A
3. C
4. D
5. B
6. A
7. A
8. D
9. C
10. B
11. C
12. C
13. D
14. C
15. C

CHAPTER 11: BUILDING RELATIONSHIPS, VALUING DIVERSITY

Challenge Yourself Quiz

LEVEL ONE

1. According to the text, college is not only about your "head" but also about your:
   A. body.
   B. heart.
   C. physical ability.
   D. finances.

2. Experts believe that intelligence is:
   A. learned.
   B. limited.
   C. narrow.
   D. multifaceted.

3. Emotional Intelligence can help you:
   A. understand people.
   B. understand yourself.
   C. deal with difficult situations.
   D. All of the above

4. There are _____ components (scales) of Emotional Intelligence.
   A. 5
   B. 4
   C. 3
   D. 8

5. Researchers believe that genes play a role in one's Emotional Intelligence, but it can also be:
   A. learned.
   B. increased.
   C. taught.
   D. All of the above

LEVEL TWO

6. If someone is optimistic and positive most of the time, they tend to have high:
   A. general mood.
   B. emotional alertness.
   C. stress management.
   D. adaptability skills.

7. According to Helen Fisher, when people are madly in love, they exhibit particular characteristics. Chelsea thinks Jack, the man she's in love with, is the most attractive man she's ever laid eyes on. Which of the following characteristic of lovers is she exhibiting?
   A. Extreme energy
   B. Imagined betterment
   C. Mood swings
   D. Interfering thoughts

8. According to the text, people who act as "mind readers" are:
   A. really helpful in identifying what is going on.
   B. described by Bach as "crazy making."
   C. extremely honest.
   D. mental negatives.

9. Bad relationships can actually:
   A. shorten your lifespan.
   B. increase your tolerance for stress.
   C. keep you focused on work to avoid thinking about the relationship.
   D. make you closer to that person if the person really needs you.

10. When relationships end, the _____ of communication between the two participants change.
    A. quality
    B. quantity
    C. quality and quantity
    D. level

LEVEL THREE

11. According to the text, appreciating diversity helps us become better citizens because:
    A. diversity is something that shows a higher level of intelligence.
    B. diversity steers away from society's "norm."
    C. diversity is what our society is based on.
    D. diversity helps us avoid stereotyping.

12. The phrase "Think globally, act locally" originally meant:
    A. global warming.
    B. taking care of your own neighborhood first.
    C. that we can't do much to affect people across the globe.
    D. doing what you can to save the environment.

13. When a couple decides to have a baby to bring themselves closer because they argue a lot, they are exhibiting a danger signal called:
    A. digging in deeper.
    B. family comes first.
    C. focusing on what is important.
    D. let's try and work it out.

14. Based on Winston Churchill's quote in this chapter, if he were alive today he would most encourage college students to get involved in:
    A. student government.
    B. service learning.
    C. foreign policy clubs.
    D. diversity groups.

15. John was very upset when his roommate borrowed his car without asking. John decided to park his car in a lot that was far away from his residence hall instead of his normal parking spot without telling his roommate. This is an example of:
    A. conflict resolution.
    B. conflict avoidance.
    C. conflict control.
    D. conflict accommodation.

Chapter 11
Answer Key

1. B

2. D

3. D

4. A

5. D

6. A

7. B

8. B

9. A

10. C

11. C

12. D

13. A

14. B

15. B

CHAPTER 12: CHOOSING A COLLEGE MAJOR AND A CAREER

Challenge Yourself Quiz

1. A SWOT analysis is a way that you can identify:
    A. successful ways of teaching.
    B. short ways of time management.
    C. strengths, weaknesses, opportunities, and threats.
    D. strengths and ways of opening thinking.

2. Which is an example of the interconnectedness of knowledge that is described in the text?
    A. Comparison and contrast exercise
    B. Course tree activity
    C. Pie chart activity
    D. Circle of Learning exercise

3. The Academic Map in the text helps identify how many colleges and universities are organized. This includes:
    A. categories that include the natural sciences, humanities, social sciences, and engineering.
    B. an organizational chart that describes who is in charge of which unit.
    C. four quadrants that list how you should choose a career.
    D. an educational organizer that will help with budgeting time.

4. Women tend to choose their major based on aptitude, while men are more influenced by:
    A. difficulty.
    B. masculinity.
    C. challenge.
    D. career advancement opportunities and salary.

5. On top of basic courses, you'll also take a concentration of courses in your academic major, so your _____ will continue to grow outward.
    A. Academic Map
    B. education knowledge
    C. level of certainty
    D. career search

LEVEL TWO

6. Andrew Carnegie, American industrialist, once said, "My heart is in the work." By this, he meant:
    A. I get emotional about my success.
    B. I have been successful beyond my wildest dreams.
    C. I am a workaholic.
    D. I am fully invested intellectually, emotionally, and psychologically in my work.

7. Research indicates that students who are left-brained tend to
    A. be more creative.
    B. study harder.
    C. not pay as close attention.
    D. choose business majors.

8. Jane's parents have encouraged her to move up from her local college to a large university and then go to a respectable law school so that she can be hired by a prestigious law firm and eventually make partner. Jane's parents are engaging in:
    A. ladder talk.
    B. encouragement.
    C. motivation.
    D. career strategies infusion.

9. To help someone understand how knowledge is interconnected, which of the following statements would you say?
    A. If you study math, you will see that it has no connection to the arts.
    B. Literature is closely connected to art by the way that it defines images.
    C. Two areas that are not clearly connected are anthropology and political science.
    D. Poetry and Physics are both a way to define and describe differences.

10. Interviews can be very intimidating, so prepare. Which of the following questions would be good to ask an interviewer?
    A. "I am not a morning person. Can I work later in the afternoon?"
    B. "What do you think that most people in your company value?"
    C. "If I only stay for six months is that okay?"
    D. "Was the last person in this job fired"?

LEVEL THREE

11. Other important suggestions for interviewing for a job in this chapter include:
    A. Be honest and admit your faults.
    B. Talk about yourself as much as possible.
    C. Don't ask questions, let the interviewer ask you.
    D. Watch for questions out of left field.

12. According to the text, "academic anatomy" can best be described as:
    A. making sure that you don't take courses that are not of interest to you.
    B. understanding how you would prioritize the way you like to work.
    C. questionnaires that can help you focus on a major or career.
    D. relating to people who are in jobs that appear interesting and stimulating.

13. Which of the following is <u>not</u> true? If you were to have an internship:
    A. you would be able to apply skills you have learned to a job.
    B. you could learn from a professional in a career with whom you would work alongside.
    C. you couldn't use this as a real experience on a résumé.
    D. you might learn that you don't like this field.

14. Generally, people with an SF psychological type would probably enjoy a career in any of the following <u>except</u>:
    A. nursing.
    B. teaching.
    C. community service.
    D. accounting.

15. According to research, which of the following statements contributes most to job satisfaction?
    A. A career where it is clear that status and salary will increase.
    B. A career where the quality of the relationship with one boss is good.
    C. A career where you are not working a sixty plus hour week.
    D. A career where you can have adventure in your job.

Chapter 12
Answer Key

1. C
2. D
3. A
4. D
5. A
6. D
7. D
8. A
9. B
10. B
11. D
12. B
13. C
14. D
15. B

CHAPTER 13: WORKING TOWARD WELLNESS

Challenge Yourself Quiz

LEVEL ONE

1. According to Chapter 13, in college, wellness is about making _____ choices.
   A. good
   B. informed
   C. informative
   D. smart

2. _____ "is a diagnosable mental, behavioral or emotional disorder that interferes with one of more major activities in life like dressing, eating or working."
   A. Anxiety
   B. Depression
   C. Mental illness
   D. Obsessive compulsive disorder

3. During college, students do:
   A. more volunteer work than in high school.
   B. mot volunteer in college.
   C. less volunteer work than in high school.
   D. three times as much volunteer work than required.

4. According to recent data, about 1,300 college students do this every year and 31,469 people try it. This statement refers to:
   A. drugs.
   B. suicide.
   C. alcohol.
   D. dropping out of school.

5. About _____ of the student body on most campuses visits the campus counseling center each year.
   A. 10%
   B. 30%
   C. 5%
   D. 50%

6. Tipper Gore, Drew Barrymore, and Carrie Fisher are mentioned in this chapter. Which of the following describes the condition they share?
    A. Generalized Anxiety Disorder
    B. Schizophrenia
    C. Obsessive Compulsive Disorder
    D. Depression

7. Which of the following does not describe a student reacting adversely to stress?
    A. Feeling irritable
    B. Having a fever over 102
    C. Experiencing stomach aches and heartburn
    D. Getting frequent colds

8. Which of the following menu items probably have the least number of calories?
    A. Hamburger and a diet coke
    B. Cheeseburger and fries
    C. Two slices of garlic bread and a soda
    D. Two slices of pizza

9. Which of the following will most likely help you to determine your level of success in college?
    A. SAT scores
    B. Initial incoming freshman placement exams
    C. Level of courses taken
    D. Your scores on the Wellness Wheel

10. Short-term stress is:
    A. worse than long-term stress.
    B. just as bad as long-term stress.
    C. in your head for about a year.
    D. what you may experience when you have to take a test.

LEVEL THREE

11. Research shows that:
    A. just 20 minutes of exercise a day can help you calm down for 24 hours.
    B. just 20 minutes of exercise a day is not enough for long term benefits.
    C. exercise alone will not help stress.
    D. if you exercise alone, you are more likely to keep it up.

12. An extraverted sensor would most likely be successful with which type of exercise?
    A. Taking leisurely walks alone
    B. Swimming laps at the pool
    C. Going to weight training classes with a friend
    D. Cycling up mountain trails

13. Which of the following is not true?
    A. Occasional binge drinking can damage the brain.
    B. Excessive drinking in college can lead to later addiction.
    C. Students generally overestimate the number of other students who use drugs.
    D. Most drinking occurs in the junior year and beyond when students are 21 or older.

14. If students want to sober up after drinking too much alcohol, they should:
    A. Drink at least three cups of coffee.
    B. Take a cold shower.
    C. Take one of the over the counter pills to stimulate the nervous system.
    D. Simply stop drinking and wait.

15. Which of the following statements about spirituality and college statements is not true?
    A. More than 75 percent of college students are interested in spirituality.
    B. About half of college students disagree with their families on religious matters.
    C. Most college students have high levels of religious tolerance.
    D. Very few college students question their own religious beliefs.

Chapter 13
Answer Key

1. B
2. C
3. C
4. B
5. A
6. D
7. B
8. A
9. D
10. D
11. A
12. C
13. D
14. D
15. D

ADDITIONAL RESOURCES

By Constance Staley

AUTHOR RECOMMENDED ADDITIONAL ACTIVITIES

Passport to Learning

By Constance Staley. Based on Jaques, D. (2000). *Learning in groups* (3rd ed.). London: Kogan Page, p. 206. Used with permission.
Recommended for pre-course planning as a possible course requirement

Group Size: Any size group
Time Required: Five minutes to collect cards at the beginning of class
Materials: Index cards, provided by students
Physical Setting: Home or residence hall
Goals: To improve attendance and encourage reading in first-year (or any) courses
In order to improve attendance, announce the first day of class that the course will use a "passport" system. If you wish, insist that no student will be admitted to each class without a "passport." At the beginning of class (and only then), students submit an index card (passport), covered front and back with notes from the day's reading assignment. Tell students that missing cards may <u>not</u> be replaced at any time during the term, that no one else may submit a card on their behalf, and that you will keep these cards (organized by student) until the final exam, when each student's stack will be returned to him or her. Students are welcome to use the entire stack during the test to maximize their performance.

Find an Expert

By Constance Staley
Recommended for Chapter 1 Building Dreams, Setting Goals as an icebreaker

Group Size: Any size group
Time Required: 15-20 minutes, followed by in-class processing and student introductions
Materials: Interview questions on following to photocopy and handout to students
Physical Setting: Classroom
Goals: To reassure beginning students that they are experts in particular areas (in fact, areas that instructors and classmates may not know much about)
Hand out the "Find an Expert" sheet following this page, one to each student, and read the instructions. Ask students to circulate to meet one another and discover what types of expertise students have cultivated before coming to college.

Variation: Add your own expertise categories, based on your particular students, institution, or location.

Find an Expert

Find someone in our group with expertise in each of the areas described. As you circulate around the room, introduce yourself, fill in your interviewee's first name below, describing your own experience as it relates and something in particular your interviewee knows about the subject that you don't. Find someone…

1. Who knows a lot about **cars**. Name: _____
_____
_____

2. Who has had a piece of **writing published**. Name: _____
_____
_____

3. Who is a **fast food** junkie. Name: _____
_____
_____

4. Who knows how **families** work as a result of having five or more siblings. Name: _____
_____
_____

5. Who knows the campus because a **friend or sibling previously attended**. Name: _____
_____
_____

6. Who's had a stellar career in **high school athletics**. Name: _____
_____
_____

7. Who's never gotten anything but **A's in math**. Name: _____
_____
_____

8. Who studied **art or dance** growing up. Name: _____
_____
_____

9. Who knows the food service industry well from working as a **server**. Name: _____
_____
_____

10. Who is a relationship expert as a result of a **long-lasting romance**. Name: _____
_____
_____

Finally, what kind of expertise do you hope to develop during your first term in college?
_____
_____

Giving Something Up To Give It All You've Got

By Constance Staley
Recommended for Chapter 1 Building Dreams, Setting Goals

Group Size: Any size group
Time Required: Approximately 20 minutes to discuss, depending on the size of the group
Materials: One index card per student
Physical Setting: Classroom (or completed as a homework assignment and brought to class)
Goals: To help students realize that achieving excellence may require making sacrifices
To emphasize managing one's time *and* achieving excellence, after describing the major assignment in your course, ask students how many of them would like to excel and achieve the best results possible. Most students will probably raise their hands. Then distribute index cards and ask students to identify what they are willing to give up in order to accomplish this goal. Continuing to "pile on," adding more and more to their already full lives, is not necessarily realistic. Getting the best results often requires eliminating something, clearing time to invest elsewhere. Are they willing to give up a hobby, pastime, leisure activity, extra hours at work, etc. in order to excel on the assignment? Students should identify their "sacrifice," write it on an index card, and submit it—not only to symbolize and publicize their personal commitment, but for discussion purposes as a group. If individuals are not willing to sacrifice anything, that response may be discussed, too.

 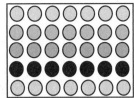

What Rules Your Life?

By Constance Staley

Recommended for Chapter 1 Building Dreams, Setting Goals
or (variation) Chapter 4 Managing Your Time and Energy

Group Size: Any size class
Time Required: May vary, depending on the amount of discussion generated
Materials: Inexpensive wooden rulers, bought in bulk, and neon sticky dots (or any color scheme) in sheets of 35 (red, orange, yellow, green, and an additional row of red on the bottom), cut into strips to give each student five different colored dots
Physical Setting: Normal classroom
Goal: To help students explore their priorities as each one relates to college success

As a class, decide what each color dot will represent, using red as the top priority in life. (Having two red dots helps students not feel guilty about putting something important in second place.) Priorities may include such things as a college education, family, spouse, children, parents, siblings, pet, job, religion, romantic partner, scholarship, athletics, and so forth. Students should place the highest priority item in their lives at the top of the ruler while <u>holding it vertically</u>, closest to the 12" mark, and then move down the ruler with other colored dots. Ask students to justify their rankings, if they're willing. How do they know a dot belongs where they've placed it? Listen to students as they discuss these items. Do their priorities shift and change? Should they? If so, in what types of circumstances? A student who is attending college to avoid a dead-end job later on in life, ironically, may be working so many hours at a dead-end job now to finance a college education (and possibly support an expensive lifestyle), that the student is putting academic success too far down the ruler (priority list), and earning a degree will be jeopardized. For many students, if they're honest, school is a lower priority than it should be. Stress the importance of prioritizing intentionally, based on long-term, rather than short-term, goals.

Variation: Base the activity on prioritizing a day's schedule with colored dots representing the most important activities to complete.

Syllabox
GES 470:
Cultural
Geography

Syllabus or Syllabox?

By Constance Staley (with thanks to Professor Mike Larkin, Department of Geography and Environmental Studies, UCCS)
Recommended for Chapter 2 Learning about Learning

Group Size: small class size because of the time investment
Time Required: may vary
Materials: small cardboard boxes, large enough to hold a CD and useful materials to introduce or demonstrate the content of a new course
Physical Setting: normal classroom
Goal: to demonstrate to students a willingness to address all learning modalities: visual, aural, read/write, kinesthetic and multimodal

Syl-la-bus [silləbəss] (plural syl-la-bi)
Definition: 1. a summary of the main topics of a course of study

Instead of the standard Read/Write syllabus students are used to, create something different. For example, for a course in cultural geography, include a CD of ethnic music you've downloaded (but be careful of downloading and music sharing rules), origami, the course schedule (as a puzzle to be fitted together), etc.

Variation: Present a very basic, "plain vanilla" Read/Write syllabus, ask students to take the VARK and discuss their results, and then ask students to create a multimodal syllabus of their own to bring and demonstrate to the class. Tell them they must justify each item they choose to include. You may be surprised to see just how creative they are and get valuable ideas for the next time you teach the course!

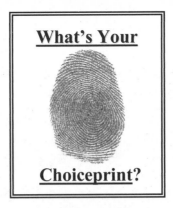

What's Your Choiceprint?

By Constance Staley

Recommended for Chapter 3 Making Use of Resources (where the "Cultivate Your Curiosity" article discusses these ideas) or possibly Chapter 4 Managing Your Time and Energy

Going to college is about a becoming part of a *community* of learners. However, with so many choices about where to live and work, which classes to take, and what activities to participate in, developing and finding *community* can be a challenge. Think about <u>all</u> the choices you've made in coming to college. When you total them up, your individual choices give you your own unique "choiceprint" that may not be identical to any other student's. After you fill out Part I, circulate and find the person in class whose "choiceprint" is most similar to yours. What else do you have in common? After you fill out Part II, discuss your responses as a group.

PART I

1. Where did you choose to live this term? _____

2. Which classes did you choose to take? _____

3. Who are the people you've chosen to be part of your small circle of friends? _____
_____

4. Which student organizations have you chosen to join? _____

5. Which campus activities will you choose to participate in this week? _____
_____

6. Which off-campus, close-by restaurants do you choose to frequent most often? _____
_____

7. Which of the available campus college success resources will you choose to use? _____
_____

8. What would you choose to do with an extra $500 if it appeared magically? _____

9. Which class would you choose *never* to miss this term? _____

10. Which of your professors will you choose to visit first during office hours? _____

PART II
Identify three choices you've made <u>today</u>, ones that you did a fair amount of thinking about. Why did you make the specific choice you made?

1. _____
_____
_____
_____
_____

2. _____
_____
_____
_____
_____

3. _____
_____
_____
_____
_____

Life is about making choices. Psychologist and professor Barry Schwartz in his book, *The Paradox of Choice: Why Less is More*, explains that in today's complex world we are continuously bombarded with choices. He describes the difference between "maximizers" and "satisficers." Maximizers don't rest until they find the best. They spend inordinate amounts of time searching for some ideal, making certain they've made the very best choice, and when they finally settle on something, they may even regret choices they passed up. "Satisficers," on the other hand, are satisfied with what's good enough, based on their most important criteria. Of course, we all do some "maximizing" and some "satisficing," but generally, which are you? For each decision you made, did you "maximize" or "satisfice" appropriately? Why or why not?

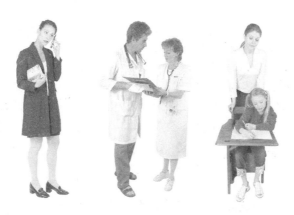

Get a Life!

By Constance Staley
**Recommended for Chapter 3 Making Use of Resources
or Chapter 12 Choosing a College Major and a Career**

Group Size: Any size group
Time Required: Out-of-class assignment in teams, followed by in-class processing
Materials: List of "Get a Life!" questions and Internet access
Physical Setting: Classroom or computer lab activity
**Goals: To help students think about their own futures and realize the investment required
to achieve and sustain "their dreams"**
Hand out the "Get a Life!" assignment on the following page and ask students to work in pairs or
trios to research the answers. They may present their profiles in class orally, in written form, or
as PowerPoint presentations. Stress accuracy, thoroughness, and creativity.

Variation: Add questions/characteristics, and be as creative as you like to help engage students
in the activity.

Get a Life!

The point of this exercise is to try on someone else's life. Work with two or three classmates to create a fictitious person. Search the Internet for answers to the following questions. Be as creative (but realistic) as you like, compile information to develop the person's personal financial profile, and present your findings to the class. Put all of your financial answers into a *monthly* average.

1. What is this person's name?
2. How old is this person?
3. Is this person male or female?
4. What is the person's marital status?
5. Does the person support others financially?
6. In which city and state does the person live? Select a place you might like to live someday.
7. If this person supports others, how much does it cost to raise one child (or more), for example, in this part of the country?
8. Where does the person live—in a house or apartment, for example? What is the average price of a house or apartment in this city?
9. If the person owns a home, what were the mortgage rates at the time? What is his or her monthly payment, including taxes and insurance?
10. What other home expenses does this person have each month? (fee for parking garage, homeowner's dues for condo, etc.)
11. What kind of car does this person drive? What year?
12. What is the average price of this car?
13. What is his or her monthly car payment?
14. What does this person spend for food each week? (self or family)
15. What are this person's average monthly utility costs (garbage removal, water, heat, etc.)?
16. If the person doesn't own a car, what are his or her transportation costs (subway, train, etc.) per month?
17. How much money does this person spend on entertainment each month? (movies, sports tickets, CDs, etc.)
18. What other monthly costs should be added in?
19. What are this person's average monthly credit card bills?
20. Is this person repaying college loans? If so, how much are those payments? Figure four or five years of college at your institution's tuition rates.
21. What is the person's occupation? Select a career you might be interested in.
22. How much education is required for this career field?
23. What is this person's monthly salary, based on average salary for this profession at this point in someone's career?
24. How much does the person invest or save each month?
25. Does this person earn enough monthly income to support his or her lifestyle? Which items in your profile may need to be adjusted?

What did you learn in researching your fictitious person? What surprised you? Did this activity change your thinking at all? Is this a career you might really be interested in? Is this a life you'd want?

From Staley, C. (2003). *50 Ways to Leave Your Lectern*. Belmont, CA: Wadsworth, pp. 120-121.
Recommended for Chapter 4 Managing Your Time and Energy

Group size: Any size class
Time required: Any portion of normal class time
Materials: Paper and writing utensil
Physical setting: Any classroom setting; however, a U-shape or circle works well
Goals: To help students organize their thoughts, present their ideas clearly, and generally hone their oral communication skills

Cut the quotations on the following pages into strips so that each student can draw one and place it face down in front of him or herself (or create your own list of quotes). Choose a student volunteer to begin the exercise. He or she should turn over the slip, read the quotation, and offer a one-minute response by first agreeing or disagreeing with the quote and then identifying two pieces of support from personal experience, course material, or other relevant information sources. When one student begins to speak, the next student to speak may turn over his or her slip and begin formulating a response. If students seem anxious about speaking in front of classmates, reassure them that everyone will start on "equal footing" and reassert the value of learning to "speak on your feet."

Variation: Identify similar individual "quotations" from your lecture, or particular important points you plan to make, and hand them out on slips before you begin. Ask students to listen for their point, and after you conclude the lecture, to agree, disagree, or comment on the point they have been dealt. If the group is large, give slips to several volunteers or "Quotefinder" designees for the class session, instead of everyone.

Time Management Quotes for "A Quote for All Reasons" Activity

Cut out the following quotes into strips to hand out to your students.

"This constant, unproductive preoccupation with all the things we have to do is the single largest consumer of time and energy." *~Kerry Gleeson*

"Life is denied by lack of attention, whether it is to cleaning windows or trying to write a masterpiece." *~Nadia Boulanger*

"Blessed are the flexible, for they shall not be bent out of shape." *~Michael McGriffy, M. D.*

"The art of resting the mind and the power of dismissing from it all care and worry is probably one of the secrets of our great men [and women]." *~Captain J. A. Hatfield*

"Time is the quality of nature that keeps events from happening all at once. Lately it doesn't seem to be working." *~Anonymous*

"Almost every project could be done better, and an infinite quantity of information is now available that could make that happen." *~David Allen*

"Rule your mind or it will rule you." *~Horace*

"Now, for many of us, there are no edges to most of our projects. Most people I know have at least half a dozen things they're trying to achieve right now, and even if they had the rest of their lives to try, they wouldn't be able to finish these to perfection." *~David Allen*

"There is one thing we can do, and the happiest people are those who can do it to the limit of their ability. We can be completely present. We can be all here. We can… give all our attention to the opportunity before us." ~*Mark Van Doren*

"There is usually an inverse proportion between how much something is on your mind and how much it's getting done." ~*David Allen*

"Vision is not enough; it must be combined with venture. It is not enough to stare up the steps; we must step up the stairs." ~*Vaclav Havel*

"A paradox has emerged in this new millennium: people have enhanced quality of life, but at the same time they are adding to their stress levels by taking on more than they have resources to handle. It's as though their eyes were bigger than their stomachs. And most people are to some degree frustrated and perplexed about how to improve the situation." ~*David Allen*

"I am rather like a mosquito in a nudist camp; I know what I want to do, but I don't know where to begin." ~*Stephen Bayne*

"Let our advance worrying become advance thinking and planning." ~*Winston Churchill*

"The middle of every successful project looks like a disaster." ~*Rosabeth Moss Cantor*

"The best place to succeed is where you are with what you have." ~*Charles Schwab*

Press Conference

By Constance Staley
Recommended for Chapter 8 Reading and Studying

Group size: Any size class
Time required: Variable
Materials: None required or index cards for students to write out questions
Physical setting: Any classroom setting
Goals: To engage students in questioning techniques as a form of classroom engagement, and to focus on speaking skills

Before beginning class (or the previous week), announce that you will hold a press conference at the end of class. The group will play the role of reporters from print media outlets of their own choosing or as assigned. (See the accompanying list on the next page.) If you wish, discuss the press conference as a communication tool, the importance of speaking skills in political or media careers, and the interests of particular outlets, based on their reading audience. You may also wish to discuss challenging situations in which public figures must communicate with care and sensitivity as they react to volatile issues. If you wish, ask students to view an upcoming press conference or show a videotaped one in class. Or use a recent, perhaps controversial, campus-related incident as a springboard. Try to make the experience as realistic as possible, using course content as the material to be covered during the press conference. Explore with students the value of asking questions in their classes and how to do so effectively.

Variation: Select a panel of student volunteers to answer questions at the press conference, or have students work in groups to generate high-quality questions.

Major Media Outlets to Accompany Press Conference Activity

Washington Post

Los Angeles Times

New York Times

Miami Herald

USA Today

New York Post

New York News

Atlanta Journal-Constitution

Dallas Morning News

Washington Times

Denver Post

Philadelphia Inquirer

Boston Globe

Chicago Tribune

Detroit Free Press

Phoenix Arizona Republic

San Francisco Chronicle

Tampa Tribune

Orlando Sentinel

Baltimore Sun

Charlotte Observer

Chicago Sun-Times

Cleveland Plain Dealer

St. Louis Post-Dispatch

Indianapolis Star

Fort Lauderdale Sun-Sentinel

Wall Street Journal

Financial Times

New York Village Voice

Army Times

Byte

Multimedia World

Fortune

Forbes

Money

People

Life

Entertainment Weekly

Rolling Stone

Vogue

Mademoiselle

Glamour

Chronicle of Higher Education

Who's to Blame?

By Constance Staley. This activity is a modern-day version of the "Drawbridge Exercise."
Recommended for Chapter 11 Managing Relationships, Valuing Diversity

Jason, a rising young executive, and Jennifer, who was finishing her master's degree in social work, had been married for a year. Although Jason had once had a serious drug problem that had gotten him in trouble with the law, he'd gotten his life back together and managed to get a good job.

One morning, Jason announced, "My company is sending me to China for six months on business. I leave on Monday. I'll be at remote sites in the countryside. I doubt I'll have cell phone coverage. But I'll send you some e-mails." He continued, "While I'm away, don't spend any time on the Internet. Plenty of marriages break up when people meet someone else online. If you do that, believe me, you're going to regret it!"

But toward the end of the six months, Jennifer began thinking about Jeff, her old college boyfriend. She went online and found his e-mail address. "Hey, great to hear from you!" Jeff replied. "I've been thinking a lot about you too lately. I just bought a new time-share condo in Las Vegas. How about coming for a visit? It'd be great to see you again!"

What a tempting invitation, Jennifer thought. Before she knew it, she had e-mailed Jeff back and bought a special $79 one-way airline ticket. *I'll have a really good time in Las Vegas with an old friend, be back in plenty of time, and Jason will never even find out.*

The week with Jeff was glorious. They saw some great shows, ate some fabulous meals, spent lots of time (and money) in the casinos, and one thing led to another. They rekindled their old romance.

But when Jennifer tried to buy a return plane ticket back home, she found that all her credit cards were maxed out. She'd gone to the ATM over and over while she was on a winning streak, and then lost it all. What was she going to do?

When Jennifer consulted Jeff, she was shocked at his reply, "Hey, you're married. This was purely physical. I'm not going to invest money in someone else's wife."

Jennifer called the airline and tried to explain things as sensitively as she could. "Look, lady, I'm sorry things didn't work out," said Jan, the person on the other end of the line. "But I can't give you a free ticket. That's all there is to it!"

In desperation, Jennifer called her best friend back home, Jessica, to ask her to wire money. Shocked, Jessica said, "You did what? You know Jason's very possessive. He's going to kill you! I don't want any part of this!" and she hung up.

Finally with time running out and her anxiety mounting, Jennifer decided to hitchhike. The trip home would be a long one. She left the hotel late that night since time was important. It was dark, and she knew it was risky, but she couldn't think of any other option.

Unfortunately, someone who called himself Jack, the sweatshirt-hooded driver of the car that picked her up, was an escaped felon who'd done hard time at a federal penitentiary. Her body was never found.

Think through all the options, and rank the following individual's responsibility from 1 (most responsible) to 6 (least responsible) for Jennifer's fate. After all class members have completed their individual rankings, discuss the exercise in groups of five students. Your group must reach a consensus, and be ready to provide a rationale for each ranking when the entire class reconvenes.

INDIVIDUAL RANKING		GROUP RANKING	
Jason, the husband	_____	Jason, the husband	_____
Jennifer, the wife	_____	Jennifer, the wife	_____
Jeff, the lover	_____	Jeff, the lover	_____
Jan, the airline employee	_____	Jan, the airline employee	_____
Jessica, the friend	_____	Jessica, the friend	_____
Jack, the escaped felon	_____	Jack, the escaped felon	_____

Is this a healthy relationship? Why or why not? What information from the story would you use to back up your answer? As a class, discuss the themes that emerge in this story that are vital to positive, fulfilling romantic relationships and themes that identify troubled relationships.

FOCUS Roadmap to College Success

"Success is a journey, not a destination." Ben Sweetland

By Constance Staley
**Recommended as an overall course activity, beginning at
Chapter 1 Building Dreams, Setting Goals**

You can't get anywhere if you don't know where you're going, right? You've begun a journey that is an investment in yourself and your own future. Your college success will be determined by the intersection of three types of goals: academic, personal, and community goals. Your teachers will identify some of these goals for you, but, you must discover and work toward these goals yourself. It's not enough to just point yourself toward your diploma four or five years from now. You must make continual progress and monitor your efforts along the way.

When you're on your way somewhere you have to pay attention: Did I make a left turn when I should have made a right one? Did I miss a piece of information on that last road sign? Is this the right exit? Which milepost am I watching for? You don't just head for a new destination and hope for the best.

In the same way, as you make your way through college, you should be asking yourself similar questions: Am I putting forth my best effort? Is this major right for me? Is the career I'm focusing on one I'm well suited for? Do I have access to friends and professors that care about my progress? Do I feel a part of my campus community?

This four-part activity will serve as your Roadmap to College Success and ask you to monitor your progress while communicating with your first-year seminar instructor all along the way. The Roadmap will ask you to complete four milepost. You will be asked to respond to an initial *challenge*, a few weeks later after your have your "bearings," to provide your *reaction* to that initial challenge, to identify the *insight* you've gained about yourself and your progress a few weeks after that, and finally, at the end of the course (or at the end of your first year of college if your instructor wishes), to list every *action* you've taken to help you succeed. Are you ready? Okay, let's go.

Milepost 1: CHALLENGE

Here's a challenge: What are your academic, personal, and community goals? Identify them now and be as specific as possible. For example, getting good grades would be a very general academic goal. Figuring out who I am would be a general personal goal, and making lots of friends would be a general community goal. General goals aren't always particularly helpful.

Examples of specific goals would be getting extra tutoring for my calculus class (academic), making an appointment to visit the Counseling Center to learn more about myself (personal), or attending three events next month to get involved on campus (community). List your goals in these three areas below, and then give/send this completed page to your first-year seminar instructor.

ACADEMIC	PERSONAL	COMMUNITY

Milepost 2: REACTION

Now that several weeks of class have gone by, it's time to react to your original goals. Were they realistic? Have you discovered some new ones? For example, perhaps you know now that tutoring is not all you'll need to be successful in your calculus class. You may need to make an appointment with your instructor to get some additional direction from him or her (academic). Perhaps when you visited the Counseling Center, you learned that you have a relationship that's getting in the way of your success to repair (personal). Perhaps you've decided that in order to pay your bills, you'll have to take on an extra job, and that attending three campus events in one month will be very difficult (community). You need to revise your goal to attending two campus events. Take a look now and provide a reaction to what you initially wrote in response to the challenge presented in Milepost 1. Revise your goals, if you need to, now that reality has set in, and send this completed page to your first-year seminar instructor.

ACADEMIC	PERSONAL	COMMUNITY

Milepost 3: INSIGHT

Now that you've handed in several papers in your classes, you've gotten your midterm exam grades back, perhaps you're beginning to feel the tug of a particular major, and you've forged some new relationships on campus, it's time for Milepost 3. Think about the insight you've gained about yourself, and list specific insights in the three areas below. Send this completed page to your first-year seminar instructor.

ACADEMIC	PERSONAL	COMMUNITY

It's now the end of your first-year seminar course (or the end of your first year of college). You've accomplished a great deal in these three areas. You're well on your way to your destination. Make a list of the ACTION you've taken that has contributed to your success, or list things you now wish you had done that would have made you more successful. Vow to do these things during your next term. Send this completed page to your first-year seminar instructor.

ACADEMIC	PERSONAL	COMMUNITY

Synthesis: Finally, react to this activity. Send your first-year seminar instructor an e-mail, or if assigned, write a synthesis paper about this assignment. Did it help you think about college as a journey? Did it help you monitor your progress? Did it help you focus and stay on course?

TYPES AND CAREERS

Prepared and © 1999 by Dr. Tom Carskadon
Dept. of Psychology, Mississippi State University
P.O. Box 6161, Mississippi State, MS 39762
(662) 325-7655 / tomcar@ra.msstate.edu
Used with permission.

- **Frequencies**. Myriad data indicate that types are very nonrandomly distributed over various jobs and career categories—i.e., in most jobs and specialties, certain types are significantly overrepresented while other types are significantly underrepresented.

- **Looking for ideas**. The 1998 MBTI Manual lists career-relevant characteristics of the different MBTI types and preferences. The earlier 1985 Manual also lists job categories rank ordered from most frequent to least frequent for each type and MBTI preference. These are good starting points for generating career possibilities to investigate and consider.

- **Unusual types in career categories**. People may be headed into careers where their types are unusual. You should not discourage them from pursuing such a career simply on the basis of their having a psychological type not often found in it; but the following questions should be posed:

  1. Do you have an accurate understanding of what the actual, day-to-day work in this field is like? Often, unusual types have misimpressions of a field; but they may perceive it accurately. Co-op programs, internships, temporary job rotations, etc. may be quite useful here.

  2. Are you willing to be a psychological "minority" in that field? Most colleagues will be quite different; the individual must be comfortable with that.

  3. Are you able and willing to change your communication style to suit the majority? Individuals with unusual types for a field have, potentially, input that is uniquely valuable; but to get it accepted, they will have to use the communication style of the majority types in that field.

  If the answer to all three questions is "yes," then do not discourage a person from entering a field where he or she will be a minority type. Data suggest that among people who choose to go into a field with full knowledge of it, unusual types in that field are just as likely to be effective in it as more frequent types are.

Using the MBTI as a screening device for hiring. To grant or den a person a job because of psychological type would be ineffective, unethical, and illegal. The MBTI should never be used for this purpose. Its proper use is for voluntary exploration of issues of placement and satisfaction, not for hiring and firing. Use it to help people determine what jobs they might be naturally suited for and enjoy; but do not restrict opportunities on the basis of type.

SELECTED ONLINE RESOURCES ON COLLEGE AND FIRST-YEAR SEMINAR TEACHING

Derek Bok Center for Teaching and Learning
     http://bokcenter.harvard.edu/icb/icb.do

Idea Center (Individual Development & Education Assessment)
     http://www.idea.ksu.edu/resources/index.html

Online Resources: Faculty Development Associates
     http://www.developfaculty.com/online/index.html

Active Learning
     http://www.active-learning-site.com

Classroom Management
     http://www.mccfl.edu/pages/1389.asp

Constructive Teaching
     http://www.2learn.ca/profgrowth/PDconstruct.asp

How People Learn
     http://www.nap.edu/html/howpeople1/index.html

Icebreakers
     http://adulted.about.com/cs/icebreakers/

Learning Style Models
- Dunn and Dunn- www.learningstyles.net
- Fender- www.ncsu.edu/effective_teaching/Learning_Styles.html
- Gregorc- www.gregorc.com
- Kolb- www.infed.org/biblio/b-explrn.htm#learning%20style
- VARK- http://www.vark-learn.com/english/index.asp

Lecturing Skills
     http://www.ferris.edu/htmls/academics/center/Teaching_and_Learning_Tips/Developing%20Effective%20Lectures/8stepstoactive.htm

Motivating Students
     http://teaching.berkeley.edu/compendium/sectionlists/sect20.html

Teaching & Learning Centers (Global)
     http://www.ku.edu/~cte/resources/websites.html

Teaching & Learning Centers (U.S.)
http://www.hofstra.edu/faculty/ctse/cte_links.cfm

Faculty Development, Honolulu Community College
http://honolulu.hawaii.edu/intranet/committees/FacDevCom/guidebk/teachtip/teachtip.htm

Good Teaching Practices: Barbara Gross Davis (*Tools for Teaching*)
http://teaching.berkeley.edu/bgd/teaching.html

National Resource Center on the Firsts-Year Experience and Students in Transition
http://www.sc.edu/fye/

Policy Center on the First-Year of College
http://www.firstyear.org/index.html

Office of Educational Development, University of California, Berkeley
http://teaching.berkeley.edu/teaching.html

Teambuildinginc.com
http://store.teambuildand First-year inginc.com/

Qualitycoach.net
http://www.qualitycoach.net/shop/shopexd.asp?id=6711

Teamwork and Teamplay
http://www.thiagi.com/book-teamwork-and-teamplay.html

RECOMMENDED READINGS: A SHORT LIST

Angelo, T. K., & Cross, K. P. (1993). *Classroom assessment techniques: A handbook for college teachers*. San Francisco: Jossey-Bass.

Bain, K. (2004). *What the best college teachers do*. Cambridge, MA: Harvard University Press.

Bean, J. (1996). *Engaging ideas: The professor's guide to integrating writing, critical thinking, and active learning in the classroo*m. San Francisco: Jossey-Bass.

Brandt, R. (1998). *Powerful learning*. Alexandria, VA: Association of Supervision and Curriculum Development.

Bransford, J. (2002). *How people learn*. Washington D. C., National Academic Press.

Brookfield, S. D. (1995). *Becoming a critically reflective teacher*. San Francisco: Jossey-Bass.

Davis, B. G. (1993). *Tools for teaching*. San Francisco: Jossey-Bass.

Erickson, B., Peters, C. B., & Strommer, D. W. (2006). *Teaching first-year college students*. San Francisco: Jossey-Bass.

Fink, D. (2003). *Creating significant learning experiences*: *An integrated approach to designing college courses*. San Francisco: Jossey-Bass.

Fleming, N. D. (2005). *Teaching and learning styles: VARK strategies*. Christchurch, NZ: Microfilm Limited.

Leamnson, R. (1999). *Thinking about teaching and learning: Developing habits of learning with first year college and university students*. Sterling, VA: Stylus.

Levine, M. (2005). *Ready or not, here life comes*. New York: Simon & Schuster.

McKeachie, W., & Svinicki, M. (2005). *McKeachie's teaching tips: Strategies, research, and theory for college and university teachers*. Boston: Houghton Mifflin.

Nathan, Rebecca. (2005). *My freshman year*. Ithaca, NY: Cornell University Press.

Nilson, L. B. (2007). *Teaching at its best: A research-based resource for college instructors*. San Francisco: Jossey-Bass.

Palmer, P. (1997). *The courage to teach: Exploring the inner landscape of a teacher's life*. San Francisco: Jossey-Bass.

Richlin, L., & Ronkowski, S. (2006). *Blueprint for learning: Creating college courses to facilitate, assess, and document learning*. Sterling, VA: Stylus.

Staley, C. (1999). *Teaching college success: The complete resource guide*. Belmont, CA: Wadsworth Publishing Company.

Staley, C. (2003). *50 ways to leave your lectern*. Belmont, CA: Wadsworth Publishing Company.

Sutherland, T., & Bonwell, C. C. (1996). *Using active learning in college classes: A range of options for faculty*. San Francisco: Jossey-Bass.

Svinicki, M. D. (2004). *Learning and motivation in the postsecondary classroom*. Bolton, MA: Anker Publishing Company.

Swing, R. (2001 & 2003). *Proving and improving: Strategies for assessing the first college year*, Vols. 1 and 2. Columbia, SC: National Resource Center for the First-Year Experience and Students in Transition.

Weimer, M. (2002). *Learner-centered teaching*. San Francisco: Jossey-Bass.

Wiggins, G., & McTighe, J. (2005). *Understanding by design*. Boston: Prentice-Hall.